ECONOMIC ANALYSIS BEYOND THE LOCAL SYSTEM

Monographs in Economic Anthropology, No. 13

Edited by
Richard E. Blanton
Peter N. Peregrine
Deborah Winslow
Thomas D. Hall

Lanham • New York • London

Copyright © 1997 by
Society for Economic Anthropology
University Press of America,® Inc.
4720 Boston Way
Lanham, Maryland 20706

3 Henrietta Street
London, WC2E 8LU England

All rights reserved
Printed in the United States of America
British Cataloging in Publication Information Available

Co-published by arrangement with the Society for Economic
Anthropology

Library of Congress Cataloging-in-Publication Data

Economic analysis beyond the local system / edited by Richard E.
Blanton ... (et al.).
    p.   cm. --(Monographs in economic anthropology ; no. 13)
Includes bibliographical references and index.
1. Economic anthropology.   I. Blanton, Richard E. II. Series.
GN448.E257   1996   306.3--dc20   96-14148 CIP

ISBN 0-7618-0341-6 (cloth: alk. ppr.)
ISBN 0-7618-0342-4 (pbk: alk. ppr.)

⊖™ The paper used in this publication meets the minimum
requirements of American National Standard for information
Sciences—Permanence of Paper for Printed Library Materials,
ANSI Z39.48—1984

Contents

**Introduction: Economic Analysis Beyond the Local System--
and Back Again**
*Richard E. Blanton, Deborah Winslow, Peter N. Peregrine,
and Thomas D. Hall*   v

**Part I: Economic Analysis Beyond the Local System:
Archaeological and Historical Perspectives**

1. Main Assumptions and Variables for Economic Analysis
Beyond the Local System
Richard E. Blanton and Peter N. Peregrine   3

2. Macro-Scale Perspectives on Settlement and Production in
Ancient Oaxaca
Gary M. Feinman   13

3. The Millennium Before the "Long Sixteenth Century:"
How Many World-Systems Were There?
Thomas D. Hall   43

4. A Local Elite and Underdevelopment in a Peripheral
Economy: Iceland in the 18th-20th Centuries
E. Paul Durrenberger   71

**Part II: Finding the Global in the Local:
Contemporary Case Studies**

5. Finding the Global in the Local
Thomas D. Hall   87

6. Emerging Linkages in the World System and the
Challenge to Economic Anthropology
Richard R. Wilk   97

7. Fertility in Maragoli: The Global and the Local
Candice Bradley   109

8. Producing Agrarian Transformation at the Indonesian Periphery
Tania Murray Li   125

9. The Invisible Peasant
Donald W. Attwood   147

10. Historical Perspectives on Long Term Change: *Compadrazgo* Choice Patterns in Rural Paraguay
Christina Bolke Turner   171

Part III: Structural Adjustment Programs: Local Contexts for Global Policy

11. Anthropology and Structural Adjustment Programs
Deborah Winslow   197

12. Local-Global Interactions in Ghana's Structural Adjustment
Gracia Clark   209

13. Household Adaptations in a Regional Urban System: The Central Valleys of Oaxaca, Mexico
Arthur D. Murphy, Mary Winter, and Earl W. Morris   235

14. Structural Adjustment, Hometowns, and Local Development in Nigeria
Lillian Trager   255

15. Rural Workers and the Re-Adjustment of Egypt's Economy: Applying Régulation Theory to Anthropology
James Toth   291

Contributors   317

Introduction

Economic Analysis Beyond the Local System--and Back Again

Richard E. Blanton
Peter N. Peregrine
Deborah Winslow
Thomas D. Hall

Until recently, it seemed that anthropology's love affair with the community study might not survive the twentieth century. Anthropologists, in general, and economic anthropologists, in particular, called for more attention to geographically larger units of data collection and analysis that would hasten the development of regional and "global" anthropology (e.g., Ekholm and Friedman 1985). Along the way, the itinerant cultural brokers of Robert Redfield's great and little traditions gave way to the central places and nested regions of G. William Skinner's and Carol Smith's regional analysis, Immanuel Wallerstein's capitalist world-system, and, more recently, Appadurai's (1993) emergent postnational order.

The push towards greater geographical inclusiveness, while contributing productive analytical insights to anthropological study, appeared to make the households, neighborhoods, and communities of traditional anthropology increasingly irrelevant or old fashioned. It is probably germane that the main theoretical inspirations for the development of a global anthropology have not come from the pens of anthropological authors as much as from those of geographers, historians, economists, and historical sociologists. Wallerstein is one obvious example, but others making important contributions include Janet Abu-Lughod, Philip Curtin, Andre Gunder Frank, Barry K. Gills, Christopher Chase-Dunn, David Wilkinson, and Thomas D. Hall, many of whom are cited in the chapters of this book.

But as we end this century, and the first century of our discipline, the tide has turned again, leading out discipline in some ways back to its origins, although back with a difference. Now, many fewer researchers, whether archaeologists, ethnohistorians, or sociocultural anthropologists, conceive of their study areas or communities in terms of only local environmental adaptation, self-sufficiency, or in terms of "pure" local cultures (Rowlands [1992] makes the same point about language study). Nevertheless, the value of local-level studies has reasserted itself as many are finding that, rather to our collective anthropological relief, global processes are, simultaneously and necessarily, local ones. Cancian (1992) has gone so far as to declare himself a "localist." As he puts it, while community studies must be broadly framed and contextualized, still,

> ...local systems have their own logic and...generalizations about local life that are derived from principles of global political economy replace the limitations of earlier community studies with a different kind of oversimilification (Cancian 1992: 2).

Similarly, Carol Smith (1984: 224) pleaded for greater attention to the "regional structures, economic and political, on which global forces play." And William Roseberry (1989: 111) argues that "...an approach that attempts to explain everything in terms of the needs or dynamics of the capitalist core, or of the system as a whole,...[is] profoundly functionalist and reductive." Roseberry (1989:120) proposes that we move beyond "spatial and layer cake metaphors" and instead study relationships that transcend spatial boundaries, including "production domains" (such as plantations), and export commodities (as in his own work in Venzuelan coffee).

Roseberry (1989:126) concludes that anthropologists will rightfully tend to privilege the local, even while specifying its connections to other arenas. We agree with his assessment, so long as conclusions drawn from local systems are effectively brought into play with the aim of developing more robust theories of the global. At present, one of economic anthropology's most important tasks is exactly this kind critical evaluation of global theory that can come only with intensive field experience in local arenas. For example, economic anthropology is able to challenge world-system theorists who mistakenly claim that the expansion of capitalism "...has led to the destruction of 'natural economy' (i.e., economies with a dominant use-value production and limited trade relations)...in Third World countries" (Evers et al. 1984: 27). We can assert that this is not always so, and, further, we make the claim that an inability to understand local systems will lead to poor characterizations of larger ones.

The Essays in This Volume

The chapters of this volume were presented at the thirteenth annual meeting of the Society for Economic Anthropology, where our goal was to explore the current range of economic anthropology's varied contributions to understanding the articulations of global and local economic processes. For those looking for ways to connect, empirically, theoretically, or methodologically, their own local work with broader processes, the meeting's papers and posters offered a rich and varied source of ideas, literature sources, techniques, and examples. We believe this richness and variety is captured in the chapters of this book.

We have divided the papers into three sections, each with its own editorial introduction. The first section investigates prehistorically- or historically-known cases, and elucidates the consequences of interactions at varying scales of regions and world-systems. Gary Feinman, who has the most local focus, nevertheless points to important consequences for social change of interregional interaction between a prehispanic Mesoamerican core zone, the Valley of Oaxaca, Mexico, and the adjacent Ejutla Valley region. Paul Durrenberger examines how Iceland's position within a growing capitalist world-system influenced regional political and economic processes. Thomas Hall's chapter takes on the highest level as he seeks to understand interactions among the pre-capitalist world-systems of Afroeurasia as a whole.

The papers in the second section present contemporary studies of local outcomes of global processes. Overall, they take the position that, to paraphrase Rick Wilk in his chapter in this section, it is important to avoid subordinating the local to the global. Furthermore, connections to the outside are often indirect, multifaceted, and complex. Candice Bradley describes how contraceptive information is reinterpreted in the "borderland between the global and the local" in Kenya. Tania Murray Li shows that it is not just top-down development but also local strategies that are responsible for the creation of new relations of production at local and regional levels in Sulawesi, Indonesia. Using the example of sugarcane farmers in western India, Donald Attwood suggests that analysts have relegated to "invisibility" precisely those peasants whose use of extralocal commercial opportunities has made it possible for them to be successful as local economic actors. On the other hand, Christina Bolke Turner shows that the riskiness of extralocal ties may inhibit vertical relations for all but the well-to-do, as seen in her study of *compadrazgo* choice in rural Paraguay. These chapters cover the globe but develop in common the idea that we should not look only at how the global affects the local, but also at how extralocal linkages are developed and manipulated by local people for their own ends.

The third section's chapters present the findings of research on the local-level consequences of the macroeconomic programs know as structural adjustment programs. Over the last few decades, structural adjustment programs have been mandated by international aid agencies for developing nations. The four chapters in this section show how apparently monolithic policies in fact vary considerably from place to place, both because of the different national contexts in which they are implemented and because of the ways in which local people respond. Gracia Clark looks at the impacts of SAPs on women traders in Ghana; Arthur Murphy, Mary Winter, and Earl Morris consider the nature of household adaptations to national economic restructuring in the Valley of Oaxaca, Mexico; Lillian Trager describes the responses to SAPs in rural Nigeria; and James Toth considers how rural workers have reacted in Egypt.

Conclusion

While it is true that ideas stemming from the growing world-system and related literatures have been of great value to the intellectual growth of economic anthropology, it is also the case that economic anthropology has much to offer in turn. In particular, economic anthropologists who combine their "localist" research agendas with global theory-building will be in the best position to counter the excessively simplistic and deterministic ideas emanating from disciplines lacking the intensive research connections to local sites. We feel that a particular strength of this volume is the diversity of local to global interactions that is presented and analyzed, and that illustrates some of the complexities of long-distance interactive processes. Any scholar trying to understand such linkages will find something of value in this collection; we all learned much about the interconnections of local and supra-local processes in the course of editing this volume, and we are sure our readers will benefit from this book as much.

References

Appadurai, Arjun
   1993 Patriotism and its Futures. *Public Culture* 5(3):411-429.

Cancian, Frank
   1992 *The Decline of Community in Zinacantan*. Stanford: Stanford University Press.

Ekholm, Kasja and Jonathan Friedman
   1985 Towards a Global Anthropology. *Critique of Anthropology* 5(1):97-119.

Evers, Has-Dieter, Wolfgang Clauss, and Diana Wong
   1984 Subsistence Reproduction: A Framework for Analysis. In *Households and the World-Economy*. Joan Smith, Immanuel Wallerstein and Hans-Dieter Evers, eds. Pp. 23-36. Beverly Hills: Sage.

Roseberry, William
   1989 Peasants and the World. In *Economic Anthropology*. Stuart Plattner, ed. Pp 109-126. Stanford: Stanford University Press.

Rowlands, Michael
   1992 Childe and the Archaeology of Freedom. In *The Archaeology of V. Gordon Childe: Contemporary Perspectives*. David R. Harris, ed. Pp. 35-50. Chicago: University of Chicago Press.

Smith, Carol A.
   1984 Local History in Global Context: Social and Economic Transitions in Western Guatemala. *Comparative Studies in Society and History* 26, 2:193-228.

Part I

Economic Analysis Beyond the Local System: Archaeological and Historical Perspectives

1

Main Assumptions and Variables for Economic Analysis Beyond the Local System

Richard E. Blanton
Peter N. Peregrine

The three papers in this section illustrate how economic analyses beyond the local system are productively applied in several situations exhibiting vastly different degrees of scale and complexity, and based on varied data sources. The examples discussed range from Gary Feinman's examination of core-periphery interactions between adjacent regions of a Mesoamerican archaic state, to Thomas Hall's consideration of the large-scale interactions of the multicultural precapitalist Afro-Eurasian world-system, to Paul Durrenberger's analysis of a local elite and underdevelopment in Iceland. The juxtaposition of these three papers, drawing from related theoretical perspectives but analyzing sharply differing kinds of social formations, gives testament to the potential advantages for economic anthropology of further development of concepts, method, and theory along these lines.

Not all economic anthropologists would agree with this conclusion. There is currently a voluminous and busy discussion, at times becoming debate, concerning the degree to which anthropologists and other social scientists would benefit from paying increased attention to long-distance interactive processes (cf. Chase-Dunn and Hall, eds 1991; Frank and Gills 1993; Hall and Chase-Dunn 1993; Peregrine and Feinman 1996; Rowlands, Larsen, and Kristiansen 1987; Schortman and Urban, eds 1992). Adams (1974), Ekholm and Friedman (1985), Kohl (1978), McNeill (1991), Schneider (1977), and Schwartz (1963) are among those arguing in favor of the adoption of some kind an approach that can avoid an excessive bounding and reification of local systems. Historically, however, anthropologists have not wholeheartedly accepted any such view, and have failed, as a result, to adequately develop concepts and theory appropriate for this scale of human action.

Why has there been so little systematic theoretical development in economic (or other) analyses beyond the local system within anthropology? Certainly abundant evidence of the importance of intergroup interaction has been available to the discipline, even in some of anthropology's earliest research reports (e.g., Wheeler 1910). Malinowski's (1922) detailed analysis of the Kula exchange system is perhaps representative of our discipline's insufficient conceptual and theoretical development in addressing extra-group social processes. Here Malinowski describes in elaborate detail a "sociological mechanism of surpassing size and complexity" (p. 510), but in his concluding comments, he adopts a more localized orientation that explains the Kula system by reference to the desire for Kula objects (Ch. 22; cf. Schwartz 1963). Malinowski's use of what may be termed an "inward-out" approach (Blanton et al. 1993:218-19), that analyzes a complex intergroup process only from the perspective of the dynamics of a local system, rather than as a social system in its own right, did not lend itself to concept formation regarding the larger interactive system as a whole.

Similarly, we find it odd that among anthropology's most highly regarded ethnographic and ethnohistorical works there can be found sophisticated analyses of the sociocultural consequences of world-system incorporation, but like Malinowski's Kula study, they fail to contribute meaningfully to theory-building and concept development regarding the extra-local system. Prominent examples of this peculiar deficiency are found in the very influential group of studies of social and cultural transformations among Native American societies caught up in the emerging European world-system (Codere 1950; Jablow 1950; Leacock 1954; Lewis 1942; Mishkin 1940; Secoy 1953). Only recently have these and related examples been recast in the more comparatively and processually-oriented conceptual framework of world-system theory (Hall 1986, 1989:Ch. 2; Kardulias 1990).

At the same time, what we view as promising conceptual frameworks for intergroup interaction research were proposed, but promptly ignored by our discipline. We include the stimulating paper by Schwartz (1963), on what he calls "systems of areal integration" in Melanesia, and Alexander Lesser's concept of "social fields" (e.g., in Mintz 1985:92-99). Wolf (1982:6, 387) effectively criticizes anthropology's tendency to view local systems as strongly bounded entities. Strangely, however, after making this argument, he reverts to a mode of production analysis, another "inward-out" analytical framework; Mintz (1977) ultimately takes a similar position in his confusing critique of Wallerstein's world-system approach. Both Wolf and Mintz seem to be carrying forward an analytical strategy that elaborated on Steward's idea of cultural core and cultural ecology (Steward 1955:37), but applied to Puerto Rico (Mintz 1956; Steward et al. 1956; Wolf 1956). Here, local ecological factors obviously could not adequately explain a social system that was extensively influenced by interactions across its boundaries. In the Puerto Rico research, a solution was developed that preserved the culture core approach, in which extra-local interaction was viewed as a source of new environmental features to which local households and communities had to adapt (e.g., in the chapters by Wolf and Mintz). Again, as with Malinowski, this approach failed to develop any new insights regarding the extra-local economic system itself.

One aspect the argumentation about economic analysis beyond the local system is the question of the applicability of Wallerstein's concept of world-system, especially regarding its suitability outside the modern capitalist world-system (e.g., Chase-Dunn and Hall 1991, 1993; Kohl 1987; Peregrine 1996; Schneider 1977)(or even within capitalism, e.g., Wolf 1982:297-98; Mintz 1977). In Schneider's (1977:26) view, a world-system perspective "pushes social science toward an understanding of change in which Western and non-Western, traditional and modern, peoples are subject, if not to similar outcomes, then at least to similar laws" (Vincent [1990:Ch. 6] arrives at a similar conclusion for political anthropology). It is not our purpose here to elaborate on the world-system debate. We suggest that a family of distinct, but related, analytical frameworks require further study and refinement, each applicable to a category of long-distance interactive system and its characteristic social processes. We would include among the most important members of this family (although others could be mentioned) the following: "Tournament of value" (Appadurai 1986:21; cf. Blanton and Taylor 1995), "interaction sphere" (e.g., Yoffee 1993; and the related concept of "peer-polity interaction" [Renfrew and Cherry, eds 1986]), "trade diaspora" (Curtin 1984), "macroregion" (Skinner 1977a, 1977b), and a "world-system theory" modified for anthropological consumption (e.g., along the lines suggested by Abu-Lughod 1989; Blanton and Feinman 1984; Chase-Dunn and Hall 1991, 1993, 1994; and Schneider 1977).

The important point is that all members of this analytical family share a set of core assumptions, and analyze the interactions among certain key variables. The main shared assumption of economic analyses beyond the local system is simply that some features of any social formation may be the result of interactions across local-system boundaries. This need not imply that extra-local interaction is necessarily always the major source of socio-cultural change (e.g., as stated in Chase-Dunn and Hall 1994:258); we avoid this kind of paradigm-promoting assertion. Rather, as we see it, the degree to which external interaction brings about change will vary in time and space. But an external interactive approach avoids the fallacy of assuming that sociocultural change will always result primarily from endogenous causal factors, an assumption found in mode of production analysis, cultural ecology, "new" archaeology, neofunctionalism, and cultural materialism, among others. An intersocietal interactive approach simply requires that the analyst remains open to the possibility that important features of social formations and their cultural codes may be consequences of the activities of social actors behaving in cross-boundary contexts.

A related assumption of economic analysis beyond the local system is that many features of multi-cultural and multi-regional systems cannot be explained only from the inward-out perspective, i.e., only as manifestations of the dynamics of the constituent local systems writ large. Instead, economic analysis beyond the local system looks at processes peculiar to intergroup interaction, processes that are monitored through the investigation of variables that describe features integral to the larger interactive systems themselves. A list of relevant variables could be lengthy, indeed, but in the papers in this section several of the most important are addressed:

(a) *Boundedness.* Boundary variables are central to analyses beyond the local system (Blanton et al. 1993:18), but are rarely systematically treated by economic anthropologists (but see Chase-Dunn and Hall 1991:8-15, and Feinman's and Hall's chapters below). The nature and degree of boundedness of social formations, i.e., the degree to which across-boundary transactions and flows of material goods and information, and migration, are hindered or facilitated, varies in time and space, with attendant consequences for freedom of choice of economic actors and degree of political centralization (e.g., Kowalewski et al. 1983), among other possible outcomes.

(b) *Control of Boundary Transactions.* Related to boundedness is the degree to which cross-boundary transactions can be controlled by political and economic actors (e.g., the monopoly controls exercised in prestige-good systems as described by Peregrine [1992]). This variable is addressed in Durrenberger's chapter on Iceland.

(c) *Non-Local Sources of Power.* The degree to which wealth, power, and prestige vis-à-vis a local group can be developed and reproduced through manipulation of cross-boundary transactions relates to political centralization variables among others (e.g., Helms 1988; Peregrine 1992; Strathern 1969).

(d) *Incorporation.* The degree and nature of local-group incorporation in larger interactive systems is highly variable, resulting in differing outcomes both for "periphery" as well as "core" components of larger systems. This variability renders problematic overly-generalized concepts such as "periphery" or "dependency" (Hall 1986, 1989; Kardulias 1990; Schortman and Urban 1994). See Hall's chapter in this section for additional comments and sources on incorporation.

(e) *Forms of Labor Control.* Local patterns of labor mobilization may be highly influenced by the demands of production destined for cross-boundary flow (e.g., Wallerstein 1974:87, passim; cf. Durrenberger's chapter below).

(f) *Intergroup Division of Labor and Territorial Production Specializations.* The degree and types of division of labor and nature of production specializations between local systems reflect, to varying degrees, each local system's role in a larger interactive arena (Skinner 1977a; Wallerstein 1974:Ch. 6). Feinman's chapter in this section addresses this issue as it applies to an archaic state in Oaxaca, Mexico.

(g) *Interregional Inequality.* The degree of inequality among interactive social formations, i.e., the degree of core-periphery hierarchy development, is expressed as the degree of between-system political and economic hegemony, unequal exchange, and differential accumulation (e.g., Chase-Dunn and Hall 1991:18-21; Ekholm and Freidman 1993; Gills and Frank 1993). We suggest the use of the concept "world-system" in cases where a core-periphery hierarchy has developed, versus "interaction sphere" in cases of roughly coequal intersocietal interaction (cf. Yoffee 1993). Wallerstein (1974:Ch.1) makes the useful distinction between world-economies, with multiple independent polities engaged in a larger economic system ("interstate systems"), and world-empires, controlled by one polity (cf. Chase-Dunn and Hall 1991:6-8).

8 Economic Analysis Beyond the Local System

These and other variables related to economic analysis beyond the local system will present many difficulties in research practice. But economic anthropology has employed or developed a host of useful strategies for analyzing more localized aspects of economic behavior. New methods, concepts, and theory are required for analysis beyond the local system, but we are confident that economic anthropologists will creatively address the challenges inherent in this domain of economic process as they have in other domains.

References

Abu-Lughod, Janet L.
   1989 *Before European Hegemony: The World System, A.D. 1250-1350.* Oxford: Oxford University Press.

Adams, Robert Mc.
   1974 Anthropological Perspectives on Ancient Trade. *Current Anthropology* 15:239-258.

Appadurai, Arjun
   1986 Introduction: Commodities and the Politics of Value. In *The Social Life of Things: Commodities in Cultural Perspective.* Arjun Appadurai, ed. Pp. 3-63. Cambridge: Cambridge University Press.

Blanton, Richard E., and Gary M. Feinman
   1984 The Mesoamerican World-system. *American Anthropologist* 86:673-682.

Blanton, Richard E., Stephen A. Kowalewski, Gary M. Feinman, and Laura M. Finsten
   1993 *Ancient Mesoamerica: A Comparison of Change in Three Regions. Second Revised Edition.* Cambridge: Cambridge University Press.

Blanton, Richard E., and Jody Taylor
   1995 Patterns of Exchange and the Social Reproduction of Pigs in Highland New Guinea: Their Relevance to Questions about the Origins and Evolution of Agriculture. *Journal of Archaeological Research* 3:113-145.

Chase-Dunn, Christopher, and Thomas D. Hall
   1991 Conceptualizing Core/Periphery Hierarchies for Comparative Study. In *Core/Periphery Relations in Precapitalist Worlds.* Christopher Chase-Dunn and Thomas D. Hall, eds. Pp. 5-44. Boulder: Westview Press.
   1993 Comparing World-systems: Concepts and Working Hypotheses. *Social Forces* 71:851-86.
   1994 The Historical Evolution of World-systems. *Sociological Inquiry* 64:3:257-80.

Chase-Dunn, Christopher, and Thomas D. Hall, eds.
  1991 *Core/Periphery Relations in Precapitalist Worlds.* Boulder: Westview Press.
Codere, Helen
  1950 *Fighting With Property: A Study of Kwakiutl Potlatching and Warfare, 1792-1930.* American Ethnological Society Monograph 18. New York: J. J. Augustin.
Curtin, Phillip
  1984 *Cross-cultural Trade in World History.* Cambridge: Cambridge University Press.
Ekholm, Kasja and Jonathan Friedman
  1985 Towards a Global Anthropology. *Critique of Anthropology* 5:97-119.
  1993 "Capital" Imperialism and Exploitation in Ancient World Systems. In *The World System: Five Hundred Years or Five Thousand?* Andre G. Frank and Barry K. Gills, eds. Pp. 59-80. London: Routledge.
Frank, Andre G. and Barry K. Gills, eds.
  1993 *The World System: Five Hundred Years or Five Thousand?* London: Routledge.
Gills, Barry K. and Andre G. Frank
  1993 The Cumulation of Accumulation. In *The World System: Five Hundred Years or Five Thousand?* Andre G. Frank and Barry K. Gills, eds. Pp. 81-114. London: Routledge.
Hall, Thomas D.
  1986 Incorporation in the World-system: Toward a Critique. *American Sociological Review* 51:390-402.
  1989 *Social Change in the Southwest, 1350-1880.* Lawrence, Kansas: University Press of Kansas.
Hall, Thomas D. and Christopher Chase-Dunn
  1993 The World-systems Perspective and Archaeology: Forward into the Past. *Journal of Archaeological Research* 1:121-43.
Helms, Mary W.
  1988 *Ulysses' Sail.* Cambridge: Cambridge University Press.
Jablow, Joseph
  1950 *The Cheyenne in Plains Indian Trade Relations, 1795-1840.* Monographs of the American Ethnological Society 19. Seattle: University of Washington Press.
Kardulias, P. Nick
  1990 Fur Production as Specialized Activity in a World System: Indians in the North American Fur Trade. *American Indian Culture and Research Journal* 14:25-60.
Kohl, Philip L.
  1978 The Balance of Trade in Southwestern Asia in the Mid-third Millennium. *Current Anthropology* 19:463-92.

1987 The Use and Abuse of World-systems Theory: The Case of the Pristine West Asian State. In *Advances in Archaeological Method and Theory, Volume 11.* Michael B. Schiffer, ed. Pp. 1-36. San Diego: Academic Press.

Kowalewski, Stephen A., Richard E. Blanton, Gary M. Feinman, and Laura M. Finsten
1983 Boundaries, Scale, and Internal Organization. *Journal of Anthropological Archaeology* 2:32-56.

Leacock, Eleanor
1954 *The Montagnais "Hunting Territory" and the Fur Trade.* American Anthropological Association Memoir 78. Menasha, Wisconsin. American Anthropological Association.

Lewis, Oscar
1942 *The Effects of White Contact Upon Blackfoot Culture: With Special Reference to the Role of the Fur Trade.* Monographs of the American Ethnological Society 6. New York: J. J. Augustin.

Malinowski, Bronislaw
1922 *Argonauts of the Western Pacific.* London: Routledge.

McNeill, William H.
1991 *The Rise of the West: A History of the Human Community.* Chicago: University of Chicago Press.

Mintz, Sidney W.
1956 Cañamelar: The Subculture of a Rural Sugar Plantation Proletariat. In *The People of Puerto Rico.* Julian Steward, et al., eds. Pp. 314-417. Urbana: University of Illinois Press.
1977 The So-called World System: Local Initiative and Local Response. *Dialectical Anthropology* 2:253-70.

Mintz, Sidney W., ed.
1985 *History, Evolution, and the Concept of Culture: Selected Papers of Alexander Lesser.* Cambridge: Cambridge University Press.

Mishkin, Bernard
1940 *Rank and Warfare Among the Plains Indians.* Monographs of the American Ethnological Society 3. Seattle: University of Washington Press.

Peregrine, Peter
1992 *Mississippian Evolution: A World-System Perspective.* Madison: Prehistory Press.
1996 Introduction: Archaeology and World-systems Theory. In *Pre-Columbian World-systems*, Peter Peregrine and Gary Feinman, eds. Pp. 1-11. Madison: Prehistory Press.

Peregrine, Peter and Gary Feinman, eds.
1996 *Pre-Columbian World-systems.* Madison: Prehistory Press.

Renfrew, Colin R. and John F. Cherry, eds.
  1986 *Peer Polity Interaction and Socio-political Change.* Cambridge: Cambridge University Press.
Rowlands, Michael, Mogens Larsen, and Kristian Kristiansen, eds.
  1987 *Centre and Periphery in the Ancient World.* Cambridge: Cambridge University Press.
Schneider, Jane
  1977 Was There a "Pre-capitalist" World-system? *Peasant Studies* 6:20-9.
Schortman, Edward M. and Patricia A. Urban
  1994 Living on the Edge: Core/Periphery Relations in Ancient Southeastern Mesoamerica. *Current Anthropology* 35:401-30.
Schortman, Edward M. and Patricia A. Urban, eds.
  1992 *Resources, Power, and Interregional Interaction.* New York: Plenum.
Schwartz, Theodore
  1963 Systems of Areal Integration: Some Considerations Based on the Admiralty Islands of Northern Melanesia. *Anthropological Forum* 1:56-97.
Secoy, Frank R.
  1953 *Changing Military Patterns on the Great Plains.* Monographs of the American Ethnological Society 21. Locust Valley, New York: J. J. Augustin.
Skinner, G. William
  1977a Regional Urbanization in Nineteenth-Century China. In *The City in Late Imperial China.* G. William Skinner, ed. Pp. 211-49. Stanford: Stanford University Press.
  1977b Cities and the Hierarchy of Local Systems. In *The City in Late Imperial China.* G. William Skinner, ed. Pp. 273-351. Stanford: Stanford University Press.
Steward, Julian H.
  1955 *Theory of Culture Change.* Urbana: University of Illinois Press.
Steward, Julian H., Robert A. Manners, Eric R. Wolf, Elena Padilla Seda, Sidney W. Mintz, and Raymond L. Scheele, eds.
  1956 *The People of Puerto Rico: A Study in Social Anthropology.* Urbana: University of Illinois Press.
Strathern, Andrew
  1969 Finance and Production: Two Strategies in New Guinea Highland Exchange Systems. *Oceania* 40:42-67.
Vincent, Joan
  1990 *Anthropology and Politics: Visions, Traditions, and Trends.* Tucson: University of Arizona Press.
Wallerstein, Immanuel
  1974 *The Modern World-system: Capitalist Agriculture and the Origins of the European World-economy in the Sixteenth Century.* New York: Academic Press.

Wheeler, Gerald C.
  1910 *The Tribe, and Intertribal Relations in Australia.* London: John Murray.
Wolf, Eric R.
  1956 San José: Subcultures of a "Traditional" Coffee Municipality. In *The People of Puerto Rico.* Julian Steward, et al., eds. Pp. 171-264. Urbana: University of Illinois Press.
  1982 *Europe and the People Without History.* Berkeley: University of California Press.
Yoffee, Norman
  1993 Mesopotamian Interaction Spheres. In *Early Stages in the Evolution of Mesopotamian Civilization.* Norman Yoffee and Jeffrey J. Clark, eds. Pp. 257-70. Tucson: University of Arizona Press.

2

Macro-Scale Perspectives on Settlement and Production in Ancient Oaxaca

Gary M. Feinman

Introduction

Eleven years ago at the Second Annual Meeting of the Society for Economic Anthropology, Richard Blanton and I (Blanton and Feinman 1984) presented a paper on the Mesoamerican world system that represents an early effort to conceptualize prehispanic Mesoamerica at the macro-regional scale. Our central conclusion was that ancient Mesoamerica could not be adequately understood if examined only at the scale of the region or polity, and that, characteristic of a world economy, systemically important economic and behavioral linkages occurred outside political boundaries. Furthermore, in contrast to Wallerstein's vision of the 16th-century world economy, many of the significant long-distance, macro-scale connections in ancient Mesoamerica were seen to involve the transfer of symbolically imbued, labor-intensive prestige goods rather than the movement of basic necessities, such as food and fuel. As with most prior and subsequent discussions of this topic (e.g. Blanton et al. 1992; Feinman and Nicholas 1991a; Pailes and Whitecotton 1979; Schortman and Urban 1987), Blanton and I drew heavily on ethnohistoric materials. However, because of the scale of inquiry and the nature of the documentary data, our empirical perspective was necessarily broad-brush, a bit anecdotal, and was focused almost exclusively on late prehispanic times.

The present examination takes a spatially narrower and explicitly more diachronic perspective. The intent is to investigate changing political and economic interconnections in ancient Mesoamerica at a scale larger than the agricultural sustaining area, the polity, or the physiographic region. Because the focus is on temporal shifts, this analysis cannot rely on documentary sources alone, and so must draw on the interpretation of the archaeological record. More specifically, the geographic focus is the Valley of Oaxaca and the neighboring region to the south, the Ejutla Valley (Figure 2.1).[1] The analytical aim is to examine the changing economic interconnections between segments or subregions of this valley system as political boundaries in the region shifted with the vacillating fortunes of the ancient polity centered at Monte Albán. Over the past twenty-plus years, Richard Blanton, Stephen Kowalewski, Laura Finsten, Linda Nicholas, and I have conducted a series of systematic archaeological surveys that have fully covered this more than 2500 km^2 study area, recording, mapping, and surface collecting thousands of archaeological sites (Blanton 1978; Blanton et al. 1982, 1993; Feinman and Nicholas 1990a; Kowalewski et al. 1989). These findings and their subsequent analysis constitute the primary empirical foundation for the present study, and much of this discussion stems directly from the thoughts, inspirations, and physical effort of my Oaxaca colleagues.[2]

Theoretical Background

At this point, the reader might fairly question why this discussion, focused on a study region that is several orders of magnitude smaller than the ancient Mesoamerica world, belongs in volume aimed at understanding past and present macro-regional processes. While admittedly this analysis is not aimed explicitly at that larger scale, the case to be examined is argued to have key theoretical implications for a suite of issues that are central to current archaeological debates concerning the study of regions and macro-regions (e.g. Chase-Dunn 1992; Chase-Dunn and Hall, eds 1991; Frank [with comments] 1993; Kohl 1989). At the most basic level, this examination, in conjunction with a series of earlier studies that also probe ancient Oaxacan economic relations (Feinman and Nicholas 1991b; Kowalewski et al. 1983; Kowalewski and Finsten 1983), illustrates how systematic archaeological observations can be used to reconstruct prehispanic patterns of production and exchange. Although many archaeologists might consider this aim obvious or trivial, it clearly is a matter of great concern to colleagues in other disciplines who also are engaged in the "world systems" debate (see for example comments in Frank 1993).

More importantly, the relations of production and exchange in the Oaxaca-Ejutla region during the prehispanic era are argued neither to be temporally constant nor directly reflective of resource distributions. The illustration of these diachronic shifts is important since it serves to dampen the implicit notion of a "natural economy" that worked in prehispanic times and was somehow conditioned principally by local resource distributions (rather than by relations of power). The findings from this study indicate that complex economic interdependencies developed early on between settlement clusters in the study region. The political relationships between these demographic clusters also appear to have been complex and variable. Thus, while important economic interconnections were not strictly local (or reflective of resource distributions), it is not a simple matter to attribute these interactions as being internal or external to a neatly defined system, polity, or region.

The nature of the relationship between extra-regional interaction and intra-regional organization also is considered. This association is found to be neither simple nor straightforward. However, the era of greatest political integration does coincide with a heightened concern for defense (boundedness) of the physiographic region (Kowalewski et al. 1983). Alternatively, the time of greatest economic dependencies, which crosscut intra-regional political divisions, is marked by heavy flows (permeability) outside the region. Both of these phases fall toward the end of the prehispanic sequence, so a general temporal trend toward greater boundary activity is evidenced, although the nature of those outside interactions shift.

This analysis therefore represents a preliminary effort to probe and empirically address the issue of "systemness" that has been raised in much recent macro-scale research (e.g. Chase-Dunn 1992, 1993). The relevant issues include: what kinds and intensities of interaction define social and economic units, do political and economic entities and boundaries necessarily overlap, how are these entities in turn then interconnected, and how do the mechanisms of interdependence vary/change over time and across space? It is not presumed that political and economic linkages were necessarily coterminous in the prehispanic world, or that physiographic boundaries necessarily define stable cultural or economic units. This investigation also takes a more continuous (in contrast to a simple binary) view of the opposition between autonomy and interdependence. Significantly, this more graduated perspective appears more in line with the complex and temporally fluid manners in which ancient Mesoamerican populations were indeed interlinked (see Marcus 1993). The aforementioned questions of "systemness" cannot be

16 *Economic Analysis Beyond the Local System*

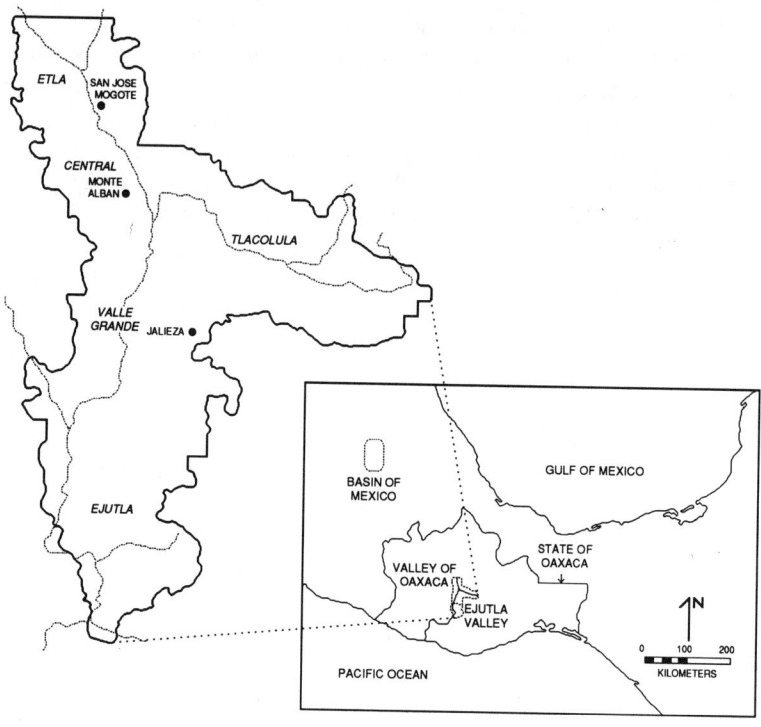

Figure 2.1: The Valleys of Oaxaca and Ejutla, with sites and places mentioned in the text.

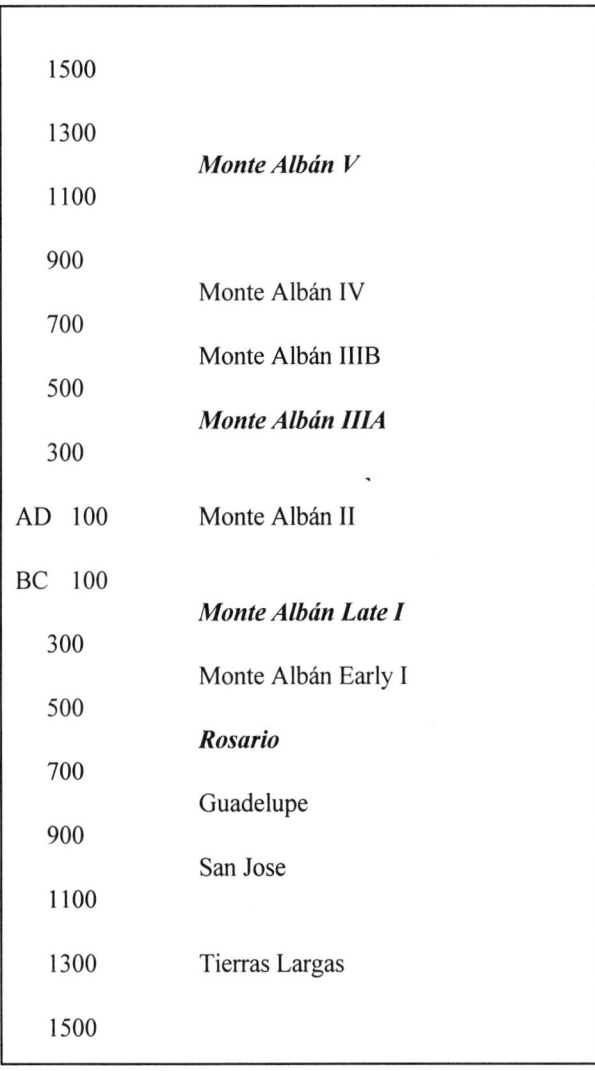

Figure 2.2: Chronological Sequence of Phases in the Central Valleys of Oaxaca, with phases under discussion in bold type.

18 *Economic Analysis Beyond the Local System*

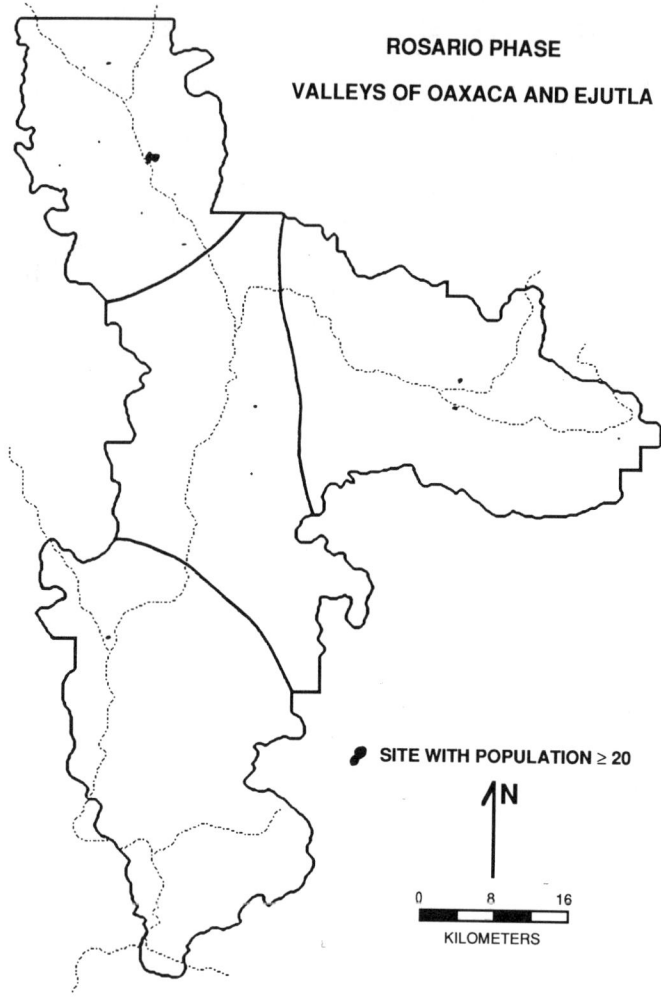

Figure 2.3: Boundaries of Rosario Phases Settlement Clusters, based on shatter zones and the location of larger sites.

adequately answered here, but by re-framing these issues they can at least be more adequately addressed.

Empirical Foundations

Given the intended focus on change in an ancient political economy, little space is devoted here to a discussion of the methodological rigors or limitations of regional archaeological survey, or a justification of the complex assumptions and tedious calculations that lie behind many of the analyses discussed, or to the elucidation of the full suite of theoretical underpinnings relevant to each synthesized investigation. Detailed discussions on these matters are readily available elsewhere (Blanton et al. 1982; Feinman and Nicholas 1987; Kowalewski et al. 1989; Nicholas 1989). Rather, this work describes and compares the shifting nature and degree of economic interdependence between spatial and political sub-units of the Valleys of Oaxaca and Ejutla during four prehispanic phases (the Rosario phase, Monte Albán Late I, Monte Albán IIIA, and Monte Albán V)(Figure 2.2). By focusing on just four phases, this analysis does not pretend to capture the full extent of diachronic complexity in ancient Oaxaca; however, the discussed chronological periods are representative of four longer temporal modes that have been used to characterize the entire prehispanic regional sequence (Kowalewski et al. 1989:507-518).

This discussion begins with the Rosario phase (Figure 2.3), which follows by roughly a millennium the advent of sedentary village life in the Valley of Oaxaca and immediately predates the foundation of hilltop Monte Albán (Flannery and Marcus, eds 1983). Although this early era is not a major focus in this paper, its examination establishes a basis for the valley-wide transitions that followed, with the establishment of the ancient Oaxacan core center at Monte Albán in period I. The size, monumentality, and geographic extent of this center expanded during the Classic period in Monte Albán IIIA. Discussion of the Rosario phase also serves to illustrate that the study region did not simply decompose (following the fall of Monte Albán) into the same spatially defined settlement sub-units that existed prior to the center's foundation. This latter point becomes clear when the organization of the region during Monte Albán V (after the decline of Monte Albán and immediately prior to Spanish conquest) is considered.

20 *Economic Analysis Beyond the Local System*

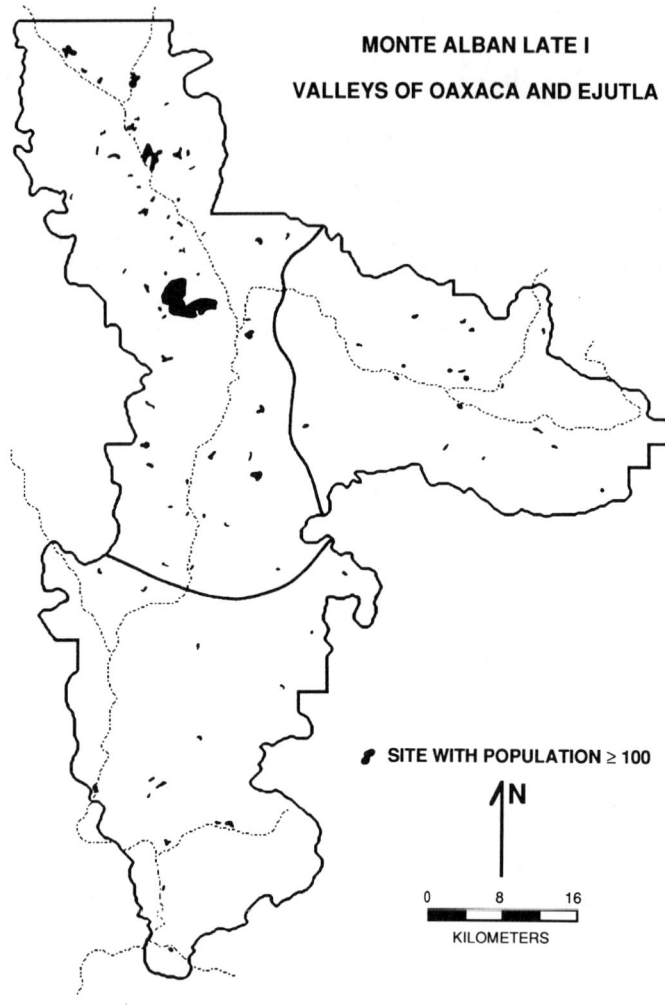

Figure 2.4: Boundaries of Monte Albán Late I Settlement Clusters, based on shatter zones and the location of large sites.

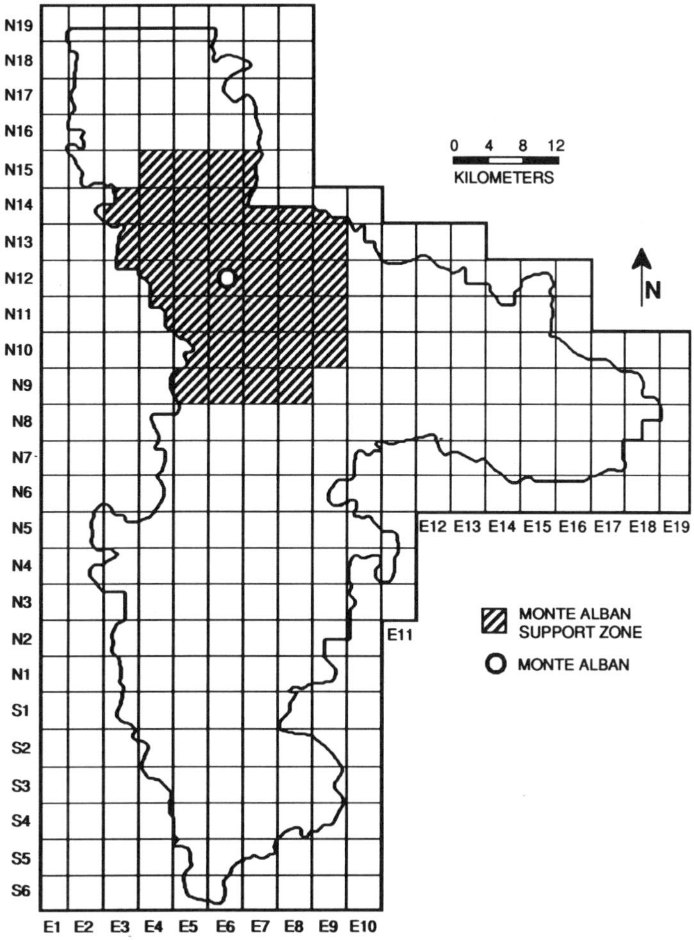

Figure 2.5: Areal Extent of Monte Albán's Agricultural Support Zone in Late I.

22 Economic Analysis Beyond the Local System

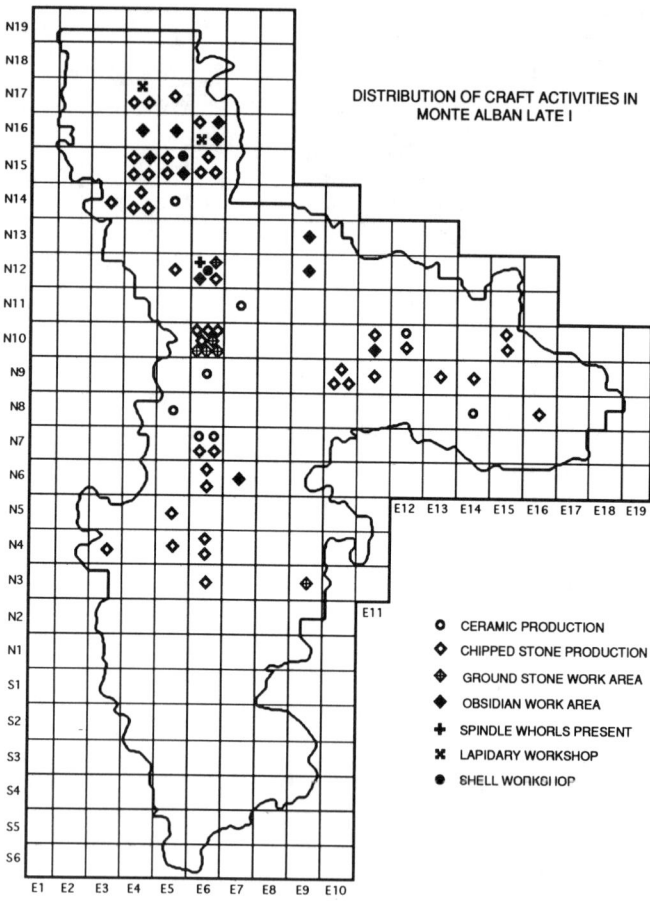

Figure 2.6: Distribution of Craft Activities in the Valleys of Oaxaca and Ejutla in Monte Albán Late I.

In its discussion of prior regional archaeological research from Oaxaca-Ejutla, this study draws most heavily on the evidence for settlement distributions and economic specialization. More specifically, to examine the former, modified nearest neighbor procedures are employed to define settlement clusters in the study region. Although the results (e.g., Figure 2.3) closely approximate prior findings (Kowalewski 1990; Kowalewski et al. 1989), minor differences in cluster definition are generated with the prior works by the secondary weight given to the distribution of population centers in this study. Previous analyses, which had slightly different analytical goals, followed strict nearest neighbor procedures more closely. Because of the interest in political units, the location of centers was considered relevant here. The examination of economic specialization draws most heavily on population-land use calculations (e.g. Feinman and Nicholas 1992a) as well as on the distributions of surface evidence for specific craft production activities, like pottery manufacture (Feinman 1980; Feinman and Nicholas 1991b, 1992b).

Rosario Phase (Middle Formative)

The settlement pattern of the Rosario phase culminated almost 1000 years during which the primate center of San José Mogote, situated in the Etla (or northern) arm of the valley dominated the region (Figure 2.1). During this millennium, demographic growth was rather slow, as settlement concentrated in and around the primate head town. Regionally, population was grouped into three settlement clusters with a sizable vacant zone in the center of the valley (Figure 2.3). The cluster around San José was much larger than the other two, making the regional demographic spread rather uneven.

Human-land calculations, which have been conducted primarily by Steve Kowalewski (1980, 1982) and Linda Nicholas (1989; cf. Feinman and Nicholas 1987, 1990b, 1992a), provide a key basis for subsequent discussions of the region's agricultural potential, the observed settlement patterns, and agricultural surpluses. In contrast to the later valley center, Monte Albán, the populace of San José Mogote could have supplied itself with sufficient food from the immediate vicinity (the land within 2-3 km of the site) (see Feinman and Nicholas 1987: Figure 4.11d). The site was situated on one of several pockets of rich alluvial land that are distributed along the valley floor (see Nicholas 1989: Figures 14.1 and 14.6). However, the lopsided population distribution in the valley was not predicated by the location of agrarian resources alone, as the other areas of productive land were sparsely settled at this time. A key point is that, not only were the agrarian resources needed to produce large agricultural surpluses located around San José Mogote, but that the human labor necessary to produce these surpluses also was concentrated around this large settlement (Feinman and Nicholas 1987).

For the most part, evidence for Rosario-phase craft specialization is skimpy and largely comes from San José Mogote. Craft production was focused on higher-status goods and ritual items, such as shell ornaments, magnetite mirrors, and perhaps decorated ceramic serving bowls, which were traded both inside and outside the study region. Access to exotic goods, such as coastal products and obsidian, as well as the information that circulated with them, may have been a factor that attracted households to cluster near San José Mogote (Feinman 1991). The explicit nature of the relationship between the settlement clusters situated in each valley arm remains sketchily known, although there are few indicators for tight economic interdependence.

Monte Albán Late I (Late Formative)

By Monte Albán Late I, several centuries later, the regional population was more than twenty-five times what it had been in the Rosario phase (Feinman and Nicholas 1990a). Monte Albán was established at the hub of the three arms of the Valley of Oaxaca in the area that formally was vacant. The core of the Monte Albán polity was the northern or Etla arm, the central area, and the northern Valle Grande (Figure 2.4). The population of this core was roughly forty times the size of the Rosario phase San José Mogote population cluster (Figure 2.3).

In Late I, most of the region's largest settlements and the sites with the most elaborate architecture were situated in the core cluster near Monte Albán. To the east, north, and south, the core area's largest sites form two rings around this central site. The outermost of these sites in the ring more-or-less define the core, as the spacing and density of settlement drops off to the south and east (Figure 2.4). Sites in the ring closest to Monte Albán lacked formal architectural groupings, while those further from the capital had unusually large amounts of construction with formal and closed plazas (Blanton 1989). Perhaps the inhabitants of the sites closer to Monte Albán generally participated in civic-ceremonial activities at the center. The latter (outer ring) sites may have served and replicated civic-ceremonial activities that were enacted at Monte Albán.

Based on land-use calculations, Monte Albán's population was too large to be adequately supported only by food grown in its immediate 2-3 km catchment area (Nicholas 1989:482, Figure 14.7). However, the site could have received sufficient foodstuffs by drawing surplus from the rest of the core zone as well. Interestingly, the core area (Figure 2.4) corresponds closely to a hypothetical transport-efficient model of the support zone—the area surrounding Monte Albán with sufficient labor and agrarian resources to provide for its inhabitants (Figure 2.5).

Most of the valley foothill or piedmont areas that experienced intensive settlement in Late I also lie within this core zone (see Kowalewski et al. 1989: Figure 6.3). In the Valley of Oaxaca, farming piedmont areas is riskier than alluvial farming. Yet with adequate moisture and labor, these areas can produce large periodic surpluses. Thus, piedmont farmers in Oaxaca would have been intermittently dependent, and then at other times able to produce large occasional agrarian surpluses. As a means of obtaining surplus production, piedmont occupation fostered increased intra-regional exchange, as areas with periodic deficits would have required occasional support from neighboring settlements where surplus production was produced (Blanton et al. 1993; Kowalewski 1980). The direction and degree of dependency would have shifted with the rainfall.

Use of the *comal*, or tortilla griddle, which signals a corresponding shift in household labor and intensification strategies (Blanton et al. 1981:71-72; Feinman 1986; Feinman et al. 1984), also was largely limited to the core zone. Elsewhere, greater tortilla consumption during Monte Albán I is argued to signal both increased labor specialization within households and a more mobile labor force that likely was producing (at least periodically) away from home (see also Isaac 1986; Winter 1984). Specialized production of basic goods, like pottery and chipped stone, also increased markedly relative to pre-Monte Albán times, with such activities found principally at settlements inside the core zone (Figure 2.6). Relative to the Rosario phase, there were major shifts in the volume and mechanisms of exchange within the core.

In contrast with the valley center, the rest of the region was less densely inhabited (Feinman and Nicholas 1990a). There was only a single large center in Tlacolula and no such places in the extreme southern arm or Ejutla (see Figure 2.4). Excluding Monte Albán, all sites positioned in defensible locations were either situated on the edge of the core zone or outside it (in Tlacolula or the southern Valle Grande). The specific nature of the relationship between the valley core and the remainder of the region (Tlacolula, southern Valle Grande, and Ejutla) remains somewhat nebulous. At this point, it seems highly unlikely that the non-core zones were entirely autonomous of Monte Albán, since there were no centers comparable to Monte Albán (in size or monumentality) elsewhere in the valley. In fact, a recent compositional analysis of period I grayware bowls indicates that ceramics made near Monte Albán were traded at least as far south as Ejutla (Banker et al. 1992). Yet, the intensity of the linkages (economic and political interdependency) between Monte Albán and the core zone were far greater than the nature of its connections to areas outside the core. Tlacolula, the southern Valle Grande, and Ejutla may have been weakly integrated into Monte Albán for reasons of defense or long distance exchange.

During Monte Albán I, new economic, political, and ideological mechanisms of integration were introduced in Oaxaca with the advent of novel funerary rituals (tombs), effigy vessels tied to supernatural forces, new public buildings, changes in storage technology, and distinct modes of exchange (Feinman et al. 1984; Flannery and Marcus.eds 1983; Kowalewski et al. 1989). Most of these changes have been noted at Monte Albán or at sites in the core zone. New data are necessary to evaluate how these strategies of interconnection may have varied in implementation over space.

Monte Albán IIIA (Early Classic)

In Monte Albán IIIA, Monte Albán politically integrated the study region to the greatest degree evidenced during the prehispanic era. The central cluster surrounding Monte Albán was larger in extent than during any other phase (Figure 2.7). Once again, this core zone was composed primarily of the central area, Etla, and now most of the region's southern arm. Ejutla remained outside this core zone, although it was no longer a sparsely inhabited frontier. The eastern (Tlacolula) arm of Oaxaca also remained outside the core cluster, but was more closely linked to it than indicated for Late I. Interestingly, Tlacolula may have been interconnected with the core through the region's second largest settlement (Jalieza), rather than directly through Monte Albán. Regionally, population was distributed more evenly than in Late I. Yet, as might be expected (given the cluster map), the lattice of centers was more intricate and multi-tiered in the core zone than in Tlacolula and Ejutla, where these subregions were dominated to a greater degree by a single center or cluster of centers.

Comparable to the period I pattern, the most transport-efficient agricultural support zones for both Monte Albán and Jalieza lie almost entirely inside the core cluster (Figure 2.8). Yet in contrast to earlier phases, there is far more evidence for craft production, and much of it occurred in the Tlacolula arm (Figure 2.9). These patterns signal increased exchange and interdependence between the settlement clusters; a point that also is evident from recent land use analyses of the valleys of Oaxaca and Ejutla (Feinman and Nicholas 1992a). In line with Blanton's (1985) more general model of highland Mesoamerican cores, agricultural production apparently was emphasized close to the urban core, while labor-intensive high-status crafts were primarily practiced at considerable distances from Monte Albán (in Tlacolula and Ejutla)(see Figure 2.9). For example, recent excavations at the Ejutla site (Feinman and Nicholas 1993), where marine shell ornaments (as well as cotton and greenstone) were worked, hint at important interpenetrating exchange links outside the valley during the Classic period.

A network of defensible hilltop terrace sites ringed roughly half of the study region in Monte Albán IIIA (Figure 2.10). Most of these sites were situated around the edge of Tlacolula, and along the eastern and western sides of the study region's southern extension. For the most part, these sites faced outside, shielding Tlacolula, Ejutla, and the southern part of the core cluster from areas beyond the valley. Yet, two lines of defensible sites also were located inside the valley. One of these subdivides Tlacolula from the eastern Valle Grande. The other separates Ejutla from the southern edge of the Valle Grande core. Both of these lines of defensible sites are almost coterminous with (and parallel) the divisions drawn between settlement clusters, and indicate that the political integration of the core cluster with the rest of the region may not have been entirely secure.

28 *Economic Analysis Beyond the Local System*

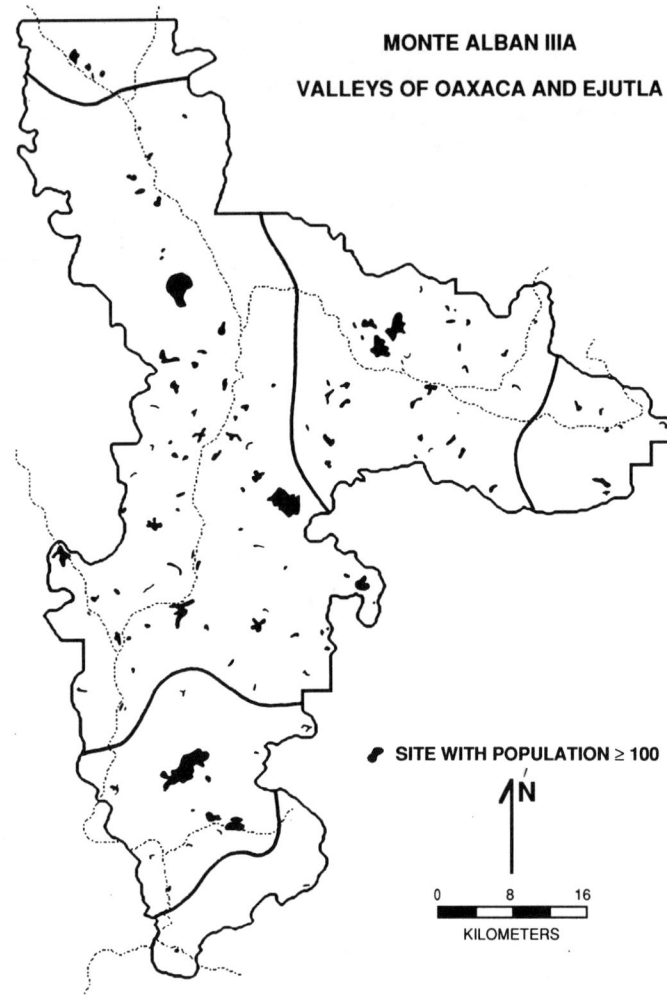

Figure 2.7: Boundaries of Monte Albán IIIA Settlement Clusters, based on shatter zones and the location of large sites.

Settlement and Production in Ancient Oaxaca 29

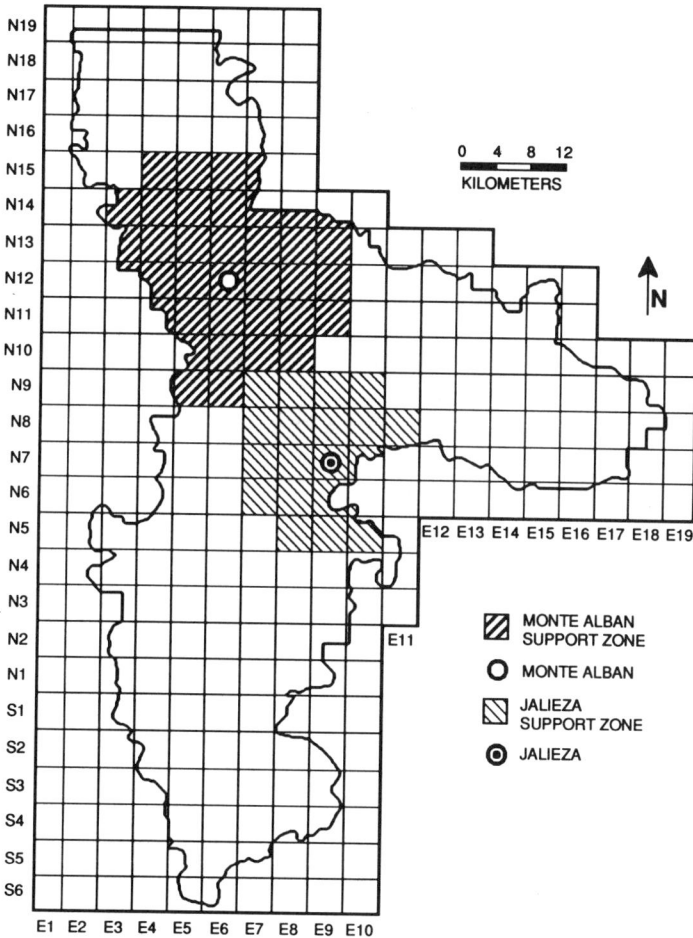

Figure 2.8: Area Extent of Agricultural Support Zones for Monte Albán and Jalieza Monte Albán IIIA.

30 *Economic Analysis Beyond the Local System*

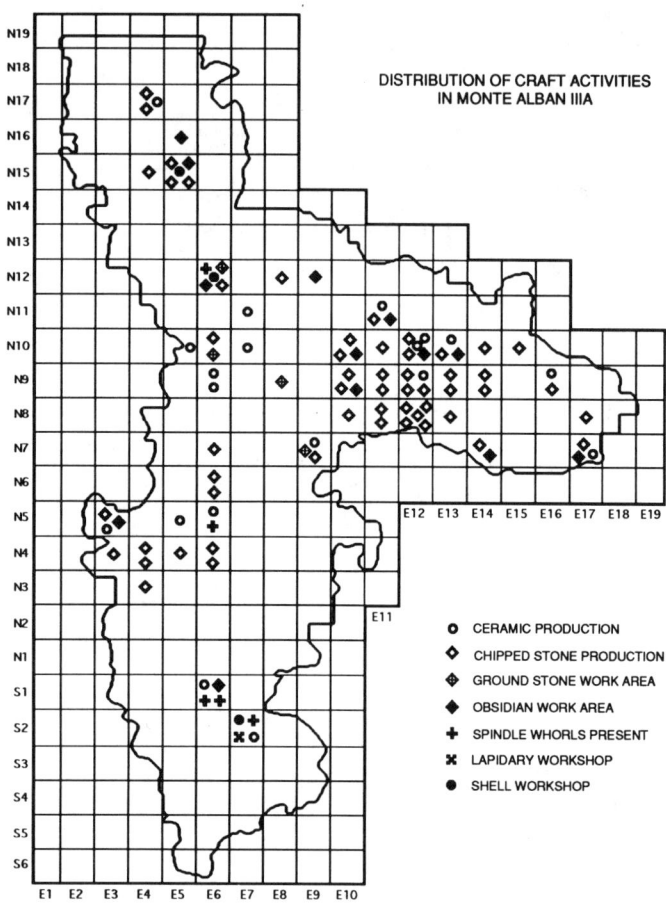

Figure 2.9: Distribution of Craft Activities in the Valleys of Oaxaca and Ejutla in Monte Albán IIIA.

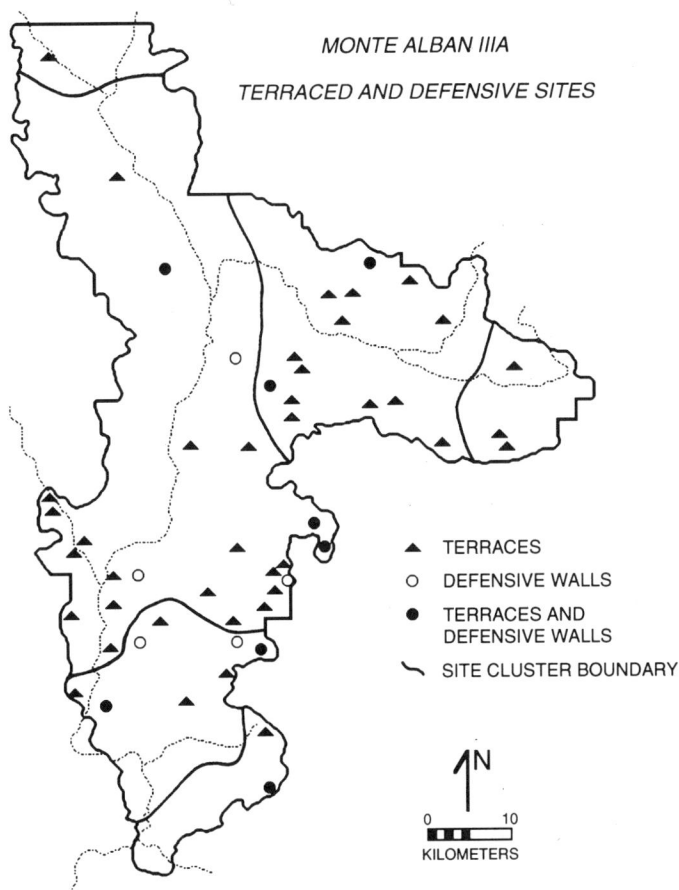

Figure 2.10: Settlement Cluster Boundaries and the Location of Hilltop Terraced and Defensive Sites in Monte Albán IIIA.

32 Economic Analysis Beyond the Local System

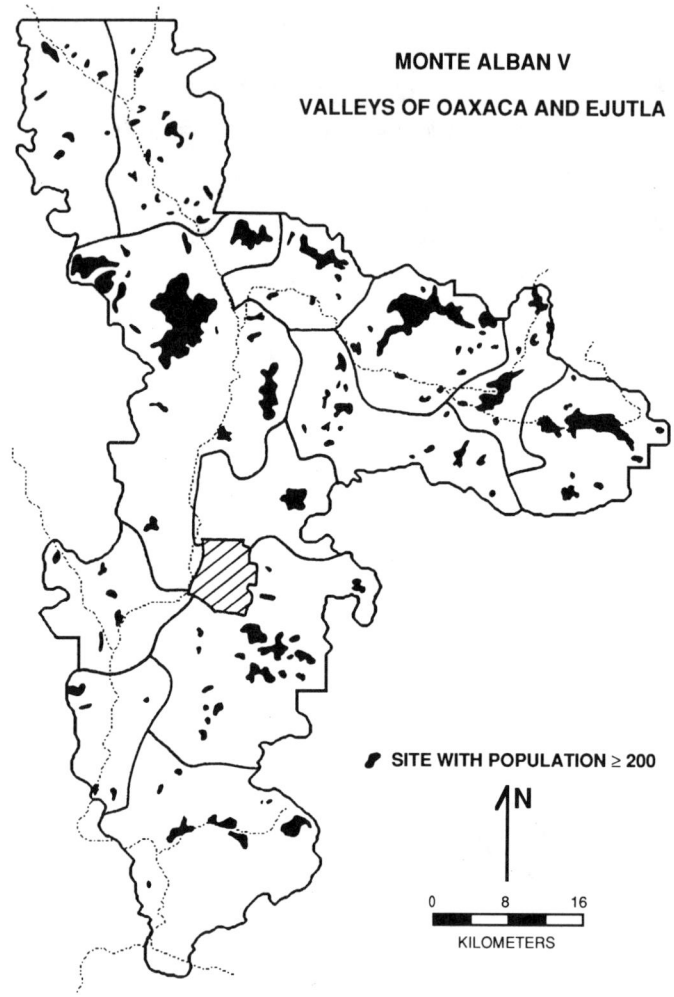

Figure 2.11: Boundaries of Monte Albán V Settlement Clusters, based on shatter zones and the location of large sites.

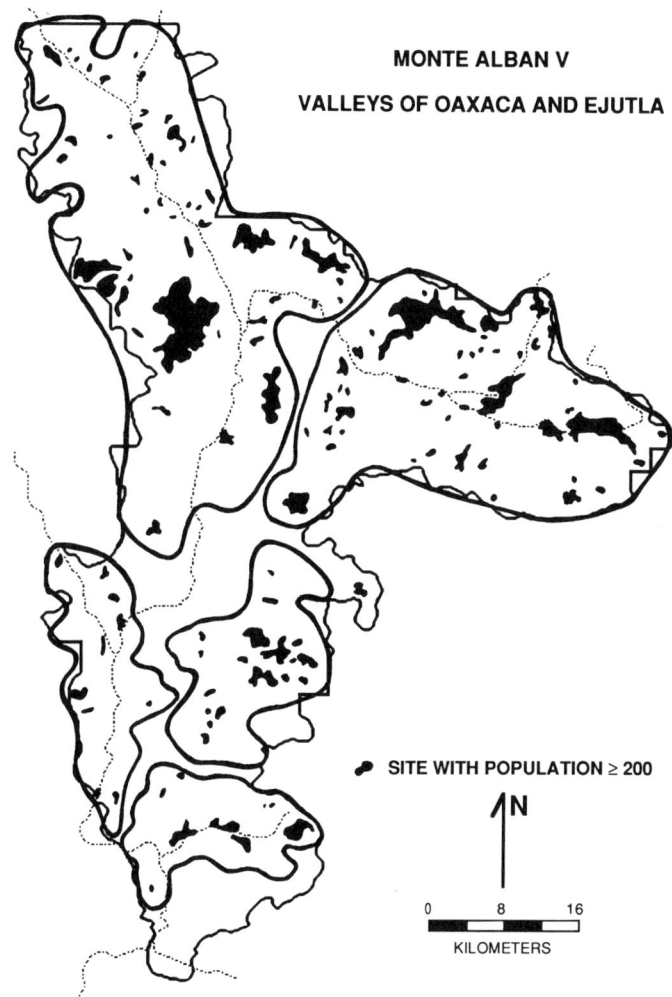

Figure 2.12: Boundaries of Five Large Monte Albán V Settlement Clusters.

34 *Economic Analysis Beyond the Local System*

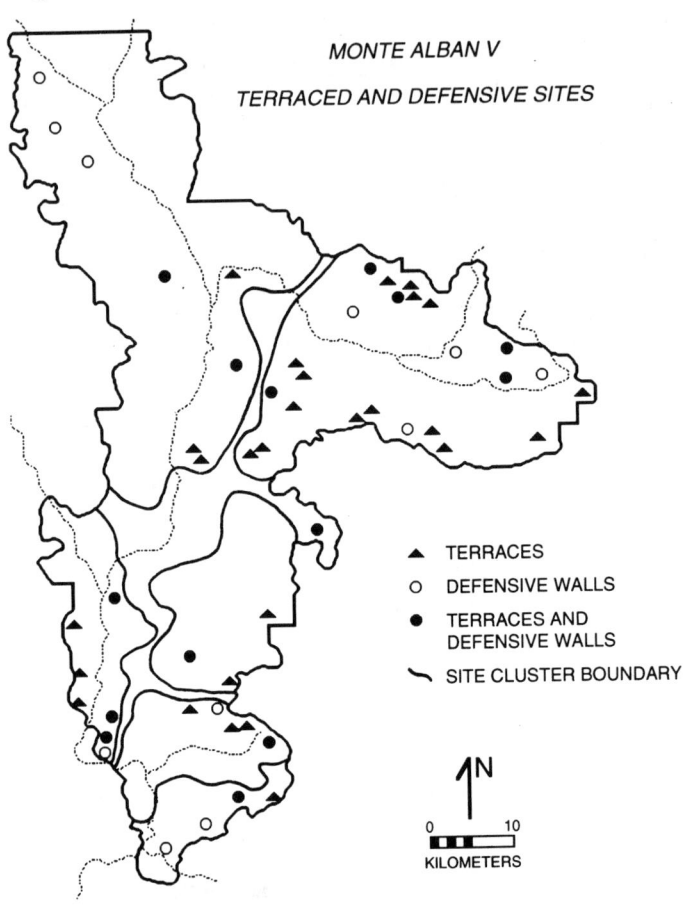

Figure 2.13: Settlement Cluster Boundaries and the Location of Hilltop Terraced and Defensive Sites in Monte Albán V.

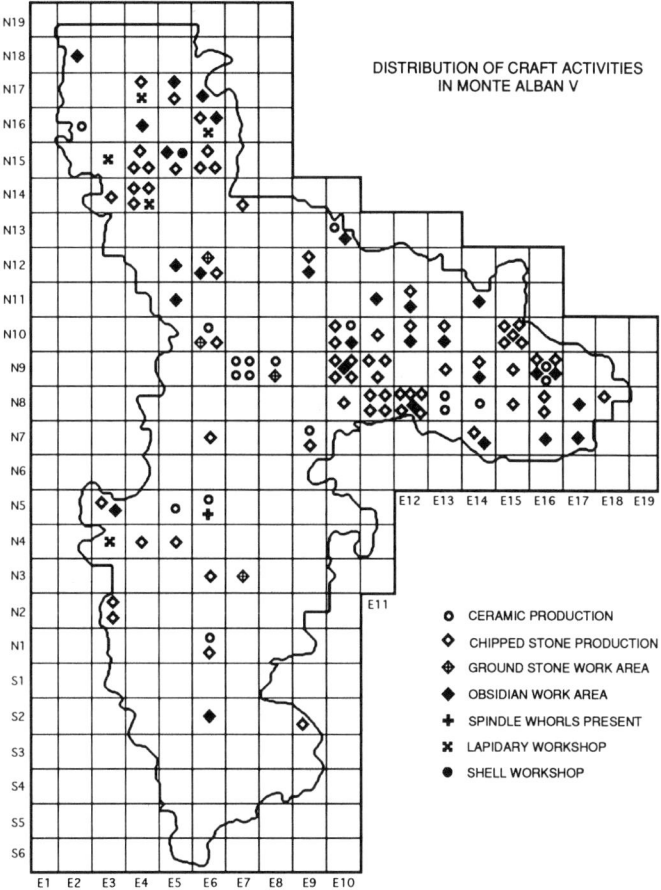

Figure 2.14: Distribution of Craft Activities in the Valleys of Oaxaca and Ejutla in Monte Albán V.

Monte Albán V (Late Postclassic)

Monte Albán V provides concrete evidence for economic interdependence cross-cutting political boundaries. In large part, this pattern becomes "visible" because the fall of Monte Albán was followed by the splintering of the region into a series of small statelets or petty kingdoms. Based on integrated analysis of ethnohistoric information, the distribution of large Monte Albán V archaeological sites, and nearest neighbor calculations, 15 settlement clusters (with an estimated mean size around 14,000 people) were defined (Figure 2.11). Yet, reflecting the political fluidity of the late prehispanic era, historical accounts also discuss confederations of these small polities around the valley's largest Monte Albán V centers, Cuilapan and Macuilxochitl (e.g. Appel 1982). A heuristic picture (Figure 2.12) of this more centralized structure, with two large clusters (surrounding the two aforementioned sites) and three small peripheral ones, can be recognized in the regional settlement pattern findings when sites are clustered using a wider nearest neighbor distance of 1500 m. A much larger percentage of the defensible sites in this phase face inward, and a considerable number sit provocatively close to the lines drawn between these larger clusters (Figure 2.13). Neither of these Monte Albán V reconstructions even remotely approximates the pre-Monte Albán organization.

Complementarity and interdependence between valley settlements, described in ethnohistoric accounts, also is rather apparent archaeologically. The bulk of the evidence for craft specialization was concentrated in the eastern part of the valley (amplifying the Classic period pattern) (Figure 2.14). These activities include the largest-scale manufacture of grayware serving bowls as well as obsidian working (the latter material is exotic to the entire region). Alternatively, the potential to generate large agricultural surpluses was greatest in the northern arm (Nicholas 1989: Table 14.14). This agrarian zone is within the Cuilapan cluster but, in contrast to earlier phases, was somewhat removed from that center itself—perhaps reflecting the reported agrarian tributes that were sent north from Oaxaca to central Mexico (Appel 1982). Agricultural surpluses also were likely channeled to Tlacolula, where periodic human-food imbalances most probably occurred (Nicholas 1989: Figure 14.9). These different production emphases between the Cuilapan and Tlacolula (focused on the site of Macuilxochitl) settlement clusters provide an empirical basis for interpenetrating accumulation—

Gills and Frank's (1991) concept for locally produced surpluses that were circulated for gain across political borders. Interpenetrating accumulation was not necessarily an emerging phenomenon in Monte Albán V (it cannot be ruled out as having existed earlier); although the volume of such interconnections was seemingly greater than in prior phases. In addition, the smaller scale of these Postclassic polities makes it easier to document archaeologically.

Monte Albán V, the phase of greatest intra-regional economic interaction was also the time when the valley's physiographic boundaries were most permeable (Kowalewski et al. 1983). The region's surrounding mountains were more densely inhabited than in earlier times (Drennan 1989; Finsten 1992), facilitating these inter-regional flows. Thus, while interpenetrating links cross-cut valley polities, the physiographic region as a whole was less clearly a discrete bounded "system" than it had been earlier.

Concluding Thoughts

The nature and configuration of subregional economic interdependencies have been shown to have shifted markedly over time in the prehispanic Valley of Oaxaca. The complexity and fluidity of these changes indicate that the patterns of specialization were neither entirely natural nor rigidly dependent on the distribution of raw resources, although agricultural production was frequently focal in Etla, as it is there today. Where possible, these regional patterns have been linked to extra-valley relations, although those interconnections are also far from simple. While status-related items tended to circulate the greatest distances in prehispanic Mesoamerica, the processing and exchange of these materials often contributed to more micro-scale economic interdependencies, as evidenced in Ejutla during Monte Albán IIIA (Feinman and Nicholas 1991a, 1991b, 1992b, 1993). Not surprisingly, this mountain-ringed study region was apparently most porous in Monte Albán V, when we have solid indications for significant economic interdependency crossing polity lines. At much smaller scales, economic linkages that cross-cut spatially defined settlement clusters existed for more basic utilitarian products, like food. Yet, how these interdependencies related to political boundaries will remain somewhat of an open question until archaeologists collect the necessary data and devise better means to define political relationships across space.

In sum, this essay has endeavored to illustrate how a macro- and multi-scale theoretical perspective, when intertwined with systematic regional-scale data collection and relational (as opposed to artifact focused) analyses, can provide complex insights into ancient political economies. The application of this approach does not imply that the macro-region is the only or the most important scale for understanding ancient Mesoamerica. Nor, does the definition of cores require the presumption that those regions necessarily had a monopoly over the technologies available to peripheral regions or that people in outlying areas had no control over their own histories. Rather, in an area like prehispanic Mesoamerica where polity dynamics were fluid and political autonomy a matter of degree (Marcus 1993), political economic theory and analysis should not be artificially constrained by the outdated notion that behavioral and cultural units were necessarily defined by static geographic features. A more dynamic perspective that analytically broaches the question of "systemness" is necessary if we are to understand long-term change in stratified societies.

Notes

1. Linda M. Nicholas prepared all of the figures included in this paper.

2. The National Science Foundation has generously supported the regional settlement pattern surveys that have been implemented in the valleys of Oaxaca and Ejutla. Necessary permissions and essential assistance were provided by the Instituto Nacional de Antropologia e Historia and the Centro Regional de Oaxaca. Thanks also are owed to all of the institutions and individuals who have facilitated the collection and analysis of information used in this research.

References

Appel, Jill
    1982 The Postclassic: A Summary of the Ethnohistoric Information Relevant to the Interpretation of Late Postclassic Settlement Pattern Data, the Central and Valle Grande Survey Zones. In *Monte Albán's Hinterland, Part I: Prehispanic Settlement Patterns of the Central and Southern Parts of the Valley of Oaxaca, Mexico*. Richard E. Blanton, Stephen A. Kowalewski, Gary M. Feinman, and Jill Appel. Pp. 139-148. Memoirs

of the Museum of Anthropology, No. 15. Ann Arbor: University of Michigan.

Banker, Sherman, Gary M. Feinman, Linda M. Nicholas, and Susan Kepecs
   1992   Compositional Variation in Ancient and Modern Oaxacan Pottery: Preliminary Perspectives. Paper presented at the 91st Annual Meeting of the American Anthropological Association, San Francisco.

Blanton, Richard E.
   1978   *Monte Albán: Settlement Patterns at the Ancient Zapotec Capital.* New York: Academic Press.
   1985   A Comparison of Early Market Systems. In *Markets and Marketing: Monographs in Economic Anthropology, No. 4.* Stuart Plattner, ed. Pp. 399-416. Lanham: University Press of America.
   1989   Continuity and Change in Public Architecture: Periods I Through V of the Valley of Oaxaca, Mexico. In *Monte Albán's Hinterland, Part II: The Prehispanic Settlement Patterns in Tlacolula, Etla, and Ocotlán, the Valley of Oaxaca, Mexico.* Stephen A. Kowalewski, Gary M. Feinman, Laura Finsten, Richard E. Blanton, and Linda M. Nicholas. Pp. 409-447. Memoirs of the Museum of Anthropology, No. 23. Ann Arbor: University of Michigan.

Blanton, Richard E. and Gary M. Feinman
   1984   The Mesoamerican World System. *American Anthropologist* 86:673-682.

Blanton, Richard E., Stephen A. Kowalewski, and Gary M. Feinman
   1992   The Mesoamerican World-system. *Review* 15:419-426.

Blanton, Richard E., Stephen A. Kowalewski, Gary M. Feinman, and Jill Appel
   1981   *Ancient Mesoamerica: A Comparison of Change in Three Regions.* Cambridge: Cambridge University Press.
   1982   *Monte Albán's Hinterland, Part I: Prehispanic Settlement Patterns of the Central and Southern Parts of the Valley of Oaxaca, Mexico.* Memoirs of the Museum of Anthropology, No. 15. Ann Arbor: University of Michigan.

Blanton, Richard E., Stephen A. Kowalewski, Gary M. Feinman, and Laura Finsten
   1993   *Ancient Mesoamerica: A Comparison of Change in Three Regions.* 2nd edition. Cambridge: Cambridge University Press.

Chase-Dunn, Christopher
   1992   The Comparative Study of World-systems. *Review* 15:313-333.
   1993   Comment on A. G. Frank, Bronze Age World System Cycles. *Current Anthropology* 34:407-408.

Chase-Dunn, Christopher, and Thomas D. Hall, eds.
   1991   *Core/Periphery Relations in Precapitalist Worlds.* Boulder, CO: Westview Press.

Drennan, Robert D.
1989 The Mountains North of the Valley. In *Monte Albán's Hinterland, Part II: The Prehispanic Settlement Patterns in Tlacolula, Etla, and Ocotlán, the Valley of Oaxaca, Mexico.* Stephen A. Kowalewski, Gary M. Feinman, Laura Finsten, Richard E. Blanton, and Linda M. Nicholas. Pp. 367-384. Memoirs of the Museum of Anthropology, No. 23. Ann Arbor: University of Michigan.

Feinman, Gary M.
1980 *The Relationship Between Administrative Organization and Ceramic Production in the Valley of Oaxaca, Mexico.* Ph.D. diss., City University of New York.
1986 The Emergence of Specialized Ceramic Production in Formative Oaxaca. In *Research in Economic Anthropology, Supplement 2: Economic Aspects of Prehispanic Highland Mexico.* Barry L. Isaac, ed. Pp. 347-373. Greenwich, CT: JAI Press.
1991 Demography, Surplus, and Inequality: Early Political Formations in Highland Mesoamerica. In *Chiefdoms: Power, Economy, and Ideology.* Timothy Earle, ed. Pp. 229-262. Cambridge: Cambridge University Press.

Feinman, Gary M., Richard E. Blanton, and Stephen A. Kowalewski
1984 Market System Development in the Prehispanic Valley of Oaxaca, Mexico. In *Trade and Exchange in Early Mesoamerica.* Kenneth G. Hirth, ed. Pp. 157-178. Albuquerque: University of New Mexico Press.

Feinman, Gary M. and Linda M. Nicholas
1987 Labor, Surplus, and Production: A Regional Analysis of Formative Oaxacan Socio-Economic Change. In *Coasts, Plains and Deserts: Essays in Honor of Reynold J. Ruppé.* Sylvia Gaines, ed. Pp. 27-50. Anthropological Research Papers, No. 38. Tempe: Arizona State University.
1990a At the Margins of the Monte Albán State: Settlement Patterns in the Ejutla Valley, Oaxaca, Mexico. *Latin American Antiquity* 1:216-246.
1990b Settlement and Land Use in Ancient Oaxaca. In *Debating Oaxaca Archaeology.* Joyce Marcus, ed. Pp. 71-113. Anthropological Papers of the Museum of Anthropology, No. 84. Ann Arbor: University of Michigan.
1991a New Perspectives on Prehispanic Highland Mesoamerica: A Macroregional Approach. *Comparative Civilizations Review* 24:13-33.
1991b The Monte Albán State: A Diachronic Perspective on an Ancient Core and its Periphery. In *Core/Periphery Relations in Precapitalist Worlds.* Christopher Chase-Dunn and Thomas D. Hall, eds. Pp. 240-276. Boulder, CO: Westview Press.
1992a Human-land Relations from an Archaeological Perspective: The Case of Ancient Oaxaca. In *Understanding Economic Process: Monographs*

in *Economic Anthropology, No. 10.* Sutti Ortiz and Susan Lees, eds. Pp. 155-178. Lanham: University Press of America
1992b Prehispanic Interregional Interaction in Southern Mexico: The Valley of Oaxaca and the Ejutla Valley. In *Resources, Power, and Interregional Interaction.* Edward Schortman and Patricia Urban, eds. Pp. 75-116. New York: Plenum Press.
1993 Shell Ornament Production in Ejutla: Implications for Highland-Coastal Interaction in Ancient Oaxaca. *Ancient Mesoamerica* 4:103-119.

Finsten, Laura M.
1992 The Mixtec Sierra: A Changing Periphery. Paper presented at the 57th Annual Meeting of the Society for American Archaeology, Pittsburgh.

Flannery, Kent V. and Joyce Marcus, eds.
1983 *The Cloud People: Divergent Evolution of the Zapotec and Mixtec Civilizations.* New York: Academic Press.

Frank, Andre Gunder
1993 Bronze Age World System Cycles (with Comments). *Current Anthropology* 34:383:429.

Gills, Barry K. and Andre Gunder Frank
1991 5000 Years of World System History: The Cumulation of Accumulation. In *Core/Periphery Relations in Precapitalist Worlds.* Christopher Chase-Dunn and Thomas D. Hall, eds. Pp. 67-112. Boulder, CO: Westview Press.

Isaac, Barry L.
1986 Introduction. In *Research in Economic Anthropology, Supplement 2: Economic Aspects of Prehispanic Highland Mexico.* Barry L. Isaac, ed. Pp. 1-19. Greenwich, CT: JAI Press.

Kohl, Philip L.
1989 The Use and Abuse of World Systems Theory: The Case of the "Pristine" West Asian State. In *Archaeological Thought in America.* C. C. Lamberg-Karlovsky, ed. Pp. 218-240. Cambridge: Cambridge University Press.

Kowalewski, Stephen A.
1980 Population-Resource Balances in Period I of Oaxaca, Mexico. *American Antiquity* 45:151-165.
1982 Population and Agricultural Potential: Early I through V. In *Monte Albán's Hinterland, Part I: The Prehispanic Settlement Patterns of the Central and Southern Parts of the Valley of Oaxaca, Mexico.* R. Blanton, S. Kowalewski, G. Feinman, and J. Appel. Pp. 149-180. Memoirs of the Museum of Anthropology, No. 15. Ann Arbor: University of Michigan.

1990 Merits of Full-Coverage Survey: Examples from the Valley of Oaxaca, Mexico. In *The Archaeology of Regions: A Case for Full-Coverage Survey.* Suzanne K. Fish and Stephen A. Kowalewski, eds. Pp. 33-85. Washington: Smithsonian.

Kowalewski, Stephen A., Richard E. Blanton, Gary M. Feinman, and Laura Finsten
    1983 Boundaries, Scale, and Internal Organization. *Journal of Anthropological Archaeology* 2:32-56.

Kowalewski, Stephen A., Gary M. Feinman, Richard E. Blanton, Laura Finsten, and Linda M. Nicholas
    1989 *Monte Albán's Hinterland, Part II: The Prehispanic Settlement Patterns in Tlacolula, Etla, and Ocotlán, the Valley of Oaxaca, Mexico.* Memoirs of the Museum of Anthropology, No. 23. Ann Arbor: University of Michigan.

Kowalewski, Stephen A. and Laura Finsten
    1983 The Economic Systems of Ancient Oaxaca: A Regional Perspective (with Comments). *Current Anthropology* 24:413-441.

Marcus, Joyce
    1993 Ancient Maya Political Organization. In *Lowland Maya Civilization in the Eighth Century A.D.* Jeremy Sabloff and John Henderson. eds. Pp. 111-183. Washington: Dumbarton Oaks.

Nicholas, Linda M.
    1989 Land Use in Prehispanic Oaxaca. In *Monte Albán's Hinterland, Part II: The Prehispanic Settlement Patterns in Tlacolula, Etla, and Ocotlán, the Valley of Oaxaca, Mexico.* Stephen A. Kowalewski, Gary M. Feinman, Laura Finsten, Richard E. Blanton, and Linda M. Nicholas. Pp. 449-505. Memoirs of the Museum of Anthropology, No. 23. Ann Arbor: University of Michigan.

Pailes, Richard, and Joseph Whitecotton
    1979 The Greater Southwest and Mesoamerican "World" System: An Exploratory Model of Frontier Relationships. In *The Frontier: Comparative Studies*, Vol. 2. William Savage and Stephen Thompson, eds. Pp. 102-121. Norman: University of Oklahoma Press.

Schortman, Edward M. and Patricia A. Urban
    1987 Modeling Interregional Interaction in Prehistory. *Advances in Archaeological Method and Theory* 11:37-95.

Winter, Marcus C.
    1984 Exchange in Formative Highland Oaxaca. In *Trade and Exchange in Early Mesoamerica.* Kenneth G. Hirth, ed. Pp. 179-214. Albuquerque: University of New Mexico Press.

3

The Millennium Before the "Long Sixteenth Century:" How Many World-Systems Were There?[1]

Thomas D. Hall

> A count should be the last stage of theoretically oriented social research, after one has got to the point where one is willing to sacrifice theoretical advance (Stinchcombe 1978:7).

Taking Arthur Stinchcombe's advice to heart has pushed me to rethink considerably the paper I originally planned. Truth in packaging requires that I make clear what is different. First, the "millennium" before Wallerstein's "long sixteenth century" (1450-1650) (Wallerstein 1974a, 1974b; Chase-Dunn 1989) is nearly two millennia. According to McNeill (1963) and Frank and Gills, eds (1993), the Afroeurasian ecumene closed sometime in the second or first century BCE (before the common era). I use Afroeurasian in place of Eurasian because parts of Africa have interacted with Eurasia for a very long time and because "Europe" is not a separate continent but a "peninsula of peninsulas" on the Eurasian landmass (Teggart 1918, 1925).[2]

Second, the counting then becomes—according to one view— incredibly easy since there was only one world-system. I must note here that the "world" in "world-system" does not mean "global" but "self-contained." Only the modern world-system is truly global—that is why Wallerstein (1974a, 1974b) used the word "world."

But third, with some conceptual legerdemain, it turns out there were many systems, but they were not quite independent. Fourth, disentangling this conceptual muddle points to potentially fruitful ways to think about other complicated interregional interactions systems (see Schortman and Urban, eds. 1992 for others). Even the terminology is disputed. Amin (1991), Wallerstein (1992, 1993), and Chase-Dunn and Hall (1991, 1992, 1993) prefer world-systems, with a hyphen and an "s." Frank (1990), Frank and Gills (1990, 1992, eds 1993), and Gills and Frank (1991,

1992) argue for no hyphen and no "s." This paper explicates these four points after briefly recapping the continuing dialogue about precapitalist world-systems.

The dialogue about precapitalist world-systems centers on whether and how the insights of Wallerstein's *Modern World-System* (Wallerstein 1974a, 1974b) can or should be extended to pre-1500 CE (Current Era) settings. While the dialogue remains far from consensus even among those who argue for such an extension of the theory, there is a growing agreement that the world-system perspective will be useful only with considerable modification to the Wallersteinian version. It should be noted that such stalwarts as Wallerstein (1990, 1992, 1993) and Amin (1991) have grave doubts about such extension. This dialog is making links with interregional interaction perspectives among archaeologists (Schortman and Urban, eds. 1992; Schortman and Urban 1992, 1994a, 1994b; Chase-Dunn 1992; Hall and Chase-Dunn 1993).

These approaches all see intersocietal interactions as a significant source of social change. This is not a return to "diffusion" as an explanation for change. Rather, it is an attempt to theorize about how states, "tribes," and other social actors themselves constitute the components of a social ecology, which itself is a major source of political, economic, cultural, and social changes. In short, the extension of world-system perspectives to precapitalist settings is one avenue toward cumulation in anthropology (and other social sciences, see Wolf 1990).

Beyond this, however, agreement dissolves rapidly and theoretical, conceptual, and empirical debates begin. In order to make sense of the cacophony I will sketch my position, then turn to a re-examination of the emergence of the Afroeurasian system, and close with some comments on the insights and conclusions derived from this exercise. I begin with a brief overview of the implications of the various approaches for defining, and thus counting, world-systems.

Bounding World-Systems

Approaches to precapitalist world-systems perspectives divide into "lumpers" and "splitters." Lumpers see only one global system far back in time (Lenski and Lenski 1987; Frank 1990, Frank and Gills 1990, 1992, eds 1993; Gills and Frank 1991, 1992). Splitters debate how many separate systems there were in both the New World (Blanton,

Kowalewski, and Feinman 1992; Upham, Feinman and Nicholas 1992, Whitecotton 1992a, 1992b) and the Old World (Chase-Dunn 1992; Chase-Dunn and Hall 1991, 1992; Abu-Lughod 1987, 1989, 1990) Wilkinson (1992, 1993a 1993b), Gills and Frank (1991, 1992), Frank and Gills (1990, 1992, eds 1993). In her one essay on the issue, Abu-Lughod straddles this gap, seeing merit in both camps (1993).

For both groups, how to specify both what constitutes a "system," without reifying it, and what bounds it remain thorny problems. The differences between the groups is the source of the two different "counts" of world-systems. For "splitters" additional issues are raised: (1) can separate world-systems interact, (2) how does one system connect or incorporate another, and (3) what constitutes incorporation?

In Chase-Dunn and Hall (1993, 1994), we examined criteria for spatially bounding intersocietal interaction networks. We argue that it is not useful to assign some forms of interaction greater importance than others. The relative importance of different types of interaction probably varies across different kinds of systems. Bounding should be inclusive enough to make comparisons across different types of system possible.

Economic, political, and information conveying (i.e., cultural) forms of interaction are important features of all world-system networks. We agree with Wallerstein (1974b, 1989) that bulk-goods exchanges are very important forms of interconnection, but agree with Schneider (1977) and Abu-Lughod (1989) that prestige-goods exchanges are also very important for the reproduction of power structures. Thus, all regularized material exchanges should be included as criteria of system boundedness. This reformulation makes it necessary to consider how relatively localized networks of bulk/goods exchange are nested within much larger networks of prestige-goods exchange in many systems. We further recognize that the luxury/bulk goods distinction is fundamentally a matter of degree and not dichotomy. The distinction can shift with changes in transportation technology. Indeed, goods that are culturally defined as valuable (luxury goods) may motivate attempts to improve costs of transportation.

We also agree with Tilly (1984:62) and Wilkinson (1987, 1988, 1991) that political interconnections are important. We propose to use the criterion of regularized political-military conflict interaction proposed by Wilkinson. This will often produce yet a different network boundary from the bulk-goods and prestige-goods networks.

Since that work was published we (Chase-Dunn and Hall 1995) are convinced that a fourth network, which we label an information network, must also be considered. While the least developed conceptually and theoretically, this may be of most interest to anthropologists. Based on our own research (Chase-Dunn and Hall n.d.) and work of Alice Willard on West Africa (1993), we argue that information flows in the form of ideologies or specific knowledge may have important consequences for system operation and change.

In most cases these four boundaries will not coincide. Typically, a world-system is delimited by nested boundaries. Generally, bulk goods will compose the smallest regional interaction net. Political-military interaction define a larger system which will include more than one bulk-goods net. Luxury goods exchanges will link even larger regions composed of smaller conflict nets (see Figure 3.1). For example, the bulk-goods net of the Roman Empire was smaller than the system of regularized military interactions. Luxury goods exchanges along the "Silk Roads" linked the Chinese, Indian, and Roman regions. These goods often served as prestige goods for Central Asian nomads (Barfield 1989; Hall 1991a, 1991b). Finally, the information network is of the same scale as the prestige goods network but does not coincide with it. Rather, it sometimes extends beyond it, as in cases of "missionaries" or "explorers" who move beyond trade connections. At other times it does not extend as far, as in cases of silent or down-the-line trade.

We propose that world-systems are constituted by all four forms of linkage. We do not claim that the networks are always nested. Indeed, the relations of these four boundary criteria remain theoretical and empirical problems. We further argue that the gradual convergence of these criteria is a major defining feature (*differentia specifica pace* Amin 1991; Wallerstein 1992, Frank and Gills, eds 1993) of the modern world-system. In earlier world-systems, these boundaries did not coincide, were typically fuzzy, and did not always change in synchronization with each other.

The use of multiple, partially autonomous boundary criteria render the concept of "systemness" problematic. We distinguish these connections from diffusion, which according to Schortman and Urban (1992) has never been well theorized. We argue that diffusion does not constitute regularized interaction, but is the limiting pole of a continuum of systemness. Our criterion for systemness is that exchanges within any one of these networks must contribute to system reproduction and/or change.

Thus, one sweet potato arriving in Hawaii does not make it part of a Peruvian world-system, nor did the short visit of Norse seamen to North America create a transatlantic system. Still, just when exchange is sufficient to constitute a system remains unclear. We argue this is both a theoretical and empirical problem that can only be resolved through further study.

This fuzziness of boundaries raises the question noted above: is it possible for separate systems to interact and remain distinct?; when do two interacting systems become one system? Wallerstein (1989; cf. Hopkins and Wallerstein 1987) argues that in the long sixteenth century, the Ottoman Empire and the nascent European world-economy were different systems, albeit ones engaged in luxury trade and armed conflict. He makes this argument on the basis of lack of heavy trade in bulk goods. By the criteria just proposed, they were part of the same military and luxury good systems, even if there was minimal bulk goods exchange as Wallerstein argues.

When do two separate systems become one larger one? Applying the criterion for systemness, when such interaction is important for system reproduction and/or change. Given the fuzziness of boundaries, however, this criterion renders initial stages of coalescence theoretically and empirically problematic. This is as it should be: the combination of formerly separate systems into one larger system is only clear after the fact. Note, too, that such combination may occur—at least initially—without awareness on the part of the actors involved, or even against their intentions.

The existence of a multi-cored system, whether generated by contact between formerly independent systems or some other mechanism, creates space for peripheral and semiperipheral actors to gain some autonomy by playing one core against another. This happened at various times in what is now the American Southwest (Hall 1989) and in southeastern Mesoamerica (Schortman and Urban 1994a, 1994b and accompanying comments, especially those of Hall 1994, Kardulias 1994, and Kohl 1994). These examples illustrate how complex such interactions can be in either ethnohistorical or archaeological settings, but also demonstrate the insights and understanding that may be gained by following this approach.

48 *Economic Analysis Beyond the Local System*

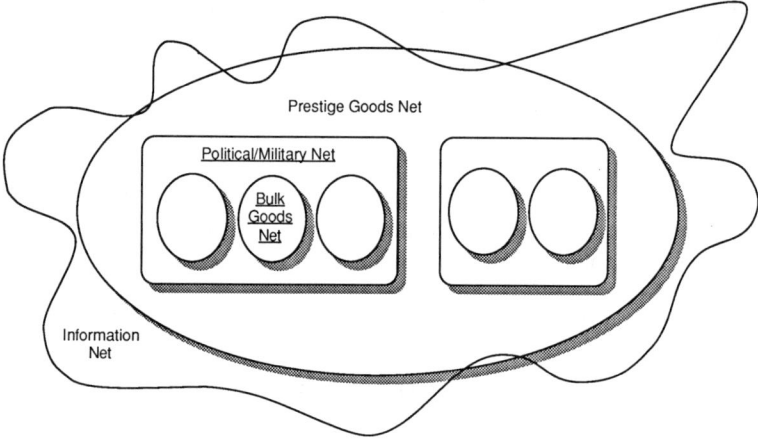

Figure 3.1: Boundaries of the Four World-System Networks.

The Millennium Before the "Long Sixteenth Century" 49

What happens when formerly distinct world-systems begin to interact regularly? I propose a provisional theoretical analysis that extends my reformulation of Wallerstein's concept of incorporation (Hall 1986, 1987, 1989). I elaborated Wallerstein's conceptualization of incorporation from a three-stage model of external arena, incorporation, and peripheralization (or the classical development of underdevelopment) (Frank 1969a, 1969b) into a continuum of incorporation that ranged from external arena through contact, then marginal, to full-blown peripheralization. I further noted that while incorporation was to a limited extent reversible, it was an asymmetrical process that tended, over time, to change toward the stronger pole of the continuum.

This modification was developed on the basis of detailed studies of how nonstate societies in what is now the American Southwest were incorporated into the capitalist world-economy over a four hundred year period. I developed this elaboration, like Wallerstein's original formulation, to describe and explain how new regions and peoples were transformed from autonomous societies into peripheral regions and actors.

The merger of two formerly distinct world-systems need not necessarily involve peripheralization of one of the formerly independent world-systems, but may, in fact, involve the transformation of two formerly unicentric world-systems into one large, multicentric world-system. Furthermore, components of the formerly independent systems may be transformed by the merger. Thus, contact along peripheral zones may transform those peripheral zones in a variety of ways, including new semiperipheral or even core zones. In what was the most dramatic such merger in world history, the Mongol Central Asian semiperiphery became for nearly a century the hegemonic core power the entire Afroeurasian world-system—but I am getting ahead of my story.

Finally, the merging of world-systems proceeds along at least three somewhat autonomous dimensions. The first of these is the trade dimension which ranges, as noted, from long-distance trade in very high value, low bulk goods to low value, high bulk goods. Second is the political/military dimension of regularized political relations, which may range from constant warfare to generalized peace. Third is the information dimension which may range from exchange of a new, easily transported technology, such as iron making (Kohl 1978), to ideologies, typically religions, which Michael Mann calls "technologies of power"

(Mann 1986), such as the spread of Islam (e.g., Willard 1993; Bentley 1993).

These three dimensions are not quite independent because intensive warfare all but obviates trade while intense trade produces a major incentive for peace. Raiding, of course, combines the two dimensions, as does the exaction of protection as was so skillfully done by Central Asian nomads for millennia (Barfield 1989). Flow of information of various sorts can promote the other interactions and is often increased by them.

Phrased alternatively, incorporation proceeds somewhat differently and somewhat independently along each of the four boundaries of world-systems. Wallerstein has focused only on the most intensive form of incorporation: intense exchange of bulk goods within one system. To be fair, this is appropriate when studying the modern world-system since, it turns out, this is one of its major distinctive features and forms the driving force behind modern world-system dynamics (Wallerstein 1993). But when studying world-systems before *circa* 1500 CE, to focus only on this type and intensity of incorporation is to miss nearly all the action and severely undercount the number of systems.

While there is much to the theoretical discussions of precapitalist world-systems (see Hall and Chase-Dunn 1994 and Chase-Dunn and Hall n.d.), this discussion is sufficient to attempt a provisional count of the world-systems in the millennium or so before the appearance of the modern world-system. Stinchcombe's (1978) admonition to count after solving theoretical problems notwithstanding, at least I can justify the way I count on theoretical grounds.

How Many World-Systems Were There?

As noted earlier, since the closing of the Afroeurasian ecumene (McNeill 1963: Ch. VII) in the centuries immediately preceding the birth of Christ, it is arguable that there has been only one such world-system. However, I will not cede to the "lumpers" so easily. Rather, I argue that there were at least three major world-systems—the Chinese, the South Asian, and the Middle Eastern—and several more minor world-systems that were involved in a long process of incorporation marked by a variety of cycles of increasing and decreasing incorporation that was only fully completed sometime in the nineteenth century.

Further, I argue that it is in the dynamics of this emerging world-system that the origins of both the modern world-system and the transformation of the tributary to the capitalist mode of production are found. So, not only did several systems merge into one, that one transformed into a social system fundamentally different from those that went before. Thus, the counting is getting complicated: at least three systems merge into one system which transforms into a fundamentally different system.

To anticipate one conclusion, or better, lesson, from this exercise: it is not the number of systems that is fundamentally important, but the complex interactions and transformations that define them. I suggest that rather than quibble about the number of systems readers consider whether or not similar processes occurred in other settings, such as the growing system of interregional interactions that arose in Mesoamerica and the Andean highlands.

A Capsule History of Afroeurasian World-Systems Since Roman-Han Times

Jerry Bentley (1993) divides this history into four eras. The opening of the ancient Silk Roads from 200 BCE to about 400 CE constitute the first period. It is notable that the Roman and Han empires rose and fell in tandem. Virulent diseases communicated along the Silk Road seem to have played a major role in the closing of this era. The second era runs from the seventh through tenth centuries. In this era, sea lanes were opened and more trade was carried overland and overseas than on the ancient Silk Roads. This blends into the third era from approximately 1000 to 1350 CE. Trade again increased over both land and sea, but the rise of nomad empires, especially the Mongol empire in the thirteenth century was even more dramatic. Finally, after a century or more of demographic recovery, the modern European era with its engulfment of the entire globe began in the late fifteenth century.

Gills and Frank (1992; Frank and Gills, eds 1993) divide this history into A (expanding) and B (contracting) phases following conventional world-system cycles theories (Goldstein 1988):

1., 2., 3., and 4. cover		1700-200 BCE
5. B: 250-200	➔	100-50 BCE
A: 100-50	➔	150-200 CE
6. B: 150-200	➔	500 CE
A: 500	➔	750-800 CE

7. B: 750-800   →   1000-1050 CE
   A: 1000-1050   →   1250-1300 CE
8. B: 1250-1300   →   1450 CE

Thus Bentley's Ancient Silk Roads period approximates Gills and Frank's periods 5 and 6; the second era, the European "Dark Ages" corresponds to period 7; the nomadic empires correspond to periods 7 and 8. Period 8 is the period most closely examined by Abu-Lughod (1989). Finally, most writers see a major shift occurring around 1000 CE (McNeill 1963, 1982; Bentley 1993; Beckwith 1987; Abu-Lughod 1989).

Sometime in the first two centuries BCE, both the Roman Empire and the Han Dynasty began to expand outward seeking outlets for products and sources of scarce material. Central Asian nomads played a crucial role in opening and maintaining this trade (Barfield 1989; Frank 1992; Hodgson 1974; Teggart 1939; McNeill 1963). In world-system terms, two formerly isolated world-systems merged at the luxury good trade level. Ideas, products, and people moved along the Silk Roads. The road over the Hindu Kush and along the Indian Ocean littoral also drew the South Asian world-system into this newly merging larger world-system, although apparently not as tightly. While this was probably not the first contact between the two world-systems at opposite ends of the Eurasian landmass, it was the first instance of sustained, direct trade, as opposed to indirect, down-the-line trade.

I should note, however, that Frank and Gills (eds 1993) argue there was another closure early in the first millennium BCE, but the evidence for that remains unclear (Frank 1993). Furthermore, if their claims are substantiated, it would strengthen the argument advanced here.

However, military activity along the frontiers of the constituent core empires had major effects on surrounding peoples. Both Rome (Dyson 1985; Mattingly 1992; Wells 1992) and China (Lattimore 1951; Barfield 1989; Fried 1952) incorporated new territories and new peoples into their systems. Many nonstate, or in a looser terminology, "tribal" peoples were drawn into local world-economies. Frontier warfare generally increased inter-tribal and state-tribal warfare (Ferguson and Whitehead 1992). Tribal peoples were often drawn into participation through prestige goods economies in which states used their monopoly of access to exotic luxury goods to influence and sometimes control local tribal leaders. The success of this technique for controlling tribal peoples further heightened the demand for luxury goods.

The Millennium Before the "Long Sixteenth Century" 53

Beside goods, technologies, and ideologies, microbes were exchanged (McNeill 1976) with devastating effects in both Rome and China. The effects of rapid die-offs accelerated, if they did not initiate, the collapse of both the Roman and Han empires. The plagues had the effects of lowering population densities well below carrying capacity and eventually all but severing the trade routes. In the above terminology, there was at best moderate luxury good coalescence/ incorporation of these three world-systems, which lasted for a few centuries and then abated significantly.

If this loosely connected system is to be counted as only one world-system, it must be characterized by one that was very loosely systemic, and then only in the luxury goods dimension. It was at best a multi-cored world-system with each of its constituent units maintaining considerable local autonomy.

Sometime in the sixth century, trade again began to develop. This time sea lanes making use of the monsoons in the Arabian Sea, the Bay of Bengal, and the South China opened additional oceanic circuits (see maps in Abu-Lughod 1989:252, 254). This allowed expansion of Indian influence into Southeast Asia, incorporating formerly isolated local world-systems directly into the South Asia world-system and indirectly into the Afroeurasian world-system. This meant, among other things, that there were alternate routes from China to the eastern Roman/Byzantine empire.

As is well known, Islam spread along these routes, serving as an ideological integrator throughout much of the new, enlarged world-system. In this phase, commerce along the Silk Roads and oceanic paths reached heretofore unprecedented levels in world history. In world-system terms the incorporation was tighter but was largely confined to the luxury goods system.

This phase of world-system merger/incorporation was both wider and deeper. As with the first phase (and probably since states first appeared) surrounding nonstate peoples were drawn into the system via warfare and trade, continuing the transformation of formerly autonomous groups into peripheral peoples. New regions were drawn into the expanding world-system. Trade with subsaharan west Africa intensified (Moseley 1992) as did trade along the east African coast. Much of southeast Asia was drawn into the system.

Western Europe, however, was a bit of an anomaly. During this period—known in Europe as the Dark Ages—incorporation into the

Afroeurasian world-system seems somewhat less than for other regions. It is not altogether clear how much less incorporated Europe was, but it seems to have been sufficiently less such that the combination of the rise of armored warriors, as protectors from raiding nomads, and the decreased access to metallic money, brought about feudalism as a response. The so-called Pirenne thesis concerning the isolation of western Europe during the Dark Ages, and throughout the first millennium CE, is considerably overstated (Randsborg 1991, 1992; Sherratt and Sherratt 1991; Sherratt 1993). This is a case where ethnocentrism, in the form of eurocentrism, has introduced a major distortion into our understanding of history. If the "Dark Ages" were, indeed, dark, they were so only for Europeans!

As noted above, *circa* 1000 CE there was a major increase in economic activity world-wide. Indeed, iron production in China reached levels not attained in England until 700 years later (McNeill 1982:26-27). Trade in Europe began to increase and western European societies began to expand, evidenced, among other things, by the crusades. This expansion gave rise to the (Afro)Eurasian world-system so brilliantly described by Janet Abu-Lughod (1989). The most notable event of this era, however, is not trade, but the merging of the second boundary criteria—political-military interaction.

The Mongol Empire for the first time united Eurasia into a single empire—although, to be sure, the merger was far from complete. Egypt and north Africa were not militarily incorporated due to the strength of the Mamlukes. Western Europe remained outside the Mongol empire, due, in part, to the inhospitality of forest zones to mounted archers (Lindner 1981, 1982) in combination with the success of armed, mounted warriors (McNeill 1963, 1964, 1982). Japan also resisted Mongol attacks, repelling Kublai's sea-borne invasion in 1281 (McNeill 1982:43) even as Baghdad fell the previous year.

Mongol unity, which lasted barely more than a century, brought major changes. Mongol unification opened the third, northern, connection between China and Europe, directly over the steppes by-passing connections through southern Iran and Iraq. The steady traffic across the steppes opened other circuits of trade: "Gradually a north-south exchange of slaves and furs for the goods of civilization supplemented the east-west flow of goods that initially sustained the caravans" (Bentley 1993:56). In Europe, increased trade began the long process of increasing the strength of merchants compared to the kings, the nobility, and the Church. The

The Millennium Before the "Long Sixteenth Century" 55

opening of pathways and increased favorability toward merchants briefly opened China, and the far east generally, to European explorers, whetting European appetites for further trade, and ultimately for more direct routes there.

Arguably, one of the most important consequences of Mongol unification was the transmission of a hitherto isolated rat-and-flea-borne steppe disease—the Black Death, or bubonic plague—to Europe and China (McNeill 1976). The Black Death first swept through Europe in 1348, ultimately killing one-third to one-half of the population, fundamentally altering relations between lord and peasant. It took Europe over a century to recover. Apparently, the plagues had nearly as dramatic effects on China.

As population slowly rebuilt in China and agriculture intensified, the bureaucrats became increasingly concerned with other threats: competing wealthy merchants and the threat of yet another steppe invasion. This led early Ming administrators to massively curtail the activities of merchants, even recalling admiral Zheng He (Cheng Ho) from his exploratory voyages to India and Africa (Levathes 1994), and to move their administrative center to the north at its present location in Beijing. This, of course, left the Indian Ocean open to European penetration with minimal opposition. Had the Chinese remained active maritime traders their clear naval superiority would doubtless have made it much harder for Europeans to gain a foothold in the Indian Ocean trade (Abu-Lughod 1989; Fitzpatrick 1992).

In world-system terms the Afroeurasian ecumene again became a single world-system at the level of luxury trade and all but a few peripheral and fewer semiperipheral areas were incorporated into the political/military system. However, this new, multi-cored world-system was especially unstable, despite being the most systemic of all Afroeurasian world-systems to date.

The new system was inherently fragile and unstable because it contradicted what Randall Collins (1978, 1981) calls the "no intervening heartland rule:" that is, the empire was too large to be maintained logistically. According to "no intervening heartland rule," when states overextend themselves by attacking opponents who are so far away that the conquering state must traverse the "heartland" of another state (either the attacked state's or some third state's), they overextend themselves logistically raising the risk of military defeat considerably, and thereby undermine the legitimacy of the ruling regime. This is why stable empires always consist of contiguous areas. (This is a powerful concept which helps explain modern failures like Vietnam, Afghanistan, and ultimately the collapse of the Soviet Union—see Collins (1986:Ch. 8) and Collins and Waller (1992).

Thus, none of the potential hegemonic core powers—the Mings, the Ottomans, or any of the local states in South Asia—could mount an expedition to conquer any of the others. Furthermore, the Mongols did not produce anything (herds, notwithstanding): they were "macroparasites" (McNeill 1980) whose wealth came from siphoning off some of the trade that traversed their territory. But this is not the only reason for instability.

The Mongol empire was an anomaly in world-system terms: it was a semiperipheral marcher state that became a core power by virtue of its middleman and military roles. The Mongols used what Barfield (1989) calls the "outer frontier strategy" too vigorously. Instead of using violence or threats of violence to exact improved terms of trade, they overshot this goal and actually conquered surrounding states (Barfield 1989, 1991). Thus, Chinggis Khan and his successors found themselves compelled to administer a state rather than milk it for tribute. In this they differed from other steppe nomads who eschewed conquest.

While it has long been observed that an empire can be built from horseback, it cannot be ruled from there-there is more to it than that. The power of Mongols derived from a kinship system that allowed easy inclusion of new members but simultaneously generated disputes over leadership upon the death of a reigning khan. To institutionalize a rule of succession would have undermined the very social features that allowed the amassing of large conquest armies. In short, Mongols could not institutionalize kinship and remain Mongols (Barfield 1989; Hall 1991a, 1991b). This is why Mongols, and steppe nomads in general, so often melded into the societies they conquered: they had to adopt sedentary state social relations in order to rule, but in doing so ceased to be Mongols (Barfield 1989, 1990, 1991).

Still, as Abu-Lughod has so persuasively argued (1989), the new Afroeurasian world-system provided the preconditions for the appearance of the modern world-system and the famous "rise of the west." The combination of internal class politics, noted above, and potential threat of repeated Mongol or steppe nomad conquest led Ming bureaucrats to move their administrative center to Beijing and severely curtail all maritime trade (Elvin 1973; Fitzpatrick 1992). Abu-Lughod (1987, 1989) argues that the west did not rise; rather, the east fell. This is something of an overstatement. The east did not so much fall as "take their ball and go home," leaving the field open to the Portuguese and Dutch who, finding the field vacant, scored "a few plays" later! This, as is well known, then allowed the development of western Europe into the core of the modern world-system.

There are two sets of supporting evidence for the foregoing analysis, both preliminary, but both suggestive of ways in which analogous processes might be investigated elsewhere. First is the evidence from Japan's rise to power. Stephen Sanderson (1994, 1995) argues that Japan is a second case of nearly independent development of capitalism. He draws parallels with England: both are islands protected from land-based invasions by natural "moats," both developed feudal systems (this applies to all of western Europe) in which states did not develop strong central power, and both were marcher states on the extreme fringes of the Afroeurasian world-system (see Chase-Dunn 1988 and 1990 on the roles of semiperipheral and march states in world-system change). Sanderson notes that Japan only lagged western European, and especially English development, by a century or two. Hence, when it was forced to participate in the modern world-system in the mid-nineteenth century, it was already well prepared to leap into capitalism.

Sanderson's argument is assailable on many grounds. That, however, is not the point here. Rather, it is suggestive of how world-systemic processes shape social change in systematic ways. Whether or not the argument survives scholarly scrutiny and public debate, it does illustrate how a world-system analysis can shed light on heretofore complex processes. The same holds for the account of the rise of the west. In his retrospective on his famous history by that title, William McNeill (1990) suggests that he should have paid more attention to the development of the ecumenes, explicitly lauding Wallerstein's work, and notes that the "rise of the west" is something of a misnomer.

The second set of evidence comes from investigations of the growth of cities throughout world history drawing on Chandler's (1987) compilation of world city populations. Wilkinson (1992, 1993a, 1993b) and Chase-Dunn and Willard (1993, 1994) have used this data to explore growth of Central Civilization and world-systems respectively. Both find compelling partial evidence for Gills' and Frank's (1992) periodization of world-system growth. In plotting growth of urban centers for central civilization and the Far East, they find a very close correlation, suggesting strong interconnections: "Anyone, even a perpetual skeptic or rabid anti-Frankian, will notice striking correspondences between the temporal rises and falls in these graphs (Chase-Dunn and Willard 1993:26). Whether this is due to participation in the same world-system, mediated by spread of disease, or due to parallel evolution is not entirely clear.

However, additional evidence points toward the world-systemic explanation. While the Far East and Central Civilization exhibit similar patterns, urban growth in India and Central Asia seldom correlates with the other two. For Central Asia, and often for northern India, this may be due the semiperipheral role played by these states. For South Asia there is the additional participation in different circuits of trade between west and east. Indeed, it is the existence since the middle of the first millennium CE of three alternative, and probably competing, routes between east and west that keeps the middle portion in turmoil.

Other factors, no doubt, also played a role. The rather formidable barriers between South and Central Asia made close connection difficult. Yet, the two regions probably had sufficient connection to prevent disease pool isolation, curtailing the dramatic effects of "virgin soil epidemics" (Crosby 1986). Developments in South Asia and Indochina are less well known than either those in Europe or in China, and are in need of extensive study. The works of Chaudhuri (1985, 1990) and Reid (1988, 1993) among others have done much to fill in the gaps, but the work is far from complete.

While this evidence is preliminary and far from conclusive, it is suggestive. Unlike Gills and Frank (1992:679-684), we do not read this as strong support for their argument. In particular the study of urban growth supports only some of their A/B phase (expanding/contracting phases) timings, noted above (Bosworth 1992, 1995). Nevertheless, the evidence is clear for a pulsating, growing, Afroeurasian world-system that served as the major social-ecological context for social change over the last two millennia or so.

So how many Afroeurasian world-systems were there? Our provisional answer is ten before the appearance of the modern world-systems:

200 BCE = 3: Central Civilization (the west), Indic, and Chinese, plus minor ones
100 BCE (*ca.*) = 1: first Afroeurasian world-system

The Millennium Before the "Long Sixteenth Century" 59

400 CE (*ca.*) = 3
600 CE (*ca.*) = 1: second Afroeurasian world-system
1000 CE (*ca.*) = 1: third Afroeurasian world-system
1250 CE (*ca.*) = 1: fourth Afroeurasian world-system
1450 CE (*ca.*) = 1: first modern world-system (mercantile capitalist)
1830 CE (*ca.*) = 1: second modern world-system (industrial capitalist)

What is important, of course, is not the number, but the recognition that there were separate systems, both contemporaneously in space, and through time. While there is certainly an argument, and even some evidence, to made for continuity among these systems, to call them one system is to obscure major, significant processes of social evolution.

Lessons from the Provisional Count of World-Systems

Given the provisional nature of this exposition and the conditional nature of much of the evidence on which it is based, "lessons" rather than "conclusions" are its appropriate products. The single most important lesson to be drawn from this exercise is to recognize that the merger of formerly autonomous world-systems is a long, complicated process that involves cyclical integration of formerly autonomous social structures. Joseph Whitecotton's (1992a, 1992b) work on the circulation of elites among Mesoamerican world-systems suggests one promising way to examine parallel processes in that region. Discussions by La Lone (1991, 1992, 1994) and others suggest other possibilities for the Andean highlands. Specifically, Mesoamerica and Andean highlands may present cases of mutually incorporating world-systems that were only partly merged with respect to luxuries and war, much of it marked by marital exchanges.

A number of other lessons derive from this exercise:

(1) There are at least four types of incorporation or merging of world-systems, which correspond to four types of boundaries: exchange of luxury goods, exchange of information, political-military interaction, and exchange of bulk goods. Furthermore, the distinction between luxury and bulk goods probably denotes the end points of a continuum of types of goods and discrete categories.

60 *Economic Analysis Beyond the Local System*

(2) The four types of boundaries and, hence, four processes of incorporation or merger, do not move together and typically do not coincide.

(3) It is only in the modern world-system, and then only in the nineteenth century, that the four boundaries do coincide.

(4) This clarifies one of the unique aspects of the modern world-system. While this does not entirely negate Amin's (1991) or Wallerstein's (1992, 1993) criteria, it does modify them considerably. It also resolves a muddle they are building: namely that virtually every characteristic they label as defining in the modern world-system is found in earlier systems.

(5) This reformulation of incorporation/merger solves Wallerstein's (1989) conundrum about the Ottoman empire being outside the modern world-system yet trading heavily with it. The merger at that point was not yet complete. The prestige goods and information exchange systems had merged, the political/military system was merging, but the bulk goods trade system remained separate.

(6) In an ironic twist, it appears that classic European feudalism, like the so-called "second serfdom" in eastern Europe half a millennium later, was a consequence of a specific type of incorporation into a larger world-system. That is, the entire Brenner debate[3] about internal and external factors in eastern European development is resolved in favor of the overarching role of the larger world-system, not Wallerstein's modern world-system, but the older Afroeurasian world-system that accounts for both the first and the second serfdom.

(7) The interrelations of plagues and demography make it clear that as societies become more and more complex, social ecology becomes increasingly important, probably more important by the dawn of the CE than the non-human ecology in shaping social change.

(8) Following the work of Ferguson and Whitehead (1992), the effects of world-system expansion and incorporation and the analysis of over two millennia of world-system history suggests that Eric Wolf's (1982) attempt to historicize "timeless" ethnography must be extended back to at least a few centuries BCE.

(9) Several issues remain unresolved: (a) Why is South Asia different? (b) When and how, precisely, does the Afroeurasian ecumene first close? (c) What is the basis of the correlation of urban growth in the Far East and Central Civilization? (d) When was the last contact between nearly equal world-systems: in the thirteenth century or the sixteenth and

seventeenth century clashes between the expanding European world-system and the Ottoman and Chinese world-systems?

(10) What is the basis of the cyclical growth and expansion of world-systems? While some of the sources of periodicity are found in complex feedback loops from social ecology to parasitology to labor relations and balances of class forces in any given mode of production, in conjuncture with geographical advantages and/or disadvantages, this explanation is far from complete. (Here there is agreement with Gills and Frank 1992:676.)

(11) While not extensively reviewed in this paper, it is clear, following the work of McNeill (1963, 1982), Bentley (1993), and Mann (1986) that the spread of world religions plays a major role in integrating world-systems. Whether Mann's analysis of religions as technologies of power is sufficient remains unclear. The persistent differences, even in the modern world-system, between the core areas corresponding to different world religions suggest continuing salience for the information network. This certainly connects with current interests in globalization (Robertson 1992).

(12) While the case for precapitalist world-system analysis is far from complete, the evidence is sufficiently strong to warrant further exploration.

In closing, let me urge those of you concerned with social, cultural, and, especially, economic "analysis beyond the local system" to consider taking precapitalist world-system analysis out for a "test drive." Whether or not you decide to "buy," you will find the view from the world-system perspective, new, interesting, insightful, and refreshing. And who knows, your "test drive" may lead to significant improvements in the model!

Notes

1.   An early version of this paper was presented at the SEA conference in 1993. Since then it became the basis for Chapter 8 of *Rise & Demise* written with Christopher Chase-Dunn. This version draws on several parts of the above manuscript and several other papers with Chase-Dunn. Along the way, we have benefited from critiques and advice of many scholars. That we have not always heeded their wisdom is not their fault.

2.   ("Ecumene" is often spelled "oikumene," as is done by Wilkinson [1992, 1993a, 1993b] and by Kroeber [1917]).

3.   Denmark (1992) reviews this controversy.

References

Abu-Lughod, Janet
  1987 The Shape of the World-system in the Thirteenth Century. *Studies in Comparative International Development* 22:3-25.
  1989 *Before European Hegemony: The World System A.D. 1250-1350.* New York: Oxford University Press.
  1990 Restructuring the Premodern World-system. *Review* 13:273-286.
  1993 Discontinuities and Persistence: One World System or A Succession of World Systems? In *The World System: Five Hundred Years or Five Thousand?* A.G. Frank and B.K. Gills, eds. Pp. 278-290. London: Routledge.

Amin, Samir
  1991 The Ancient World-systems versus the Modern Capitalist World-system. *Review* 14:349-385.

Barfield, Thomas J.
  1989 *The Perilous Frontier.* London: Blackwell.
  1990 Tribe and State Relations: The Inner Asian Perspective. In *Tribe and State Formation in the Middle East.* Philip S. Khoury and Joseph Kostiner, eds. Pp. 153-182. Berkeley: University of California Press.
  1991 Inner Asia and Cycles of Power in China's Imperial Dynastic History. In *Rulers from the Steppe: State Formation on the Eurasian Periphery.* Gary Seaman and Daniel Marks, eds. Pp. 21-62. Los Angeles, CA: Ethnographics Press, Center for Visual Anthropology, University of Southern California.

Beckwith, Christopher I.
  1987 *The Tibetan Empire in Central Asia.* Bloomington: Indiana University Press.

Bentley, Jerry H.
  1993 *Old World Encounters: Cross-cultural Contacts and Exchanges in Pre-Modern Times.* Oxford: Oxford University Press.

Blanton, Richard, Stephen Kowalewski and Gary Feinman
  1992 The Mesoamerican World-system. *Review* 15:419-426.

Bosworth, Andrew
  1992 World Cities and Economic Cycles: Testing Barry Gills and Andre Gunder Frank's A and B Phases. Paper presented at the International Studies Association meeting, Vancouver, BC, May.
  1995 World Cities and World Economic Cycles. In *Civilizations and World-systems: Two Approaches to the Study of World-historical Change.* S.K. Sanderson, ed. Pp. 206-227. Walnut Creek, CA: Altamira Press.

Chandler, Tertius
  1987 *Four Thousand years of Urban Growth: An Historical Census.* Lewiston, NY: Edwin Mellon Press.

Chase-Dunn, Christopher
  1988 Comparing World Systems: Toward a Theory of Semiperipheral Development. *Comparative Civilizations Review* 19:29-66.
  1989 *Global Formation: Structures of the World-economy.* London: Basil Blackwell.
  1990 Resistance to Imperialism: Semiperipheral Actors. *Review* 13:1-31.
  1992 The Comparative Study of World-systems. *Review* 15:313-333.
Chase-Dunn, Christopher and Thomas D. Hall
  1991 Conceptualizing Core/Periphery Hierarchies for Comparative Study. In *Core/Periphery Relations in Precapitalist Worlds.* C. Chase-Dunn and T.D. Hall, eds. Pp. 5-44. Boulder: Westview Press.
  1992 World-systems and Modes of Production: Toward the Comparative Study of Transformations. *Humboldt Journal of Social Relations* 18:81-117.
  1993 Comparing World-systems: Concepts and Working Hypotheses. *Social Forces* 71:851-886.
  1994 The Historical Evolution of World-systems. *Sociological Inquiry* 64:257-280.
  1995 "Rethinking the Evolution of World-systems—Another Round." Paper presented at World System History: The Social Science of Long Term Change, University of Lund, Sweden, March 25-28.
  n.d. *Rise and Demise: Comparing World-systems.* Boulder: Westview Press.
Chase-Dunn, Christopher and Alice Willard
  1993 "Systems of Cities and World-systems: Settlement Size Hierarchies and Cycles of Political Centralization, 2000 BC -1988 AD." Paper presented at International Studies Association, Acapulco, March.
  1994 Cities in the Central Political/Military Network Since CE 1200: Size Hierarchy and Domination. *Comparative Civilizations Review* 30:104-132.
Chaudhuri, K. N.
  1985 *Trade and Civilisation in the Indian Ocean: An Economic History from the Rise of Islam to 1750.* Cambridge: Cambridge University Press.
  1990 *Asia before Europe: Economy and Civilisation of the Indian Ocean from the Rise of Islam to 1750.* Cambridge: Cambridge University Press.
Collins, Randall
  1978 Some Principles of Long-term Social Change: The Territorial Power of States. In *Research in Social Movements, Conflicts, and Change.* Louis Kriesberg, ed. Pp. 1-34. Greenwich, CT: JAI Press.
  1981 Long-term Social Change and The Territorial Power of States. In *Sociology Since Midcentury.* Randall Collins, ed. Pp. 71-106. New York: Academic Press.

1986 *Weberian Sociological Theory.* Cambridge: Cambridge University Press.

Collins, Randall and David Waller

1992 What Theories Predicted the State Breakdown and Revolution of the Soviet Bloc? In *The Transformation of European Communist Societies, Research in Social Movements, Conflicts and Change, Vol 1,.* Louis Kreisberg and David R. Segal, eds. Pp. 31-47. Greenwich, CT: JAI Press.

Crosby, Alfred W.

1986 *Ecological Imperialism: The Biological Expansion of Europe, 900-1900.* New York: Cambridge University Press.

Denemark, Robert A.

1992 Core-periphery Trade: the Debate with Brenner over the Nature of the Link and its Lessons. *Humboldt Journal of Social Relations* 18:119-145.

Dyson, Stephen L.

1985 *The Creation of the Roman Frontier.* Princeton: Princeton University Press.

Elvin, Mark

1973 *The Pattern of the Chinese Past.* Stanford: Stanford University Press.

Ferguson, R. Brian, and Neil L. Whitehead

1992 The Violent Edge of Empire. In *War in the Tribal Zone.* R. B. Ferguson and N. L. Whitehead, eds. Pp. 1-30. Santa Fe, New Mexico: School of American Research Press.

Fitzpatrick, John

1992 The Middle Kingdom, the Middle Sea and the Geographical Pivot of History. *Review* 15:477-521.

Frank, Andre Gunder

1969a *Capitalism and Underdevelopment in Latin America: Historical Studies of Chile and Brazil.* Rev. ed. New York: Monthly Review Press.

1969b *Latin America: Underdevelopment or Revolution.* New York: Monthly Review Press.

1990 A Theoretical Introduction to 5,000 Years of World System History. *Review* 13:155-248.

1992 *The Centrality of Central Asia.* Comparative Asian Studies, 8. Amsterdam: Vrije Universiteit Press for Center for Asian Studies Amsterdam (CASA).

1993 The Bronze Age World System and its Cycles. *Current Anthropology* 34:383-413.

Frank, Andre Gunder and Barry K. Gills
  1990 The Cumulation of Accumulation: Theses and Research Agenda for 5000 Years of World System History. *Dialectical Anthropology* 15:19-42.
  1992 The Five Thousand Year World System: An Interdisciplinary Introduction. *Humboldt Journal of Social Relations* 18:1-79 (Reprinted In *The World System: Five Hundred Years or Five Thousand?* A.G. Frank and B.K. Gills, eds. Pp. 3-55).
Frank, Andre Gunder and Barry K. Gills, eds.
  1993 *The World System: Five Hundred Years or Five Thousand?* London: Routledge.
Fried, Morton
  1952 Land Tenure, Geography and Ecology in the Contact of Cultures. *American Journal of Economics and Sociology* 11:391-412.
Gills, Barry K. and Andre Gunder Frank
  1991 5000 Years of World System History: The Cumulation of Accumulation. In *Core/Periphery Relations in Precapitalist Worlds.* C. Chase-Dunn and T.D. Hall, eds. Pp. 67-112. Boulder: Westview Press.
  1992 World System Cycles, Crises, and Hegemonial Shifts, 1700 B.C. to 1700 A.D. *Review* 15:621-687.
Goldstein, Joshua
  1988 *Long Cycles: Prosperity and War in the Modern Age.* New Haven: Yale University Press.
Hall, Thomas D.
  1986 Incorporation in the World-system: Toward A Critique. *American Sociological Review* 51:390-402.
  1987 Native Americans and Incorporation: Patterns and Problems. *American Indian Culture and Research Journal* 11:1-30.
  1989 *Social Change in the Southwest, 1350-1880.* Lawrence, KS: University Press of Kansas.
  1991a The Role of Nomads in Core/Periphery Relations. In *Core/Periphery Relations in Precapitalist Worlds.* C. Chase-Dunn and T.D. Hall, eds. Pp. 212-239. Boulder: Westview Press.
  1991b Civilizational Change: The Role of Nomads. *Comparative Civilizations Review* 24:34-57.
  1994 Comment on Edward Schortman and Patricia Urban's "Living on the Edge: Core/Periphery Relations in Ancient Southeast Mesoamerica." *Current Anthropology* 35:415-416.
Hall, Thomas D. and Christopher Chase-Dunn
  1993 The World-systems Perspective and Archaeology: Forward into the Past. *Journal of Archaeological Research* 1:121-143.
  1994 Forward into the Past: World-systems Before 1500. *Sociological Forum* 9:295-306.

Hodgson, Marshall G.S.
  1974 *The Venture of Islam.* 3 Volumes. Chicago: University of Chicago Press.
Hopkins, Terence K., and Wallerstein, Immanuel
  1987 Capitalism and the Incorporation of New Zones into the World-economy. *Review* 10:763-779.
Kardulias, P. Nick
  1994 Comment on Edward Schortman and Patricia Urban's "Living on the Edge: Core/Periphery Relations in Ancient Southeast Mesoamerica." *Current Anthropology* 35:416.
Kohl, Philip L.
  1978 The Balance of Trade in Southwestern Asia in the Mid-third Millennium B.C. *Current Anthropology* 19:463-492.
  1994 Comment on Edward Schortman and Patricia Urban's "Living on the Edge: Core/Periphery Relations in Ancient Southeast Mesoamerica." *Current Anthropology* 35:416-417.
Kroeber, Alfred L.
  1917 The Superorganic. *American Anthropologist* 19:163-213.
La Lone, Darrell E.
  1991 The Development of State Production Enclaves in the Inca Empire. Paper presented at the annual meeting of the Society for Economic Anthropology, Bloomington, Indiana, April.
  1992 Social Negotiation, Geopolitics, and World-Systems: Three Perspectives for Exploring Inca State Expansion. Paper presented at the annual meeting of the Andeanist Society Meeting, Champaign, Illinois, March.
  1994 An Andean World-System: Production Transformations Under the Inka Empire. In *The Economic Anthropology of the State.* E.M. Brumfiel, ed. Monographs in Economic Anthropology, No. 11. Pp. 17-41. Lanham: University Press of America.
Lattimore, Owen
  1951 [1940] *Inner Asian Frontiers,* 2nd ed. Boston: Beacon Press.
Lenski, Gerhard and Jean Lenski
  1987 *Human Societies,* 5th ed. New York: McGraw-Hill.
Levathes, Louise
  1994 *When China Ruled the Seas: The Treasure Fleet of the Dragon Throne, 1405-33.* New York: Simon & Schuster.
Lindner, Rudi Paul
  1981 Nomadism, Horses and Huns. *Past & Present* 92:3-19.
  1982 What was a Nomadic Tribe? *Comparative Studies in Society and History* 24:689-711.
Mann, Michael
  1986 *The Sources of Social Power: A History of Power from the Beginning to A.D. 1760.* Cambridge: Cambridge University Press.

Mattingly, D. J.
   1992 War and Peace in Roman North Africa: Observations and Models of State-tribe Interaction. In *War in the Tribal Zone.* R.B. Ferguson and N.L. Whitehead, eds. Pp. 31-60. Santa Fe, New Mexico: School of American Research Press.

McNeill, William H.
   1963 *The Rise of the West: A History of the Human Community.* Chicago: University of Chicago Press.
   1964 *Europe's Steppe Frontier, 1500-1800.* Chicago: University of Chicago Press.
   1976 *Plagues and Peoples.* Garden City, New York: Doubleday.
   1980 *The Human Condition: An Ecological and Historical View.* Princeton: Princeton University Press.
   1982 *The Pursuit of Power: Technology, Armed Force, and Society since A.D. 1000.* Chicago: University of Chicago Press.
   1990 The Rise of the West after Twenty-five Years. *Journal of World History* 1:1-21. (Reprinted as new preface to 1991 printing of *The Rise of the West,* Chicago: University of Chicago Press).

Moseley, Katherine P.
   1992 Caravel and Caravan: West Africa and the World-economies ca. 900-1900 A.D. *Review* 15:523-555.

Randsborg, Klavs
   1991 *The First Millennium A.D. in Europe and the Mediterranean: An Archaeological Essay.* Cambridge: Cambridge University Press.
   1992 Barbarians, Classical Antiquity and the Rise of Western Europe: An Archaeological Essay. *Past & Present* 137:8-24.

Reid, Anthony
   1988 *Southeast Asia in the Age of Commerce, 1450-1680 Vol. 1: The Lands Below the Winds.* New Haven: Yale University Press.
   1993 *Southeast Asia in the Age of Commerce, 1450-1680 Vol. 2: Expansion and Crisis.* New Haven: Yale University Press.

Robertson, Roland
   1992 *Globalization: Social Theory and Global Culture.* Newbury Park, CA: Sage Press.

Sanderson, Stephen K.
   1994 The Transition from Feudalism to Capitalism: The Theoretical Significance of the Japanese Case. *Review* 27:15-55.
   1995 *Social Transformations: A General Theory of Historical Development.* London: Basil Blackwell.

Schneider, Jane
   1977 Was There a Pre-Capitalist World-system? *Peasant Studies* 6:20-29.

Schortman, Edward M. and Patricia. A. Urban, eds.
   1992 *Resources, Power, and Interregional Interaction.* New York: Plenum Press.

Schortman, Edward M. and Patricia. A. Urban
   1992 The Place of Interaction Studies in Archaeological Thought. In *Resources, Power, and Interregional Interaction*. E.M. Schortman and P.A. Urban, eds. Pp. 3-21. New York: Plenum Press.
   1994a Living on the Edge: Core/Periphery Relations in Ancient Southeast Mesoamerica. *Current Anthropology* 35:401-430.
   1994b Reply. *Current Anthropology* 35:421-426.
Sherratt, Andrew G.
   1993 What Would a Bronze Age World System Look Like? Relations Between Temperate Europe and the Mediterranean in Later Prehistory. *Journal of European Archaeology* 1:1-57.
Sherratt, E. S. and Andrew G. Sherratt
   1991 From Luxuries to Commodities: The Nature of Mediterranean Bronze Age Trading Systems. In *Bronze Age Trade in the Mediterranean*. Studies in Mediterranean Archaeology, 90. N. Gale, ed. Pp. 351-386. Jonsered: Paul Anströms Förlag.
Stinchcombe, Arthur
   1978 *Theoretical Methods in Social History*. New York: Academic Press.
Teggart, Frederick J.
   1918 *The Processes of History*. New Haven: Yale University Press. (Reprinted University of California Press 1942, and Peter Smith 1972).
   1925 *Theory of History*. New Haven: Yale University Press. (Reprinted University of California Press 1942, and Peter Smith 1972).
   1939 *Rome and China: A Study of Correlations in Historical Events*. Berkeley: University of California Press.
Tilly, Charles
   1984 *Big Structures, Large Processes, Huge Comparisons*. New York: Russell Sage.
Upham, Steadman, Gary Feinman, and Linda Nicholas
   1992 New Perspectives on the Southwest and Highland Mesoamerica: A Macroregional Approach. *Review* 15:427-451.
Wallerstein, Immanuel
   1974a The Rise and Future Demise of the World Capitalist System: Concepts for Comparative Analysis. *Comparative Studies in Society and History* 16:387-415.
   1974b *The Modern World-system: Capitalist Agriculture and the Origins of European World-economy in the Sixteenth Century*. New York: Academic Press.
   1989 *The Modern World-system III: The Second Era of Great Expansion of the Capitalist World-economy, 1730-1840s*. New York: Academic Press.
   1990 World-system Analysis: The Second Phase. *Review* 13:287-293.
   1992 The West, Capitalism, and the Modern World-system. *Review* 15:561-619.

The Millennium Before the "Long Sixteenth Century" 69

1993 World System vs. World-systems. In *The World System: Five Hundred Years or Five Thousand?* A.G. Frank and B.K. Gills, eds. Pp. 291-296. London: Routledge.

1995 Hold the Tiller Firm: On Method and the Unit of Analysis. In *Civilizations and World-systems: Two Approaches to the Study of World-Historical Change*. S.K. Sanderson, ed. Pp. 225-233. Walnut Creek, CA: Altamira Press.

Wells, Peter S.

1992 Tradition, Identity, and Change Beyond the Roman Frontier. In *Resources, Power, and Interregional Interaction*. E.M. Schortman and P.A. Urban, eds. Pp. 175-188. New York: Plenum Press.

Whitecotton, Joseph W.

1992a Culture and Exchange in Postclassic Oaxaca: A World-system Perspective. In *Resources, Power, and Interregional Interaction*. E.M. Schortman and P.A. Urban, eds. Pp. 51-74. New York: Plenum Press.

1992b Precapitalist Elites in the Mesoamerican World-system. Paper presented at annual meeting of the Social Science History Association, Chicago, November 1992.

Wilkinson, David

1987 Central Civilization. *Comparative Civilization Review* 17:31-59.

1988 Universal Empires: Pathos and Engineering. *Comparative Civilizations Review* 18:22-44.

1991 Core, Peripheries, and Civilizations. In *Core/Periphery Relations in Precapitalist Worlds*. C. Chase-Dunn and T. D. Hall, eds. Pp. 113-166. Boulder: Westview Press.

1992 Cities, Civilizations and Oikumenes: I. *Comparative Civilizations Review* 27:51-87.

1993a Cities, Civilizations and Oikumenes: II. *Comparative Civilizations Review* 28:41-72.

1993b Civilizations, Cores, World-economies and Oikumenes. In *The World System: Five Hundred Years or Five Thousand?* A.G. Frank and B.K. Gills, eds. Pp. 221-246. London: Routledge.

Willard, Alice

1993 Gold, Islam and Camels: The Transformative Effects of Trade and Ideology. *Comparative Civilizations Review* 28:80-105.

Wolf, Eric R.

1982 *Europe and the People Without History*. Berkeley: University of California Press.

1990 Distinguished Lecture: Facing Power—Old Insights, New Questions. *American Anthropologist* 92:586-596.

4

A Local Elite and Underdevelopment in a Peripheral Economy: Iceland in the 18th-20th Centuries

E. Paul Durrenberger

Introduction

Iceland's small homogeneous island population lends itself to the myth of uniqueness propagated by its nationalist rhetoric, itself a function of its classically peripheral position in the world economy as a colony of Denmark until the middle of the twentieth century. Iceland's economy and political rhetoric alike are examples of general patterns that can be observed clearly in other parts of the world.

Given that Iceland exhibits the classic pattern of the core-periphery relationship, in this paper I discuss the place of local elites and how they protected an old system to defend their interests in it, thus delaying the process of development rather than encouraging it. In other words, the same elite that was espousing a nationalist independence rhetoric was at the same time acting against the economic interests of most of their countrymen to protect their own. I argue, though, that this was not a consequence of Icelandic culture or any local dynamic, but rather of Iceland's place in a dynamic global political and economic system.

As Chirot (1986:4) points out, until very recently, "all states were controlled by and organized for the benefit of a very small elite" to extract surpluses from the general population to allow the elites the means with which maintain their control. The idea of states' exercising power for the sake of their majorities does not change this relationship. Much of the elite's room for maneuver is determined by the position of their country in the world system. A state's position in the world economy—its degree of centrality or peripherality—is defined by its political and military power, its degree of economic development, and the degree to which its economy is dependent on exporting raw materials. Dependency on export of primary products blocks the development of diversified economies so that it is impossible for capital to move from one sector to another to adjust to differential price levels (Chirot 1986:97-99).

On the basis of these criteria, Chirot (1986) classifies Denmark as belonging to the minor core during the first decade and a half of the twentieth century. Like the overseas English settler colonies of Australia, Canada, and New Zealand, it was dependent on a few primary exports but had a highly advanced agriculture to capitalize internal industrialization. By the turn of the century Denmark had no need of Iceland's agricultural product.

In general, the position of local elites depends on their control of the supply of raw material they export. They therefore have an interest in maintaining their economy in the same condition. Even in "an independent peripheral state, local elites making a living from the export trade and enjoying well-established connections with traders in core economies had every incentive to maintain export economies even in times of trouble. That was where their investments, knowledge, and power lay—not in risky new economic diversification ventures" (Chirot 1986:100).

One contrast between colonial and independent peripheral countries is that independent countries can base general infrastructural development on even a single export while colonies lack the political means to do so (Chirot 1986:105). After Iceland became independent in 1944, it directed national policy to the development of infrastructure for the fishing industry.

In peripheral countries, Chirot (1986) continues, landowners, government officials, and investors are the elite while a new middle class of merchants, intellectuals, and civil service people develops to replace the old middle class of small landowners and officials. A new lower middle class of small merchants, and artisans and a new working class of workers in enclave cities develop. Iceland provides an example of such class development as it shifted from agricultural to fisheries exports with independence, and even before as people in increasing numbers voted with their feet to abandon the impoverishment of the countryside and move to the burgeoning fishing villages and the primate city of Reykjavík.

Wallerstein and other world systems analysts have pointed out that in peripheral areas, economic forces are not primary. "In the periphery extra-economic coercion plays a much greater part in production

A Local Elite and Underdevelopment 73

relations," as Chase-Dunn (1989:23) puts it. Just as serfdom developed in Poland to control labor to produce commodities to export to Western European core areas (Chase-Dunn 1989:29) an Icelandic elite tried to maintain control of agricultural labor to guarantee its continued role in trading relationships with Denmark. Chase-Dunn characterizes the periphery as the locus of labor intensive production with low wages or coerced and relatively unskilled labor (1989:39, 50, 121). In his terms, Iceland under Denmark was more like a tributary than a capitalist state.

Speaking of the development of the capitalist world system, Chase-Dunn (1989:180) argues that the first comparative advantage in production was revealed in the Netherlands' capture of a large share of the herring fisheries and the European market for fish early in the development of European capitalism, a movement to which Denmark responded by trying to close Iceland off with a trade monopoly.

Contextualizing Icelandic independence and economic development in terms of a world systems perspective not only shows us how it is one example of a much broader and general process but also urges us to look at global as well as local conditions. To understand the power and position of the local elite, we need to contextualize it in terms of Danish and world history.

History

Chase-Dunn dates the beginning of the capitalist world system to Europe's emergence from feudalism from 1450 to 1640. The Netherlands developed hegemony from 1640 to 1815 when Great Britain took over. In 1917 the United States became dominant. As English and German traders set up operations in Iceland to export fish, the Danes restricted trade opportunities and finally in 1602 initiated a complete monopoly of trade with Iceland. Until 1787, when the monopoly was lifted, only those with license from the Danish king could trade with Iceland. Some argued that fisheries would divert labor from farmers, decrease production, and if fisheries failed, there would not be sufficient food to support the population. Others argued that as long as imports from England and Holland could supply food in return for fish, agriculture in Iceland was not important. The monopoly did not allow this debate to continue. Under the monopoly the price of imports rose and the price of exports remained constant. Even so, there was strong demand for fish products and the price for them was greater relative to agricultural products, mainly lamb and wool.

Even though fish prices declined, there was even more emphasis on providing fish and there was a constant push to take advantage of this opportunity by developing fisheries. The problem was that fisheries competed with farmers for labor. If people could earn a living fishing, there would be no one to do the seasonal work of bringing in hay and tending sheep for farmers.

In 1848, when the City Council of Copenhagen, with a large crowd behind it, demanded increased popular participation in government, the king agreed, formed a new cabinet, including leaders of the opposition, and promised to promulgate a constitution. A democratically elected assembly met, and in 1849 a new constitution was ratified and the absolute rule of the Danish king came to a formal end. These changes had little consequence for the elite in Denmark, but they provided a rhetoric of individual liberty and independence for Icelandic students there.

The entities of the monarchy had been held together only by their personal relations with the king himself. There was a core kingdom in the area of today's Denmark with the half Danish speaking-half German speaking Duchy of Schleswig, and two German Duchies of which the king was a duke, the colonies in the Virgin Islands and Greenland, and the two dependencies of the Faeroe Islands and Iceland. The residents of these places were no longer subjects of the king, but citizens of a state. The three duchies were taken by a German army after a short war in 1864. The Danes did not see the integration of the dependencies in the Atlantic important as they contributed little to the Danish economy and no other state claimed them. It was clear to the Faeroese and Icelanders, though, that because of their small numbers, they would have no weight in a Danish parliament.

Today, the "struggle" for independence in Iceland is depicted as long, arduous, and heroic. In fact, as Halfdanarson (1991) shows, it was none of these as there was no opposition. In 1874, after the Danish parliament agreed to subsidize the administration in Iceland, the King of Denmark promulgated a constitution for Iceland which granted it a parliament with limited legislative power. The executive was in Danish hands and the King had veto power over the parliament. In 1904 Denmark granted Iceland home rule, and sovereignty over internal affairs in 1918, and in 1944, Iceland declared itself an independent republic when Denmark was occupied by the Germans in World War II.

Political Economy in Iceland

From medieval times the criterion for participation in civil society had been ownership of sufficient means to support dependents. The same criterion defined households and their heads, whether male or female, as independent. Heads of independent farming households were known as *bændur* (sing., *bóndi*). The medieval period closed decisively in 1264 when, after some decades of internecine fighting, the last remaining chieftain surrendered his authority to the King of Norway to become his earl. In 1380 Iceland went with Norway under Danish rule. After the end of the medieval period there was a group of administrators, religious functionaries, and merchants. Everyone else was a dependent of a householder.

Iceland was divided into administrative districts called *sýslur* (sing. *sýsla*). Further subdivisions were the 18 townships called *hreppar* (sing., *hreppur*), each with a magistrate. *Hreppar* were responsible for the welfare of their residents. A person without means was dependent on this unit for support. Thus, the farmers of each township were very selective about whom they allowed to join their units and tried to bar those who they might have to maintain. Cross-cutting the *hreppar* lines were parish lines of churches. There was an administrative settlement at Reykjavík, but no towns or even villages. The settlement pattern was dispersed farming households.

People often left their homes after they were confirmed in the Icelandic church about age 14 to work on others' farms until men could gain sufficient means to head their own households as independent farmers or until women married independent farmers. People got married in their late 20's or early 30's. By the time they were 40, according to the census of 1850, most males were independent farmers. Because there were more females than males, a larger portion of women remained perpetual servants and unmarried.

Ideologically, the period between childhood and independence was viewed as an apprenticeship being a farmer or farmer's wife. By law, these servants were as children to their masters, who could discipline them as children. Servants were prohibited from traveling without permission. While the ideology made this out as an apprenticeship system, from 1783 the law required that all of those who were not independent farmers had to make annual labor contracts as servants with independent farmers. This law was promulgated specifically to put an end to migratory day labor which would raise the cost of labor for independent farmers (Halfdanarson 1991:61-65).

Sometime after the medieval period, the meaning of the term "farmer" was broadened to include those who did not own their farms but rented from others or had other access to land. The semantic range of the term was thus broadened beyond landowners, and makes subsequent social and class analysis difficult. This is analogous to the current American usage of the term "businessman" to refer to people whose business interests range from those of Andrew Carnegie to the owners of a "mom and pop" store, to a farmer. In other words, it has no analytical coherence. Independent farmers could be of different scales, control different ranges of resources, and be at correspondingly different levels of prosperity.

Icelandic laws limited production to farms and made the family the unit of farming and labor. Everyone who was not an independent farmer was subject to an independent farmer. Thus, there was no "national level" or "community level," only the "household level." In the household, the head was in control. Labor discipline was private and the cost of social control was minimal. Thus, Denmark had to make no investment in political or economic infrastructure. Both were unified in the farming household.

The law defined two spheres: public and private. In the public sphere all was egalitarian. The participants were independent farmers. In the private sphere, everything was hierarchical and patriarchal (Halfdanarson 1991:65). It is no wonder that the sagas of medieval Iceland held interest for this elite—they ratified the values they enshrined in law as a self-perpetuating system of household economies that benefited themselves.

In addition to independent farmers and their dependents, there were lodgers and cottagers, households without access to land. These existed as separate units under the sponsorship of a farmer and the other members of the *hreppur*, the commune, but owned no land and paid rent to the farmer. Whether to sponsor such a household was not a decision the farmer could take alone because the dependent people, having no access to resources, were liable to become wards of the commune as a whole. If such a household failed, the commune could break up the household and redistribute its people. The main difference between lodgers and cottagers was that cottagers were more common in the western part of Iceland and depended more on fishing, working primarily on farmers' boats. They usually had families but no servants. According to the census of 1703, lodgers were mainly close to inland farms and often composed of single unmarried individuals, a majority of whom were women. Some lodgers were married but about half were headed by females, whereas about 17 percent of cottager households were headed by women. There were also unmarried unattached work people who worked by the day and usually lived close to the sea. Thus, the major socio-economic categories were independent farmers, lodgers and cottagers, dependent workpeople, and paupers who were the responsibility of the communes (Magnússon 1985:29-34).

From the time of the first settlement of Iceland in the 9th century, grass was the basis of the agrarian economy. Farmers harvested grass from nearby fields to make hay to feed their cows and sheep during the winters and in the summers took sheep to graze the common lands in the hills and grazed cows closer to home. The prosperity of the farm depended on its livestock and the size of the herd depended on the grass a farmer could lay up for winter. The amount of grass depended on the amount of land a farmer controlled and the amount of labor he could amass to work it, especially during the intense haying period at the end of summer.

In early medieval times large landowners used slaves, but when some people began to offer to do seasonal work because they had less than sufficient land to support their households, landowners freed their slaves and began to rely on seasonal labor. Making *hreppar*, townships, responsible for the people in them guaranteed the preservation of a supply of labor even if the landowners did not support workers directly during the winter. It spread the costs of labor over the entire community. The 19th century labor laws in effect returned Icelandic farmers to their early medieval state—having to support sufficient labor for their farms throughout the year in order to guarantee access to labor when they needed it.

The difference was that in the 19th century, farming was not the only possible occupation. Fishing had always been an integral part of farm operations, and farmers owned the shores and hence controlled access to the sea. Fishing operations were part of the annual round of farming chores. Only foreigners in the 19th century used sailing smacks offshore to catch fish to sell in other lands. Salted cod entered the European market from Denmark. Farmers traded their cod to Danish merchants for flour, tobacco, sugar, fish hooks, line, rope, and manufactured goods. Spain and Portugal purchased salted Icelandic cod via Denmark.

These alternatives were sufficient to threaten the system the independent farmers favored. But population increase was just as important.

A period of population growth began in the 1820's. The first response was to increase the number of farms by various measures from tenancy to claiming land in marginal areas. This expansion came to an end by the middle of the 19th century because some could not support themselves, and because of sheep epidemics. In 1840, 34 percent of men between the ages of 30 and 34 were dependent as were 20 percent of men from the ages of 35-39. In 1890, 56 percent of men from 30 to 34 were dependent (an increase of 22 percent) and 36 percent of the men from 35-39 (an increase of 16 percent). During these fifty years, the percentage of dependency of men increased a total of 38 percent. The system in which a dependent male could hope to some day control his own farm had changed to one in which increasing numbers of men were never able to look forward to independence. Meanwhile, the number of cottagers, married couples with independent households but without farms, grew. Throughout the 19th century, the Icelandic Parliament, which represented the landed elite, passed laws to restrain the growth of cottagers, to make them liable to means tests, and to forbid them to settle on the coast. Landowners, acting through Parliament, wanted to preserve their own labor supply and keep people off the *hreppar* rolls. The lawmakers repeated the old argument that while a fisherman might be able to support a family some years, fishing was risky and not a stable, long-term means of support for a household.

Those people who had no place in the farming economy, and who could not establish new farms, along with those who could never hope to gain access to farms, either emigrated to North America or to the coasts to become cottagers in spite of the laws. They still relied on haymaking work during the summer for wages but flocked to the shore to participate in the developing fishing industry. They were no longer subject to the control of farmers and raised their children in very different environments than before (Halfdanarson 1991:113).

The trade monopoly with Denmark was rescinded in 1787 and all Danish subjects, not just those with royal licenses, were allowed to trade with Iceland, but foreigners (English and Dutch) were still banned from commerce with Iceland until after 1816 when they were allowed to trade but subjected to discouraging differential taxation. While there were Icelanders who traded, they were dependent on Danish merchants and

A Local Elite and Underdevelopment 79

were parts of their operations (Magnússon 1985:41) in accordance with the general pattern Chirot (1986) outlined. Some of these began to invest, often with Danish merchants, in decked sailing smacks. They created a demand for labor and the option was attractive to people who had less than sufficient means to support their households—lodgers, cottagers, dependents, and paupers. It was not until 1905 when steam trawlers began to be used that fishing supplied year round work for fishermen (Magnússon 1985:89). Thus there emerged an alternative commercial elite with interests in fishing opposed to the landowning elite.

From 1776 to 1787 the Danish crown subsidized the Royal Trade Company to teach Icelanders how to better exploit their fishery resources. Icelandic landowners resisted because they feared they would lose control of their labor (Magnússon 1985:50).

The farmers argued for greater local autonomy to control matters in their own *hreppar*, their own communes. An 1853 petition deplores the unorderly conditions and argues that power should be in the hands of a committee elected from the commune's "most respectable men." Halfdanarson (1991) notes the irony that it was these same farmers who championed oppression in their own districts who favored individual liberty, free trade, and independence from Denmark.

In 1851 the Danish government forbade officials from sitting in Parliament, making it clear that administrators were to serve the crown. The role thus left empty was filled by the intellectuals, lawyers, and students, creating a new political category, a new upper middle class as Chirot (1986:111) calls it. Farmers wanted independence not for development or free trade, as some of these new leaders argued, but to restrain individualism and control labor (Halfdanarson 1991:99).

From 1783 to 1863 workpeople not in service were outlawed. In 1861 the Icelandic Parliament passed a law giving commune officials the right to decide who could and could not be a cottager; the King added a provision that if they were rejected, cottagers could appeal to the justice of the county or the prefect of the district because, he argued, "Icelanders are not particularly liberal in deciding cases of this nature . . ." (Halfdanarson 1991:154).

In 1863 the law was changed to exempt those with five cow-values, above a given age, or with some years already served. The Icelandic Parliament passed a law in 1808 that declared that cottagers would have to own a cow or six ewes. In 1863 they passed a law that cottagers had to get permission from local authorities to settle. In 1887 cottage dwelling was forbidden in rural areas, indicating a distinction between the countryside and the beginnings of fishing communities along the shores. Cottage dwellers were required to cultivate a minimum area of land.

Recognizing the problem of greater population than could be supported on the land, the farmers argued for population control by legislation to prohibit marriage between people who could not support themselves. Until the middle of the 19th century, local authorities in communes, *hreppar*, had issued marriage licenses and controlled who could marry. About mid-century, central authorities took over this function. From 1847 to 1865 there were petitions and acts from the Icelandic Parliament to this effect, all rejected by the Danish government and crown. The Danish government rejected an 1861 bill in the Icelandic Parliament that gave farmers the right to discipline their dependents. The Danish government argued that dependents had right to due process and could not be treated as children (Halfdanarson 1991:150-151).

Conclusions

In Iceland, a local elite designed a self perpetuating social and economic system within the Danish state. When the Danes tried to loosen the local landowning elite's hold over the people by centralizing authority for deciding marriages and residence, the farmers protested. When demographic and economic conditions led to the development of a market for Icelandic fish, the farmers did all in their power to prevent the formation of a fishing labor force that would compete for their labor supply and control of it.

In fact, Iceland never repealed the labor laws; Icelanders simply violated them until they lost their force. Some of the farmers began to invest in the new technology of fishing, decked smacks, as others followed, they began to demand labor to process and catch fish and workers could find work in the burgeoning coastal fishing villages as well as Reykjavík with its fleet of steam trawlers and fish processing industry.

As Denmark was incorporated into a wider sphere, its absolute monarchy was replaced by a nation state which redefined relations among its component parts, not only the various possessions but the individual and the state, and provided a context for Icelandic independence. Though farmers strove to perpetuate their hold over the economy, they failed and industrial fishing became the backbone of the

A Local Elite and Underdevelopment 81

national economy. It was the international linkages that Danish commerce established with Spain and Portugal as buyers of salted fish that laid the foundation for this development against the will of the powerful local elite.

Iceland is an example of peripheral backwardness, but, for a century or so, at least, not because the Danes made it so, but because the Icelandic elite demanded it to serve their interests. But this elite owed its existence to Danish policy that created it and defined its interests. The Danish trade monopoly created the autonomous Icelandic form as the primary social, economic, and political unit in the interests of the Danish tributary system. Danish policy defined the interests of the farmers and the system in which they operated. So, in the longer run, it is wrong to suppose that local Icelandic choices, culture, and decisions were instrumental or causative. At least they must be set within the operational context of Danish colonial and foreign policy as well as Danish history.

Denmark withdrew Iceland from the emerging Dutch-English-Hansiatic league fish trade to keep its rich fishery under its own control. The Danish crown did this by means of a trade monopoly that restricted imports. Iceland developed as a periphery to Denmark sharing a classical pattern of political and economic structures common throughout other peripheral areas.

In response to Danish policy a local farming elite developed a system of self contained farms in Iceland and opposed the development of fishing which would threaten its secure and enforced supply of cheap labor. This set fishing interests against farming interests just as in Chile different mining interests were in opposition. Capitalists with interests in copper mines wanted to tax the more profitable nitrate mining sector to underwrite infrastructure developments to aid them in a period of declining prices and support to their competition for export markets. Copper mining interests wanted to use public funds to increase their efficiency and improve their competitive position in the global system. Because nitrate mining was profitable under current circumstances, the nitrate interests did not see this as advantageous, so there was fierce competition within the periphery because of the different points of intersection and fortunes in the world market (Chase-Dunn 1989:122-123).

Likewise, there has always been a similar competition between interests of fishing and farming in Iceland. As long as farmers controlled the terms of trade, the fishing industry remained stagnant so that farmers would be insured a supply of captive labor at cheap rates. Icelandic farming interests therefore resisted attempts to develop fisheries. With the loss of indirect Danish supports, and independence, this faction finally lost to the fisheries sector.

By the same token, it was connections well beyond this local system, the connections of capital and markets, as well as militaries, that provided the ingredients for economic independence that gave political independence meaning in 1944. As the Danes began to modernize and develop, they set the conditions for Icelandic independence. Finally it was conditions beyond Danish control, occupation by Germany in World War II, and the occupation of Iceland by British and then American troops, that pushed Iceland into independence. Given independence and population growth along with new sources of outside capital provided by international events, the new government focused its efforts on the development of industrial fishing and infrastructure to support it.

The trade monopoly organized Iceland for mercantile purposes, as a tributary state, but its organization outlived its usefulness and became a hindrance to organizing for capitalism. The monopoly created the Icelandic class of farmers with their own entrenched interests and power to defend them versus fisheries. This resistance to development can be read as local, as the consequence of Icelandic conditions and Icelandic mentalities only if we ignore history and context. If we place Iceland in its historical and geo-political context, we see that this "backwardness" was not a local dynamic, and certainly not culturally determined, but part of a larger Danish and international system, a part of an embracing world political and economic system.

References

Chase-Dunn, Christopher
    1989 *Global Formation: Structures of the World Economy.* Cambridge: Basil Blackwell.
Chirot, Daniel
    1986 *Social Change in the Modern Era.* New York: Harcourt Brace Jovanovich.
Halfdanarson, Gudmundur
    1991 *Old Provinces, Modern Nations: Political Responses to State Integration in Late Nineteenth and Early Twentieth-Century Iceland and* Brittany. Ph.D. diss., Cornell University.

Magnússon, Magnús S.
1985 *Iceland in Transition: Labour and Socio-economic Change before 1940.* Lund: Eknomisk-Historiska Föreningen.

Part II

Finding the Global in the Local: Contemporary Case Studies

5

Finding the Global in the Local

Thomas D. Hall

Too often analysis moves from larger to local processes, working deductively, to the neglect of the equally important inductive linkage from the local to the global. The papers in this section reverse this tendency and use analyses of local processes and events to explore the effects and reactions to global processes and events. Some of the papers, especially Richard Wilk's, address local-supra-local linkage head on and in depth; others address it through their analyses of case materials.

What I argue here is that world-system analysis, when done well does both, using each approach not only as a corrective for the other, but also as a fertile source for further theoretical development at each level of analysis. A key point I wish to make is that each of these papers individually, but even more so as a collection, are rich sources for improved theorizing about world-systemic processes. To explicate how this is so it is necessary to review briefly some of the recent developments in world-system theory, and their linkages to anthropological thinking.

Eric Wolf suggests that interest in world-system theory is one form of reborn diffusionism (1990:588). While true, there is more to it than this. World-system theory or, better, perspective, is one of many potential ways of cumulating anthropological knowledge and building explanations for cultural phenomena (Wolf 1990:594). This potential has been most strongly developed with respect to the effects of colonialism. The relations among theories of colonialism, dependency, and world-systems theory have been discussed in detail in a variety of places (Chirot and Hall 1982; Shannon 1989; Chase-Dunn 1989; Martin 1994).

In *Europe and the People Without History* (1982), Eric Wolf spoke eloquently and at length about the distortions introduced into anthropological theory through insufficient attention to colonial processes. Janet Abu-Lughod (1989) argues for twelfth-, thirteenth-, and fourteenth-century roots for the modern world-system, deeper than Wallerstein originally proposed. She also argues that the entire conception of the "rise of the west" is mistaken, and suggests that the "east fell" or, at least, withdrew (Abu-Lughod 1989, 1993).

Archaeologists, in particular, have found considerable potential in world-system theory but have been dissatisfied with the results (Hall and Chase-Dunn 1993). All have recognized, to some degree, that world-system theory cannot be applied wholesale to precapitalist settings. Pailes and Whitecotton (1975, 1979) were the first to modify world-system theory for use in precapitalist settings. Jane Schneider (1977) wrote one of the most insightful critiques, questioning Wallerstein's emphasis on bulk to the neglect of luxury goods. Blanton and Feinman (1984) and Santley and Alexander (1992) have also made important critical statements.

More recently, Chase-Dunn and Hall (1991, 1993, 1994) have argued that in order to be useful in precapitalist settings many of the assumptions of the theory of the modern world-system (Wallerstein 1974a, 1974b, 1979, 1980, 1984, 1989, 1991) must be transformed into empirical questions. Andre Gunder Frank and Barry K. Gills (1992; eds 1993) have made similar arguments about "the 5000 year world system." In the process, they extend and elaborate Wolf's basic argument to all of human history since the appearance of the first states some five thousand years ago.

One of the more ironic critiques of world-system theory has been that it is too Eurocentric, focused as it is on the growth and expansion of the western European world-economy that has come to encompass the entire planet. In all fairness to Wallerstein this critique, while in many ways incisive, is misdirected. He never claimed his theory had universal applicability. Rather, he only claimed that it applied to the modern world, that is the last half millennium. This is why he has strong doubts about extending world-system history so far back in time (Wallerstein 1992, 1993, 1995).

A more precise way of rephrasing the critique would be to say that world-system theory is "corecentric," focussing on core development, and "statecentric," tending to ignore nonstate societies. These tendencies have given the impression that peripheral areas and peoples are victims rather than actors. While partially correct, today this criticism is somewhat misleading. The basic story had to be told (Wallerstein 1974b, 1980, 1989) before the nuances, wrinkles, tangents, and anomalies could be addressed. In my own work, I have been highly critical of the neglect of mainstream world-system analysts of nonstate and peripheral peoples

(1983, 1985, 1986, 1989b). I argue that if there is, indeed, a world-system, its effects should not only be visible in far peripheries, but that it is precisely in far peripheries that certain effects and reactions will be most readily visible. My critique of Wallerstein's concept of incorporation was based on the study of peoples in what we know today as the American Southwest (Hall 1986, 1987, 1989a).

Kathryn Ward has pioneered similar critiques of world-system theory for neglecting gender (Ward 1984, 1993; ed. 1990). This work is important to several of the papers in this sections. Others have written case studies that offer fine-grained analyses of the complex functioning of the world-system with respect to: slavery (Morrissey 1989; Tomich 1990), agrarian capitalism (McMichael 1984; So 1986), and relationships of nonstate peoples to the modern and ancient world-systems (Baugh 1991; Hall 1989a; Harris 1990; Kardulias 1990; Mathien and McGuire eds 1986; Meyer 1990, 1991, 1994; Peregrine 1992).

A number of other studies bear more directly on "modern" or "state-centered" topics, which could be useful background to more localized studies. Bunker (1987) and Troillot (1988) have analyzed peasant societies in global perspective. Suter (1992) looks at debt cycles, while Foran (1993) studied the Iranian revolution. The collection edited by Smith et al. (1988) delves into racism and sexism from a number of interesting angles. Goodman et al. (1992) make connections to disease in ways that call to mind the role of disease in the history of Afroeurasia (McNeill 1976; Hall, this volume, Part I). These are only some of the new areas which world-system analysts have explored (for a more complete review see Chase-Dunn and Grimes 1995).

Even culture has begun to gain some attention, although most of the work focuses on culture as a consumption good in modern societies (e.g., Bergesen 1990, 1991, 1992, 1995; Kiser and Drass 1987). This newer work goes beyond what Wilk argues is Wallerstein's (1990) too cursory treatment. Bradley et al. (1990) connect world-system theory, history, and cultural change in insightful ways, beginning some of the work Wilk suggests should be done.

Richard Wilk's paper, in my view, nicely complements the pleas I make here and in my previous chapter, and the comments made by Blanton and Peregrine, to give the world-system perspective serious consideration. Wilk discusses three founding assumptions—the dichotomy of autonomy and dependence, the impact myth, and functional integration—which have blocked economic anthropologists from addressing the complexities of globalization. The contribution that economic anthropologists, indeed all anthropologists, can make to anthropology and world-system analyses is, as Wilk says, "to re-problematize the relationship between cultural production and economic integration in a comparative framework." Only by comparative study of the myriad manifestations of world-system processes in local events can we hope to find the underlying processes that create this tremendous variety of local responses to globalization.

Each of the remaining papers in this section either contribute directly to world-system theorizing, or supply data and analyses from which to make such contributions. Candice Bradley's paper on the acceptance of contraception in Maragoli between 1976 and 1989 demonstrates the utility of looking into the center from the periphery to discover new forms of colonialism (invasion of women's bodies in the form of contraceptives) and how local ideas transform those attempts, giving women a modicum of power over them. Significantly, she suggests ways in which postcolonial analysis can improve world-system and demographic theorizing, and ultimately maybe do something useful for the people we so often study.

Tania Li's paper on tree farming in the upland peripheries of Sulawesi, Indonesia, provides a nearly paradigmatic model of how to analyze the interconnections of the global and the local. The "uneven, but not random" privatization of land is due to a change in mode of production, which entails changes in gender, family, political, and economic relations. While this is clearly a case of incorporation into the world-economy, this account is not what Wilk calls an "impact myth." Rather, it is a story of continuing transformation as the degree and type of incorporation shifts with changes in the world-economy. Here the local actors are not lost to global forces, but attempt to adjust these forces in creative ways. As Li notes, the story is far from over.

Donald Attwood uses his studies of rural Maharashtra to unpack what we mean by peasants and just what it is they do. What he argues is that they do lots of things, that they have done them sometimes for long periods, but changed them often. The arrival of Europeans is another "impact myth"—commercialization is ancient, corroborating for South Asia what I argued in my chapter about all of Afroeurasia. He begins converting an old dichotomy, subsistence vs. commodity production, into a mixture of both that varies along a continuum of proportions. Finally, he notes, most explicitly in his list of five factors that blocked peasant

Finding the Global in the Local 91

"self-transformation," that many of the factors that shaped peasant life were both external and noneconomic. Implying, in short, that their economic patterns were in large part a creative reaction to externally imposed constraints. Thus, he demonstrates, like Tania Li and Candice Bradley, but on a larger scale, the myriad reactions of local producers to varying degrees and types of incorporation into the assorted world-systems.

Christina Turner again changes scale and gives a narrow, ethnographic account of villagers of Ñu Pyajhu Guazú, Paraguay, especially their fictive kinship system. This ethnography, however, differs from older, garden variety ethnographies in that it gives center stage to external constraints on action. In particular, she argues that the local *compadrazgo* choices are a means of minimizing risks inherent in living in a volatile environment subject to rapid market fluctuations and political instability. In short, *compadrazgo* has been a creative adaptation to changes originating externally. Turner notes toward the end of her paper that this system may be beginning to change due to stronger incorporation into the national and global system via improved roads and the expected arrival of electrical power.

Several of these papers are couched in terms that are critical of world-system and other macro theories. Most are "friendly critiques," that is, critiques whose intent is not to demolish the macro theory, but to modify, extend, amend, or otherwise improve it. In this sense all these papers are potential contributors to an improved world-system theory. Collectively, they demonstrate a number of ways local and supra-local processes can be linked empirically and theoretically to provide a richer understanding of economic, political, and cultural processes.

They also show ways to use a world-system perspective to go beyond the local system and to respond to Wolf's call for cumulation in anthropology (1990). To do so, however, requires the analyst to go beyond the classic statements of world-system theory, and to explore the numerous studies that have built on the original statements. Four works make useful starting points: Christopher Chase-Dunn and Peter Grimes's (1995) recent summary of world-system research; Christopher Chase-Dunn's (1989) masterful summary of world-system research; William Martin's (1994) sweeping history of world-system thinking; and Giovanni Arrighi's (1994) restatement of modern world-system history. Thereafter any of the growing number of specific studies, a few of which have been mentioned here, provide more locally rooted models. In summary, in going "beyond the local system," ask not what world-system theory can do for you, but what you can do for world-system theorizing.

References

Abu-Lughod, Janet
1989 *Before European Hegemony: The World System A.D. 1250-1350.* New York: Oxford University Press.
1993 Discontinuities and Persistence: One World System or a Succession of World Systems? In *The World System: Five Hundred Years or Five Thousand?* A.G. Frank and B.K. Gills, eds. Pp. 278-290. London: Routledge.
Arrighi, Giovanni
1994 *The Long Twentieth Century.* London: Verso Press.
Baugh, Timothy
1991 Ecology and Exchange: The Dynamics of Plains-Pueblo Interaction. In *Farmers, Hunters, and Colonists: Interaction Between the Southwest and the Southern Plains.* K.A. Spielmann, ed. Pp. 102-107. Tucson: University of Arizona Press.
Bergesen, Albert
1990 Turning World System Theory on its Head. *Theory, Culture & Society* 7:67-81.
1991 The Semiotics of New York's Artistic Hegemony. In *Cities in the World-system.* R. Kasaba, ed. Pp. 121-132. New York: Greenwood Press.
1992 Godzilla, Durkheim, and the World-system. *Humboldt Journal of Social Relations* 18:195-216.
1995 Postmodernism: A World System Explanation. *Protosoziologie* 7:54-59, 304-305.
Blanton, Richard and Gary Feinman
1984 The Mesoamerican World System. *American Anthropologist* 86:673-682.
Bradley, Candice, Carmella Moore, Michael Burton and Douglas White
1990 A Cross-cultural Historical Study of Subsistence Change. *American Anthropologist* 92:447-457.
Bunker, Stephen
1987 *Peasants Against the State.* Champaign-Urbana: University of Illinois Press.
Chase-Dunn, Christopher
1989 *Global Formation: Structures of the World-economy.* London: Basil Blackwell.
Chase-Dunn, Christopher and Peter Grimes
1995 World-systems analysis. *Annual Review of Sociology* 21:387-427.

Chase-Dunn, Christopher and Thomas D. Hall
1991 Conceptualizing Core/Periphery Hierarchies for Comparative Study. In *Core/Periphery Relations in Precapitalist Worlds*. C. Chase-Dunn and T.D. Hall, eds. Pp. 5-44. Boulder: Westview Press.
1993 Comparing World-systems: Concepts and Working Hypotheses. *Social Forces* 71:851-886.
1994 The Historical Evolution of World-systems. *Sociological Inquiry* 64:257-280.

Chirot, Daniel and Thomas D. Hall
1982 World-system Theory. *Annual Review of Sociology* 8:81-106.

Foran, John
1993 *Fragile Resistance: Social Transformation in Iran from 1500 to the Revolution*. Boulder, CO: Westview Press.

Frank, Andre Gunder and Barry K. Gills
1992 The Five Thousand Year World System: An Interdisciplinary Introduction. *Humboldt Journal of Social Relations* 18:1-79 (Reprinted In *The World System: Five Hundred Years or Five Thousand?* A.G. Frank and B.K. Gills, eds. Pp. 3-55).

Frank, Andre Gunder and Barry K. Gills, eds.
1993 *The World System: Five Hundred Years or Five Thousand?* London: Routledge.

Goodman, Alan H., D. L. Martin, and G. J. Armelagos
1992 Health, Economic Change, and Regional Political Economics Relations: Examples from Prehistory. *MASCA Research Papers in Science and Archaeology* 9:51-60.

Hall, Thomas D.
1983 Peripheries, Regions of Refuge, and Nonstate Societies: Toward A Theory of Reactive Social Change. *Social Science Quarterly* 64:582-597.
1985 Is Historical Sociology of Peripheral Regions Peripheral? *California Sociologist* 8(1-2):281-304. [Reprinted as 1989b].
1986 Incorporation in the World-system: Toward A Critique. *American Sociological Review* 51:390-402.
1987 Native Americans and Incorporation: Patterns and Problems. *American Indian Culture and Research Journal* 11:1-30.
1989 *Social Change in the Southwest, 1350-1880*. Lawrence: University Press of Kansas.
1989b Is Historical Sociology of Peripheral Regions Peripheral? In *Studies of Development and Change in the Modern World*. M. T. Martin and T. R. Kandal, eds. Pp. 349-372. Oxford: Oxford University Press.

Hall, Thomas D. and Christopher Chase-Dunn
1993 The World-systems Perspective and Archaeology: Forward into the Past. *Journal of Archaeological Research* 1:121-143.

Harris, Betty J.
   1990 Ethnicity and Gender in the Global Periphery: A Comparison of Basotho and Navajo Women. *American Indian Culture and Research Journal* 14:15-38.
Kardulias, P. Nick
   1990 Fur Production as a Specialized Activity in a World System: Indians in the North American Fur Trade. *American Indian Culture and Research Journal* 14:25-60.
Kiser, Edgar and Kriss A. Drass
   1987 Changes in the Core of the World-system and the Production of Utopian Literature in Great Britain and the United States, 1883-1975. *American Sociological Review* 52:286-293.
Martin, William G.
   1994 The World-systems Perspective in Perspective: Assessing the Attempt to Move Beyond Nineteenth-century Eurocentric Conceptions. *Review* 17:145-185.
Mathien, Frances Joan and Randall McGuire, eds.
   1986 *Ripples in the Chichimec Sea: Consideration of Southwestern-Mesoamerican Interactions.* Carbondale, IL: Southern Illinois University Press.
McMichael, Philip
   1984 *Settlers and the Agrarian Question: Foundations of Capitalism in Colonial Australia.* Cambridge: Cambridge University Press.
McNeill, William H.
   1976 *Plagues and Peoples.* Garden City, New York: Doubleday.
Meyer, Melissa L.
   1990 Signatures and Thumbprints: Ethnicity Among the White Earth Anishinaabeg, 1889-1920. *Social Science History* 14:305-345.
   1991 "We Cannot Get a Living as We Used To:" Dispossession and the White Earth Anishinaabeg, 1889-1920. *American Historical Review* 96:368-394.
   1994 *The White Earth Tragedy: Ethnicity and Dispossession at a Minnesota Anishinaabe Reservation, 1889-1920.* Lincoln: University of Nebraska Press.
Morrissey, Marietta
   1989 *Slave Women in the New World: Gender Stratification in the Caribbean.* Lawrence: University Press of Kansas.
Pailes, Richard A. and Joseph W. Whitecotton
   1975 Greater Southwest and Mesoamerican World-systems. Paper presented at the Southwestern Anthropological Association meeting, Santa Fe, March.
   1979 The Greater Southwest and the Mesoamerican "World" System: An Exploratory Model of Frontier Relationships. In *The Frontier:*

Comparative Studies, Vol. 2, W. W. Savage, Jr. and S. I. Thompson, eds. Pp. 105-121. Norman: University of Oklahoma Press.

Peregrine, Peter N.
1992 *Mississippian Evolution: A World-system Perspective.* Monographs in World Archaeology, 9. Madison: Prehistory Press.

Santley, Robert S. and Rani T. Alexander
1992 The Political Economy of Core-periphery Systems. In *Resources, Power, and Interregional Interaction,* E.M. Schortman and P.A. Urban, eds. Pp. 23-59. New York: Plenum Press.

Schneider, Jane
1977 Was There a Pre-Capitalist World-system? *Peasant Studies* 6:20-29 (Reprinted In C. Chase-Dunn and T. D. Hall, *Core/Periphery Relations in Precapitalist Worlds,* Pp. 45-66. Boulder: Westview Press).

Shannon, T. R.
1989 *An Introduction to the World-system Perspective.* Boulder: Westview Press.

Smith, Joan, Collins, Jane Hopkins, Terence K., and Muhammed, Akhbar
1988 *Racism, Sexism and the World-system.* New York: Greenwood Press.

So, Alvin
1986 *The South China Silk District: Local Historical Transformation and World-system Theory.* New York: State University of New York Press.

Suter, Christian
1992 *Debt Cycles in the World-economy: Foreign Loans, Financial Crises, and Debt Settlements, 1820-1990.* Boulder: Westview Press.

Tomich, Dale W.
1990 *Slavery in the Circuit of Sugar: Martinique and the World Economy, 1830-1848.* Baltimore: Johns Hopkins University Press.

Troillot, Michel-Rolph
1988 *Peasants and Capital: Domenica in the World Economy.* Baltimore: Johns Hopkins University Press.

Wallerstein, Immanuel
1974a The Rise and Future Demise of the World Capitalist System: Concepts for Comparative Analysis. *Comparative Studies in Society and History* 16:387-415.
1974b *The Modern World-system: Capitalist Agriculture and the Origins of European World-economy in the Sixteenth Century.* New York: Academic Press.
1979 *The Capitalist World-economy.* Cambridge: Cambridge University Press.
1980 *The Modern World-system II: Mercantilism and the Consolidation of the European World-economy, 1600-1750.* New York: Academic Press.
1984 *The Politics of the World-economy: The States, the Movements, and the Civilizations.* Cambridge: Cambridge University Press.

1989 *The Modern World-system III: The Second Era of Great Expansion of the Capitalist World-economy, 1730-1840s.* New York: Academic Press.
1990 World-system Analysis: The Second Phase. *Review* 13:287-293.
1991 *Geopolitics and Geoculture: Essays on the Changing World-system.* Cambridge: Cambridge University Press.
1992 The West, Capitalism, and the Modern World-system. *Review* 15:561-619.
1993 World System vs. World-systems. In *The World System: Five Hundred Years or Five Thousand?* A. G. Frank and B. K. Gills, eds. Pp. 291-296. London: Routledge.
1995 Hold the Tiller Firm: On Method and the Unit of Analysis. In *Civilization and World-systems: Two Approaches to World-historical Change.* Stephen K. Sanderson, ed. Pp. 225-233. Walnut Creek, CA: Altamira Press.

Ward, Kathryn B.
1984 *Women in the World System.* New York: Praeger.
1993 Reconceptualizing World-system Theory to Include Women. In *Theory on Gender/Feminism on Theory.* P. England, ed. Pp. 43-68. New York: Aldine.

Ward, Kathryn B., ed.
1990 *Women Workers and Global Restructuring.* Ithaca, NY: ILR Press.

Wolf, Eric R.
1982 *Europe and the People Without History.* Berkeley: University of California Press.
1990 Distinguished Lecture: Facing Power—Old Insights, New Questions. *American Anthropologist* 92:586-596.

6

Emerging Linkages in the World System and the Challenge to Economic Anthropology[1]

Richard R. Wilk

It is already almost an academic cliché that the world is increasingly integrated, that the global economy is now mirrored by global culture and global structures of power. This acceptance is reflected in terms like "transnational," "diaspora" and "cosmopolitan." Whole journals, like *Diaspora, Theory, Culture & Society,* and *Public Culture* have staked out global culture as their territory, and anthropologists like Arjun Appadurai and Ulf Hannerz have helped colonize the subject. But though economic anthropologists embraced the economic and historical aspects of World Systems Theory long ago, and were in the vanguard of anthropological investigation of global interconnections, I find that we are lagging far behind in extending our topical reach to include global *culture*.

Over the last few years, I have been doing research on consumer goods in Belize, on flows of money, people and media in and out of the country, and the relationship between Belize's economic position in the world and its cultural identities (Wilk 1993). As I have pursued these topics, I have found myself drawn further and further away from what is conventionally recognized as economic anthropology. And this bothers me. Because I think that what I am doing is very much economic anthropology, and that the literature I am reading would benefit a great deal from what economic anthropologists have to offer. So this paper is a result of being bothered, of having a nagging feeling that something is wrong, and of trying to find the itch. In it I am trying to explain *why* economic anthropology is often so marginal to issues of global cultural integration, mass consumption, national economic policies, and global flows of people, money and commodities.

I do not intend to single any individuals out for blame or praise. I don't think that economic anthropology's failure in embracing global culture is anyone's fault. Instead our problem with this topic stems from some very fundamental assumptions we continue to make about the relationships between what we call "culture" and "the economy." Though we have long ago left the world of isolated peasants and tribes behind, we still carry basic terms and concepts that were forged in the village, out into a world of MTV, Free Trade Agreements, and ethnic cleansing.

Setting the Stage: The World We Have Lost

Anthropologists like Appadurai, Hannerz and Friedman tell us that global trends include both unification and fragmentation; that economic, social, political and economic changes are increasingly disarticulated. Friedman (1992) interprets fragmentation as the backwash from the passing of global hegemony; the old cultural order with its northern metropoles and neo-colonies is falling apart, to be replaced by a new multicentric disorder. Appadurai (1990) portrays a process of "deterritorialization;" no longer tied to particular locations or to each other, cultural and economic processes flow through mobile terrains which he calls *finanscapes, mediascapes* and *ethnoscapes* (among others). Hannerz (1987; 1990) describes a world of creolization, where the boundaries between existing cultural units shift, dissolve and are reconstituted anew, where rootless transnational cosmopolitans build cultural capital negotiable in every locale. Hannerz is ready to throw away the previous "natural" order of cultural units and boundaries, and substitute cultural flows and processes of transformation.

The core issue in the literature on globalization is the *relationship between culture and the economy.* The question is about how greater economic and electronic integration are affecting culture and social organization. These are the classic issues—the central problematics—of economic anthropology. Why don't we have a collective voice in debates about the effects of economic globalization on local cultural processes? For the last 50 years we have been writing detailed case studies of how regions, communities, and ethnic groups are affected by economic integration. Why have these studies remain unlinked, isolated from each other, and ignored in the wider debates and in other disciplines?

I would argue that our attempts to use world systems theory to provide that integration have been mostly futile (with perhaps the partial exception of Wolf's *Europe and the People Without History*). This failure is partially a result of our tendency to depend on Wallerstein's conservative formulation of the theory, a version that subordinates local to global, culture to the economy, and agency to structure, placing the very concept of an anthropological economics in the intellectual periphery, or maybe off the map entirely. Wallerstein presumes the answer to most of the questions we think are worth investigating; his most recent writing reduces culture to false consciousness, a system that contains contradictions, transforms hierarchy into difference, motivates people to work, and blinds them to growing inequities and global deterioration (Wallerstein 1990, cf. Boyne 1990).

We might be tempted to debate Wallerstein, and perhaps follow Albert Bergesen (1990), to "turn world system theory on its head" and reverse Wallerstein's model. Bergesen argues that in reality the social and political determine the economic; the expansion of the world economy results from prior political and cultural expansion. But hold on a minute—isn't this what economic anthropology has been discussing since Malinowski? Didn't we learn 20 years ago that arguing the absolute priority of culture or economy was a futile chicken and egg hunt? We have so much of substance to offer in this debate, why has the message failed to get through?

Three Weak Foundations

Autonomy and Dependence

I want to focus on three collective sins—problems that have prevented economic anthropology from stepping out onto the center of the stage where global culture and economy are being debated. I am not doing this to point fingers; I include myself in any collective guilt. The issues I raise are ones that lie more in our collective unconscious, institutionalized in our categories and vocabularies, than in anyone's conscious daily practice.

The first problem is what I call the *polarization of autonomy and dependence;* the tendency to create ideal types at the extremes of a continuum. In this case we place absolute economic autonomy at one end and a totally open, highly dependent system at the other. It is easy to find examples of this at all levels of analysis, from the household to the nation state. The classic formulation is that once upon a time (always before the ethnographer arrived) these people were isolated and independent, where today they are drawn into the interdependent market economy (see the preface to Wilk 1991 for an extended critique). Or we can play it in reverse; once upon a time all these families worked together and were interdependent, but now they have been fragmented and are isolated from each other.

In the real ethnographic present, however, most households, communities and regions balance self-provisioning and production for exchange. The extreme cases are the ones that are easy to think with— they appear implicitly as ideal types in most comparative anthropological discussions. On one end you have total self-provisioning, and at the other you have total dependency on exchange, but like "primitive communism" or the "primordial horde," or "group marriage," the extremes are mostly ethnographic fictions. They don't exist in the human species. We know of no society where households are completely autonomous. If nothing else, a household is not genetically isolated—it cannot produce its own children. Lévi-Strauss sees this as the primordial exchange relationship, as if households could otherwise be economically viable. The converse, a household which produces nothing that it consumes, in which all relationships are commodified, is equally impossible. Even in the consensual households which I studied in California—up to eight unrelated college students sharing a house, there were all kinds of non-commodified relationships, and many kinds of self-provisioning work. Mowing the lawn or fixing the roof can be marginalized by defining it as "housework," but this does not make the problem go away.

In most cases, even in a fully capitalist and modern society, the issue for studying households is one of degree. What are the proportions of goods and services provided by the household for the household, and what proportion of labor is devoted to production for exchange? What kinds of relationships do households have with each other, what do they get out of it? In many cases the ideal types at the extremes guide and inform the questions we ask; we are always pushing our cases towards one extreme or the other. (Here I would point at Sahlins' *Stone Age Economics* as a major influence in building these oppositions into the very vocabulary with which we discuss the "domestic mode of production" and types of reciprocity.)

If we shift scale and think about countries—modern nation states, we find the same problems. Again there are evolutionary and primordialist assumptions, and the extremes are imaginary debating tools, which in practice get in the way of our analysis. The precapitalist condition is usually depicted as one of complete autonomy, the fully modern one as total interdependence. Economists tend to view anything which impedes the growth of interdependence as an inhibition of free trade. Periods when interdependence declines are considered recessions or depressions. To neoclassical economists, the logic of exchange and efficiency will always produce more interdependence through the mechanism of specialization and comparative advantage. But the end result is not specified—is it supposed to be total interdependence? Every country producing just one or two goods for which it has comparative advantage, and buying everything else from others? Again, the extreme cases are fictitious,

The reality of the world is the territory in between. The polar types, and the evolutionary framework in which they are embedded, keep us from fully engaging the complex relationships between autonomy and dependency. Data on world trade do not support simple linear models, but show instead a lot of temporal variation in the autonomy of local systems.

The Impact Myth

This brings me to a second weak foundation that makes it difficult for economic anthropology to engage global problems. Here the ideas derive originally from unilinear evolutionism and the modernization theory of the 1950s and 1960s. The problem emerges clearly in the classic ethnographic story which I call an *impact myth*: First, you had some original or aboriginal culture. Then, there was some drastic external economic or political impact which transformed their productive system. Finally, you end up with a new cultural form that is dramatically different from the original state. You can repeat the story several times if you have good historical material.

I do not deny that from these stories we have extracted a lot of important generalizations about processes of monetization, proletarianization, social circumscription, and resettlement. But there are two crucial problems with the ways we tell this story. First is the starting point, the semi-mythical "before time," of pristinity. Much recent ethnohistory and critical anthropology has questioned the accuracy of ethnographic reconstructions of precapitalist or precolonial times, casting them as rationalist, romantic or orientalist projections (Thomas 1992). Second, there is the assumption of a sequence of order/disorder/order, that once the political/economic/cultural worlds were in harmony; they were integrated. Disorder, disarticulation, conflict and dysfunction are then explained as the result of impact, and are thereby implied to be unnatural or anomalous or temporary.

Order thereby becomes the natural state of things. Unless something comes along to cause disruption, there will be an equilibrium. This is not the same as the much-criticized tendency of classical British social anthropology to assume functional integration (see below). Most anthropologists have long since discarded the idea that every action or institution or custom has its function, and every functional requirement is met by some social or economic agent. The impact myth is more subtle and pervasive, but also more reasonable (on the face of it). It is often a simple product of the short time horizons of non-literate peoples, or the limitations of documentary resources. We usually cannot tell what kinds of changes were taking place before the time we are studying. But whether we intend them to or not, our accounts often downplay the possible chaos or disorder of earlier times, and we thereby allow our work to fall into the classical form of the impact myth.

Functional Integration

This brings me to charge number three: our habit of accepting the untested premise of functional integration. The idealized autonomous village was one where things worked, where Julian Steward could find balance and equilibrium as the economy was integrated with the political system, reflected and maintained by culture. Within the economy, production, exchange and consumption were functionally articulated into a single closed system, a rationalized loop.

Economic anthropologists have heaped all kinds of criticism and ridicule on this model over the last twenty years (and even long before— the critics are too numerous to mention here, though Raymond Firth was certainly a pioneer). What is distressing is that many of its vestiges still hang on, particularly in the ways that we think about cause and effect, and connections between different elements of society.

The hermetic, balanced cultural system never existed, and its functional integration was never more than partial. The village model is particularly damaging to an anthropology of global systems because of what it says about the relationship between production and consumption, economy and culture. The functional model leads us to expect spatial and temporal isomorphism between all these components. When the economy changes, so does culture. Where there are economic boundaries, we should find cultural boundaries. The social context of production should also be the social context of consumption.

We thereby naturalize and primordialize ethnic and tribal boundaries, claiming they are somehow natural expressions of underlying economic units. But in fact most of those boundaries are anything but natural; they are political, intentional, pragmatic and contested.

Wallerstein makes a similar error when he argues for a tight functional integration between culture and the global economic system (1990). The literature on globalism is full of imaginary functional linkages; people look at evidence for one kind of global linkages, and then assume correspondences in other areas (e.g., global economic integration will lead to global cultural integration, global media will lead to global consumerism, global migration will lead to ethnic fragmentation). A more realistic approach is the one taken by Mintz in *Sweetness and Power,* where he describes connections and circuits, but never implies that the economic connections between Caribbean slaves and European nobility were mirrored by cultural connections, or even mutual awareness.

An Example

I have often wrestled with all three of these problems in my own fieldwork in Belize. Lately I have been working on local and global connections, and have found myself especially vexed by the false dichotomy of autonomy and dependence.

Many Belizeans seem preoccupied with issues of local autonomy, of dependence on foreigners, and the impending loss of local culture. They sometimes sound like the anthropologists of the 1960s, always insisting that Belize is becoming more dependent all the time, and that the invasion of foreign money, tourists, immigrants and media are transforming a once stable, just and self-reliant society into a suburb of Los Angeles. In other words, outmoded anthropology has largely become folk-knowledge among the people we study.

To summarize a book length manuscript in a few words—the folk explanation of cultural dependence and autonomy just isn't so. In fact, a better case can be made for the opposite, that as the Belizean economy has become more open, more dependent, less autonomous, Belizean cultural production has become more intensive. As the economic and social boundaries have come down, as Belizeans themselves have become extremely mobile, something called "Belizean culture" has finally emerged and has acquired a distinctive and widespread meaning and following.

When I began to visit Belize in the early 1970s, people carefully explained to me that the local Afro-Creole people were culturally "really" British or Caribbean. The Hispanic communities were "just Mestizos" like Guatemalans or Mexicans. The only people in the country who were widely acknowledged to have a culture were marginalized minority immigrants—Kekchi, Mopan, Garinagu and Mennonites—all of whom were known to keep to their own communities, to have distinctive ways of life, their own languages, foods and religions.

When I asked about "Belizean Food," people laughed at me, or looked puzzled, as if I had named an imaginary animal in a list of known species. In those days when I looked for Belizean gifts for my friends in the U.S.—there were simply no local, distinctive or emblematic objects one could take home to prove that one had been to a place called "Belize." Only stamps, coins and bottles of "local" Belikin beer; brewed next to the Belize City airport by an American, in a Canadian brewery using Dutch malt concentrate and English bottles. *I* found something quite special and distinctive there, but there were no public symbols, no public discussions about that distinction.

About the only other people who seemed to believe in something called Belizean culture were politicians. Prime Minister George Price gave many speeches about the need to develop a Belizean culture that would bring together the country's diverse ethnic groups, sometimes hinting at American-style syncretism, but more recently favoring the pluralist metaphor of the stewpot over the blender (Judd 1989).

Today the quaint, isolated, autonomous place I once knew, a country with no self-consciousness, has changed dramatically. Belize is awash with emblematic locally produced goods—woodcrafts, hot pepper sauces, dolls and dresses. There is a literally booming local music industry, boasting its own fusion of traditional Garifuna drums with Caribbean tunes, now marketed in America and England. A Belizean cuisine has appeared and now almost every local eatery is advertising "authentic Belizean food." There is a touring national dance troupe, a national theater movement, a historical society that is designating and protecting landmarks and choosing national heros. There are now self-consciously Belizean painters producing oils of village life, Belizean poets, and there is contention for the position of the great Belizean novel. Belize has become a cultural place.

The point is that the articulation between the economy and cultural representations is not direct; it is complex and often runs directly counter to expectations generated by traditional anthropological models. In Belize, greater economic integration has led to much more conscious cultural production and certain kinds of cultural autonomy. In colonial times the country was much more self-sufficient, according to my analysis of customs records, but there was very little local cultural production. And this is not something new, unique to the era of jet travel and satellite TV. The relationship between cultural identification and political/economic autonomy has always been problematic, far from what we would expect based on polarized evolutionary models.

My own ethnohistoric work with the Kekchi in Belize began as a simple impact myth (Wilk 1991). Here were these isolated autonomous subsistence oriented communities, with their age-old Kekchi culture. Along came cash crops and wage labor, and suddenly their culture had to adapt; Kekchi culture as an autonomous and distinctive entity seemed to be on the way out. Historical perspective shows just how wrong this model was. I witnessed only the most recent of many episodes of Kekchi participation in a global system of production and consumption.

And the interesting thing was that the times when Kekchi culture appeared most stable, when aspects of daily life became central to Kekchi cultural identity, were the times of most rapid economic and political change, not the times of economic stability. Corn swidden farming and communal labor became essential parts of Kekchi cultural identity during the late 19th century when they became workers on coffee plantations, not during the Classic period. The cargo system and communal landholding became traditions in the 1920s when they produced bananas for Standard Fruit. And in the last 15 years, again under pressure, tradition is solidifying once again and new kinds of uniformity are emerging.

Conclusion

When I read a version of this paper at the annual SEA meetings in 1993, many people in the audience were angry. Some felt that I was just dredging up old complaints and critiques that had been addressed long ago (by people wiser and better read than myself!). I do not claim that my criticisms here are original, but I think most of us underestimate how deeply these problems are embedded in our practice. I think they are particularly damaging at this point in time, because they are binding our feet to the ground when we should be leaping into new topics and taking center stage in academic debates from which economic anthropology is now mostly missing. The connections between economic life and the political and cultural order are the very heart of economic anthropology, and we are in a very strong position to use our traditional strengths on the issues raised by global interdependence.

The papers in this volume represent a new kind of engagement with the problem of world cultural systems, and go a long way towards answering some of my complaints. As Hall argues in the previous chapter, there are strong foundations within world-systems theory, on which economic anthropology can build. I would argue that our central goal must be to re-problematize the relationship between cultural production and economic integration in a comparative framework. Otherwise we will be frustrated in our attempts to build "economic analysis beyond the local system," without merely duplicating macroeconomics or old evolutionary models of modernization.

Notes

1. A preliminary draft of this paper was presented at the 13th annual meeting of the Society for Economic Anthropology, Durham, NH 1993. I appreciate the assistance of Anne Pyburn in writing this paper; James Carrier also offered useful comments on an earlier draft. Some of the comments from the audience at the SEA meetings were also very useful. The research in Belize discussed here was supported by a grant from the Wenner-Gren Foundation for Anthropological Research, and a Fulbright Fellowship.

References

Appadurai, Arjun
    1990 Difference in the Global Cultural Economy. *Public Culture* 2(2):1-24.
Bergesen, Albert
    1990 Turning World System Theory on its Head. *Theory, Culture & Society* 7:67-81.
Boyne, Roy
    1990 Culture and the World System. *Theory, Culture & Society* 7:57-62.

Friedman, Jonathan
  1992 The Past in the Future: History and the Politics of Identity. *American Anthropologist* 94(4):837-859.
Hannerz, Ulf
  1987 The World in Creolization. *Africa* 57(4): 546-559.
  1990 Cosmopolitans and Locals in World Culture. *Theory, Culture & Society* 7:237-251.
Judd, Karen
  1989 Who Will Define Us? Creole History and Identity in Belize. Paper presented at the Annual Meeting of the American Anthropological Association, Washington, D.C..
Mintz, Sidney W.
  1985 *Sweetness and Power: The Place of Sugar in Modern History.* New York: Penguin Books.
Sahlins, Marshall
  1972 *Stone Age Economics.* London: Tavistock Publications.
Thomas, Nicholas
  1992 The Inversion of Tradition. *American Ethnologist* 19(2): 213-233.
Wallerstein, I.
  1990 Culture as the Ideological Battleground of the World System. *Theory, Culture & Society* 7:31-55.
Wolf, Eric R.
  1982 *Europe and the People without History.* Berkeley: University of California Press.
Wilk, Richard
  1991 *Household Ecology.* Tucson: University of Arizona Press.
  1993 Beauty and the Feast: Official and Visceral Nationalism in Belize. *Ethnos* 58:3-4: 294-317.

7

Fertility in Maragoli: The Global and the Local

Candice Bradley

This paper locates the study of fertility and fertility decline in Africa in postcolonial perspective. This perspective emphasizes the interplay of power, information, and knowledge between the global, capitalist world-system and local, marginalized places. The local place explored in this paper is Igunga Sublocation, in the Maragoli region of western Kenya.[1] Like many other parts of Kenya, Maragoli is in the throes of rapid fertility decline (Table 7.1). This paper focuses on the adoption of contraception in Igunga, and on individual and historical relationships which may influence people's contraceptive choices.

Most demographic research, including my own in Maragoli, is ultimately grounded in modernization theory. Classical modernization theory imagines a world with two kinds of nation-states: those which are modern, and those which are modernizing. Countries which are not modern are thought to be moving inevitably toward modernization, as they adopt new technology and abandon traditions which keep them from full participation in a capitalist market economy (Bradley, in press). Modernization theory typically attributes the causes of underdevelopment to internal factors, and as such "Third World societies needed to overcome the traditionalism of their social structures, cultural values, and political institutions" (Shannon 1989:4-5).

Although classical modernization theory has been rejected in virtually all social science disciplines, aspects of most contemporary theories of fertility decline contain its underlying assumptions. Theories of fertility decline which emphasize the distribution of contraceptives, improvements in health care, equitable education and women's status, reversals in wealth flows, and the dissemination of information, are all grounded in modernization theory. In these models, modernization, westernization, technological improvements and/or economic development—including increased educational or economic opportunities—ultimately raise women's status and lower fertility. As such, most contemporary demographic theorizing contends that, and brings evidence to bear on the notion that, progress, particularly for women, brings about fertility decline. These assumptions are not necessarily inappropriate, and indeed much of this research has led to viable population policy (Bradley 1995; Brass and Jolly 1993; Caldwell 1982; Dow et al. 1994; Handwerker 1989, 1991, 1993; LeVine et al. 1991; Watkins 1991; van de Walle and Foster 1990).

	Ssennyonga (1976)	Bradley (1989)
Dependency Ratio	134.0	118.3*
Crude Birth Rate (per 1000)	49.4	44.5
Crude Death Rate (per 1000)	14.3	12.2
Total Fertility Rate	8.6	7.1**
Percent Contracepting	1.0	31.0**
(n)	(398)	(303)

(* $p < .05$; ** January 1991 data)

Table 7.1: Igunga Sublocation Population Statistics.

The assumptions of modernization theory often pervade models of fertility decline which claim to reject it. Typical critiques of modernization theory are that it is functionalist, ahistorical, and blames underdevelopment on the victim. World-systems theory differs from modernization theory in its emphasis on global relationships, especially an international division of labor, in which historical processes result in differential development of some nation-states relative to others. The marginalized zones, or periphery, of the world system include classes, genders and ethnic groups whose marginalization serves the ends of the capitalist world-economy, yet may resist its intrusion (Wallerstein 1974, Shannon 1989).

However, modernization theory's assumptions are not absent from demographic theorizing within the world-systems approach, nor from feminist perspectives on the "Third World" which are informed by world-systems theory and its predecessor, dependency theory. These perspectives often contend that economic and technological development, underdevelopment, modernization, or the intrusion of the capitalist world-system lower women's status and result in higher fertility in peripheral regions of the world-economy. Researchers using this model argue that women have no other choices but to keep fertility high. Again, fertility and women's status are inversely related.

Like world-systems theory, a postcolonial perspective considers the world as a single economic, political and ecological system with an international division of labor. However, a postcolonial perspective recognizes multiple forms of imperialism which continue after the abolition of de facto colonies. Colonization established with economic power and force gives way in the postcolonial period to new forms of imperialism (Said 1993). These may include economic intrusion, but have also discussed women as "the last colony" (Mies et al. 1988), the technologization of reproduction as "colonized seeds" (Shiva 1994), and the continuation of colonial ideas in "colonized minds" (Ngugi 1986). In postcolonial imperialism, the agents of transformation are information and knowledge (Said 1993).

It is not necessary to adopt anti-quantitative, interpretive or postmodern methodologies to see these forces at work. Watkins (1991), for example, describes the importance of the spread of information about contraception in the process of fertility decline. Caldwell (1982) has discussed the impact of informational resources, such as pictures of westernized nuclear families in African schoolchildren's textbooks. Feminist perspectives such as Greenhalgh's (1994) paper on controlling births and bodies in China is another example, as is Tsing's (1993) discussion of resistance to government birth control programs among Meratus Dayaks and Bledsoe's (1990) discussion of why condoms are not more popular in African cultures.

The dissemination and adoption of contraception is a ripe area for considering the connection between the global world-economy and the peoples in "out of the way places" (Tsing 1993). We can choose to conceptualize contraception as we currently do, in terms of demand, supply and unmet need. We can also conceptualize fertility in terms of informational and ideological postcolonizing of peoples in the periphery.

I have chosen to talk about contraception and fertility decline in Maragoli as two separate tales. The first is the story of fertility decline and marginalization in Igunga, which describes the transformation of this sublocation from a place where only one percent contracept to a place where nearly a third do. Here, I present the factors which predict contraceptive use in Igunga Sublocation. The second is a postcolonial story, describing what I see as the reasons Igunga women have opted for injections over other forms of family planning.

Fertility Decline and Marginality in Maragoli

Igunga Sublocation was transformed between 1976 and 1989 from a place where 99 percent of the women did not use contraception, to a place where nearly a third used it. Total fertility rates in Igunga declined from 8.6 in 1976 to 7.1 in 1991. This evidence, and other data collected in Igunga between 1988 and 1991, parallels national-level data in Kenya, Botswana and Zimbabwe which have begun the transition toward lower fertility (see Table 7.2).

Survey Years	1976-79	1984²	1989-90	1993
Kenya, TFR	7.9	7.7	6.7	5.4
% Contracepting	---	---	27	33
Western Province, TFR	8.6	7.9	8.1	---
% Contracepting	---	---	---	25.6
Kakamega Dist., TFR	8.7	9.2	7.0	---
Igunga Sublocation	8.6	---	7.0	---
% Contracepting	1	---	31.9	---
sample size	398	---	303	---

Table 7.2: Total Fertility Rates and Current Contraceptive Use.[3]

Maragoli is the place-name for this part of western Kenya, the homeland of the Logoli. The Logoli are one of seventeen Luyia-speaking sub-nations of the Abaluyia. The Abaluyia number about a million and are the second largest ethnic group in Kenya. The Logoli are patrilineal, patrilocal horticulturalists who grow maize and beans, and who keep some cattle. Nearly 4,000 people live in Igunga.

Igunga is located on a murram road about 100 kilometers from the Uganda border. In this part of Kenya, one has the sense of being at the edge of the world-system. There is no electricity, no television, and only a few telephones in Igunga. Like the rest of western Kenya, Igunga is a source of labor for other, more industrialized parts of Kenya. Long-distance migration is therefore a historical pattern, contributing to a high proportion of female headed households (> 50 percent). Some people are fortunate to have teaching or other government jobs, but other kinds of local wage work--weeding, or transporting maize to the mill--pay very

Fertility in Maragoli 113

little. Igunga homesteads average less than a hectare per household, and agricultural yields cannot support a family for the entire year. Thus, survival in Igunga depends in part on earnings and remittances, and hunger is a way of life (Munroe et al. 1969).

Tsing (1993:xi) defines "marginality" as "distinctive and unequal subject positions within common fields of power and knowledge." Tsing's example is the Meratus Dayaks of Borneo, where she found marginality to be more than an "ethnographic feature," but rather a way to break open the gulf between the regions of the world-system, to understand the interaction between colonized and colonizer, and the "key to reformulating cultural theory" (Tsing 1993:13).

Like that of the Meratus Dayaks, Maragoli's marginality in the capitalist world-economy has been long-term. It was rarely contacted by Europeans before the 20th century, although there were people in regions to the north who were taken by Arab traders into the global slave trade. During the colonial era Maragoli was squeezed for land, labor and resources, including gold (Wagner 1949, 1956). Even after Kenya's independence, western Kenya continued to be underdeveloped relative to Kenya's central regions (Leo 1984).

In the local economy, however, Igunga is centrally located, and has been for at least a century. Igunga is within walking distance of two growing urban centers, including Mbale, the Vihiga District headquarters. In 1937, Mbale was the largest market center in what was then North Kavirondo District. It abutted a main motor road, and included many stores, tearooms, tailor shops, butchers' shops and stalls (Wagner 1956:166). On Saturdays, hundreds of marketers, mostly women, would come from all over western Kenya to buy and sell such items as maize, pots, groundnuts, sugar cane and firewood. Imported clothes, toiletries, tinned food, sewing machines and tools were also available. Nowadays, Mbale is but one of several urban centers in Western Province, but by no means the largest. It has a hotel, a women's hospital, and dozens of small shops in rows of permanent buildings.

Some researchers have explained Maragoli's historically high fertility in terms of marginality. Ssennyonga (1978) argued, for example, that in 1976 the Logoli had few options other than bearing children to compensate for their poverty. Ssennyonga focused his ethnographic lens on growing differentiation with Igunga, with a wealthy "roadside elite" who did not need to limit births, and a "downhill" underclass needing high fertility for survival. The economic and reproductive positions of both the roadside elite and the downhill people were explained as outcomes of colonial-era policies which were exploitive and pronatalist (Ssennyonga 1978). Many researchers, including Ssennyonga, define Maragoli as a bedroom community of Nairobi, Kisumu, Naivasha, and other relatively distant (i.e., not a daily commute) wage-labor destinations.

Ssennyonga's (1978) explanation of Maragoli's high fertility was similar to arguments later made by feminist world-system theorists. Kathryn Ward (1993), for example, argued that women's status in peripheral nations generally declines with world-system intrusion, and as a consequence fertility rises. Ward hypothesizes that the reason fertility goes up is because women use children and childbearing as one means of achieving status and power where other options are limited. This is because men generally have more control over socioeconomic resources introduced by foreign investors. Men also gain greater access to and control over monetarized and industrial sectors of the economy, though she and others later acknowledge that differential access to opportunities between men and women in the informal sector are also important (Ward 1993, see also Staudt 1976, 1979).

It would therefore make sense that increasing centrality of Kenya into the world-economy would result in lower fertility in Kenya overall, and in Maragoli in particular. Indeed, the first three African nations to turn the corner toward lower fertility--Kenya, Zimbabwe and Botswana--have been relatively stable economically in the African continent and have been able to provide near-universal education to women (van de Walle and Foster 1990). It may be, however, that the decline in fertility in these nations is also a barometer of their ascent from the margins of the world economy (in other words, the causal arrows go in the opposite direction). Improved position in the world-system should theoretically result in lower fertility and higher women's status, as long as this improved position was accompanied internally by the expansion of economic opportunities (Dow et al. 1994).

The quantitative findings from Igunga do indeed suggest a relationship between women's empowerment and the choice to contracept. I have reported elsewhere about changes in Igunga between 1976 and 1989, and about differences between Igunga women who contracept and those who do not.[4] During that thirteen year period, education in Igunga became more equitable between the genders, as it did in much of Kenya. The quantitative findings, based on survey data from

303 women between the ages of 15 and 49 (Ndege 1993, Bradley and Ndege forthcoming, Bradley forthcoming, Bradley 1995) suggest that women's empowerment, when combined with education, is an important predictor of contraception.

Empowering activities are defined as those activities in which a woman acts in her own right. Some authors refer to this as agency (Karp 1986), autonomy, or the condition of women. A woman who is empowered may control or influence social, political and economic decision making, both within and beyond the household (Bradley 1995, Handwerker 1989, 1991, 1993).

In Igunga, a woman who is educated is in a better position to access opportunities which are empowering to her (Table 7.3). The opportunities, or forms of empowerment, that seem to make a difference in who contracepts are banking, belonging to a cooperative, and obtaining credit. These are relatively new activities for women in western Kenya. Although women had informal cooperatives in the past, only after independence was membership in formal cooperatives opened to women (Nasimiyu, in press). Women's access to credit and agricultural training were limited even recently (Staudt 1976, 1979). Some women, particularly older ones, are empowered by activities that were traditionally limited to men, including owning land and cattle.

Variable	Parameter estimate	Standard error	T	P-value
Constant	-2.339	0.578	-4.148	0.000
Age	0.041	0.017	2.407	0.016
Years Educated x New Forms of Power	0.072	0.018	3.940	0.000

(N=293; Hosmer-Lemeshow statistic: 5.460; p-value: 0.71; df: 8)

Table 7.3: Logistic Regression Analysis Predictors of Current Contraceptive Use.

The Idea That Redeems: Choosing Contraception

The difference between the world-systems perspective discussed above and the postcolonial one I now propose is in the location of the colony. Those of us who do research on fertility in the developing world are accustomed to thinking about it in terms of salesmanship and distribution. The task at hand is to locate and create a market for contraceptives, to deliver them, and to continue an educational process toward their proper use. This is an internal colony. As the title of a book by Ngugi wa Thiong'o (1986) suggests about the postcolonial era, the retention, transmission and adoption of ideas is a colony of the "mind."

Ngugi wa Thiong'o talked about decolonizing the mind in the context of the languages of African literature. In *Culture and Imperialism*, Said (1993) argues that imperialism is an "idea"--much like the "idea that redeems" in Conrad's (1989 [1902]) *Heart of Darkness*. A colonized mind, both of the colonizer and the colonized, carries outdated assumptions of the colonial era. One of these is that Africa is empty in the middle, that in a sense there is "nobody home." This assumption is alluded to in *Heart of Darkness* when Marlow stares at the map of Africa (Conrad 1989:33), and was part of the ideology in Berlin in 1884 when Africa was carved up amongst the European nations. If there is nothing there, we are free to carve up, settle, Christianize and commodify.

The adoption of contraceptives requires not only the spread of new ideas (Watkins 1991) but also their incorporation into the body. Shiva (1994:129), an ecological feminist, argues that "the interior spaces of the bodies of women, plants and animals" is a new sort of colony, of which genetic engineering is the best example. The link to contraception is obvious, since contraceptives are placed within the body and transform it. Obviously this body is not empty; there is already somebody at home, and this person can choose to resist.

The problem with contraception is that people resist it. This was true when Mamdani (1973) wrote about Indian families piling contraceptives up in decorative stacks on the shelf, and it was true in when Tsing (1993) found birth control pills manufactured in California lined up as decorations in Borneo. Both communities rejected the pills for different reasons. The Meratus Dayaks were coerced to use contraceptives by the government, who threatened to deny them an election. To resolve the problem, the community selected women who volunteered to pretend to use contraception. Both communities ultimately found new uses for the pills, far beyond any original intent of the manufacturer and out of control as far as population policy was concerned. Finally, the Meratus Dayaks had come to regard the birth control pills as health aids. Tsing writes:

Fertility in Maragoli 117

The pills I knew in the United States as artifacts of medical science had been transformed by Indonesian state discourse into an icon of bureaucratic order, and transformed again...into the daily health-promoting herbal tonics of folk medicine (Tsing 1993:105).

Although entertaining examples, these are not merely strange cases in the lore of contraceptive reinterpretation. All contraceptives are reinterpreted, however subtly. The adoption of contraception, and the turn toward lower fertility, represents not only the adoption of new ideas, but at some level their transformation. The idea that redeems becomes ideas that redeem, and these ideas differ between the core and the margins of the world-system.

An example of subtle reinterpretation in Igunga is the preference for injections over other forms of birth control (see Table 7.4). Commonly discussed rationales for the preference for injection in Africa are that they do not require daily remembering, and are also an effective birth control that can be taken without relatives finding out.

Nevertheless, injection has been part of the cultural landscape in Igunga, as well as other parts of Africa, for decades. Vaughan (1991) argues that a "needle mentality" developed in Africa during a yaws epidemic in the 1920's. This needle mentality was of great concern to physicians working in Africa during the early part of the century. A physician named W.T.C. Berry who worked in Nyasaland in the 1930's wrote the following:

> Many patients in Nyasaland, I discovered, were dissatisfied unless they were given some sort of injection. Among the hundreds of sick, partially sick and others with backs rheumaticky and aching from the heavy toil of breaking up the soil with hand tools, enquiry as to what might be wrong with them often elicited, not a direct reply, but the single word 'Jackson!' Anthropologists of the future may report folklore telling of a wondrous healer, one Jack, whose skill was only surpassed by his sons! To spare their disillusion let it be said at once that this word is a relic of the reference once paid to the dramatic response of yaws, which used to be very prevalent, to treatment by arsenicals, which had been given by injection. 'Jackson' was a corruption of the world 'injection' . . . (Vaughn 1991:48).

The needle mentality is alive and well in Igunga, and is evident in the number of antibiotic injections given by medical doctors in clinics, whether or not the patient has an illness that is amenable to treatment with antibiotics. Patients are nevertheless pleased when they come away from a clinic having been injected; it is what they expect in a cure.

Injections are so popular that there is a minor industry of quacks, or "local doctors," who specialize in "treating" people with injections. These practitioners have been talked about in Kenya because they reuse needles and are thus suspected of spreading AIDS. They are probably far more dangerous and insidious in the spread of HIV than the widely popularized "circumcision knife." Educated people in the village also suspected that the "medicines" injected by the local doctors were useless, outdated, and perhaps even dangerous. But there nevertheless was a lively market for these specialists and their injections in the village.

I was personally surprised by the comfort people in Igunga had with injections when I took insulin shots in front of my field staff. Although I often stuck the needles in strange places (my stomach for example) there was rarely any reaction.

Thus, injections are part of shared colonial history in Africa. It should not be surprising that they are the often leading choice of contraception, especially among those with less education.

Methods	Number	Percent	Years Schooling
Injection	24	7.9	6.46
Pill	18	5.9	7.35
Rhythm	13	4.3	6.15
Traditional	13	4.3	5.54
I.U.D.	11	3.6	8.55
T.L./Vasectomy	10	3.3	7.30
Condoms	5	1.7	8.60
Abstinence	1	0.3	7.00
Other (foam, tablets, etc.)	1	0.3	7.00
All Methods	96*	31.6	7.06

(*96 users from a random sample of 303 Igunga women. Mean education for the 207 non-users is 6.10 years.)

Table 7.4: Family Planning Methods, Igunga, 1989-90.

Conclusion

When we talk about fertility transition, we generally accept the revolutionary nature of the change from high to lower fertility. We tend to think of the causes of the change as being, as Tsing (1993) states about marginality, features of the society. One could argue that changes in characteristics of women, including their empowerment and education, could also be thought of as features of the society.

The acceptance of contraception in Maragoli during the years between 1976 and 1989 represents more than a set of changes in features of the society. It is the hallmark of a transformation at the borderland between the global and the local. It is about the triumph of ideas. It is not merely enough, however, that the information gets there and is spread, but that it gets there and is interpreted. How it is interpreted in the local place is what ultimately determines whether contraceptives are used, and which ones are used. It may also have something to do with what "other" kinds of uses or meanings become attached to the contraceptives.

In the last analysis, I hope to have demonstrated that the perspectives discussed in this paper are not ultimately incompatible. I believe that modernization theory underlies most demographic theorizing about fertility. I have also argued that postcolonial and world-systems perspectives emphasizing the tensions and interactions between the local and the global place can also illuminate our understanding of the process of fertility decline.

Acknowledgements

Funding for the research leading to this paper came from the National Science Foundation, the Wenner-Gren Foundation, Fulbright-Hays and the Ford Foundation. I would like to thank Susan Watkins, Thomas Hall, W. Penn Handwerker, James Onyango Ndege, my colleagues at the Population Studies and Research Institute of the University of Nairobi, the Population Studies Center at the University of Pennsylvania, and Caroline Makinson of the Andrew W. Mellon Foundation.

Notes

1. The research discussed here took place in Igunga Sublocation, West Maragoli Location, in what is now Vihiga District's Sabatia Division.
2. Since no Igunga survey was conducted in 1984 or 1993, no sample sizes are presented for these columns. The other data are from national-level statistics.
3. Sources for this table include Bradley (1995) NCPD (1989, 1993), Ndege (1993), Omurundo (1989), and Ssennyonga (1978).

4. Over a two year period between 1988 and 1991, a University of Nairobi graduate student and I did two censuses in Maragoli, collected socioeconomic, health, and fertility data in a focused sample of 24 households, and ran a survey of 303 women between the ages of 15 and 49 (Ndege 1993; Bradley and Ndege in press; Bradley in press, 1995). These findings were compared to a similar study done in Igunga Sublocation in the 1970s (Ssennyonga 1978), and thus represent a longitudinal study of a sublocation in the throes of fertility decline.

References

Bledsoe, Caroline
   1990 The Politics of AIDS, Condoms, and Heterosexual Relations in Africa: Recent Evidence from the Local Print Media. In *Births and Power*. W. Penn Handwerker, ed. Pp. 197-223. Boulder, CO: Westview Press.
Bradley, Candice
   in press Declining Fertility and Wealth Flows in Maragoli. In *African Families and the Crisis of Social Change*. T.S. Weisner, C. Bradley and P. Kilbride, eds. Westport, CT: Greenwood.
   1995 Women's Empowerment and Fertility Decline in Western Kenya. In *The Anthropology of Fertility: Remaking Demographic Analysis*. S. Greenhalgh, ed. Cambridge: Cambridge University Press (in press).
Bradley, Candice and James Onyango Ndege
   in press Fertility Decline in a Maragoli Sublocation. In *Ecological and Cultural Change and Human Development in Western Kenya and Western Province*. J. Akong'a, A.B.C. Ocholla-Ayayo, and S. Wandibba, eds. Nairobi, Kenya: G.S. Were Press.
Brass, William and Carole L. Jolly, eds.
   1993 *Population Dynamics of Kenya*. Washington D.C.: National Academy Press.
Caldwell, John
   1982 *Theory of Fertility Decline*. London: Academic.
Conrad, Joseph
   1989[1902] *Heart of Darkness*. London: Penguin.
Dow, Thomas, Linda Archer, Shanyisa Khasiani, and John Kekovole
   1994 Wealth Flow and Fertility Decline in Rural Kenya, 1981-92. *Population and Development Review* 20(2):343-364.
Greenhalgh, Susan
   1994 Controlling Births and Bodies in Village China. *American Ethnologist* 21(1):3-30.
Handwerker, W. Penn
   1989 *Women's Power and Social Revolutions*. Newbury Park, CA: Sage.
   1991 Women's Power and Fertility Transition: The Cases of Africa and the Caribbean. *Population and Environment* 13(1):55-78.

1993 Empowerment and Fertility Transition on Antigua, WI: Education, Employment, and the Moral Economy of Childbearing. *Human Organization* 52(1):41-52.
Karp, Ivan
1986 Agency and Social Theory: A Review of Anthony Giddens. *American Ethnologist* 13(Feb.):131-137.
Leo, Christopher
1984 *Land and Class in Kenya*. Toronto: University of Toronto Press.
LeVine, Robert, Sarah LeVine, Amy Richman, F. Medardo Tapia Uribe, Clara Sunderland Correa, and Patrice M. Miller
1991 Women's Schooling and Child Care in the Demographic Transition: A Mexican Case Study. *Population and Development Review* 17(3): 459-496.
Mamdani, Mahmood
1973 *The Myth of Population Control: Family, Caste and Class in an Indian Village*. New York: Monthly Review Press.
Mies, Maria, Veronika Bennholdt-Thomsen, and Claudia von Werlhof
1988 *Women: The Last Colony*. London: Atlantic Highlands.
Munroe, Robert H., Ruth L. Munroe, Sara Nerlove, and Robert E. Daniels
1969 Effects of Population Density on Food Concerns in Three East African Societies. *Journal of Health and Social Behavior* 10:161-171.
Nasimiyu, Ruth
in press Changing Women's Rights over Property in Western Kenya. In *African Families and the Crisis of Social Change*. T.S. Weisner, C. Bradley and P. Kilbride, eds. Westport, CT: Greenwood Press.
National Council for Population and Development (NCPD)
1989 *Kenya Demographic and Health Survey*. Nairobi, Kenya: Central Bureau of Statistics.
1993 *Kenya Demographic and Health Survey. Preliminary Report*. Nairobi, Kenya: Central Bureau of Statistics.
Ndege, James Onyango
1993 *Correlations and Determinants of Interspousal Communication about Family Planning in Kenya: A Case Study of Sabatia Division, Kakamega District*. M.A. thesis, University of Nairobi.
Ngugi wa Thiong'o
1986 *Decolonising the Mind: The Politics of Language in African Literature*. London: James Curry.
Omurundo, John Kwendo
1989 *Infant/Child Mortality and Fertility Differentials in Western Province: A Divisional Level Analysis*. MSc thesis, Population Studies and Research Institute, University of Nairobi.
Said, Edward
1993 *Culture and Imperialism*. New York: Vintage Books.

Shannon, Thomas Richard
   1989 *An Introduction to the World-system Perspective.* Boulder, CO: Westview Press.
Shiva, Vandana
   1994 The Seed and the Earth. In *Close to Home: Women Reconnect Ecology, Health and Development Worldwide.* V. Shiva, ed. Pp. 128-143. Philadelphia, PA: New Society Publishers.
Ssennyonga, Joseph
   1978 *Population Growth and Cultural Inventory: The Maragoli Case.* Ph.D. diss., University of Sussex.
Staudt, Katherine
   1976 *Agricultural Policy, Political Power, and Women Farmers in Western Kenya.* Ph.D. diss., University of Wisconsin, Madison.
   1979 Rural Women Leaders: Late Colonial and Contemporary Contexts. *Rural Africana* 3:5-21.
Tsing, Anna Lowenhaupt
   1993 *In The Realm of the Diamond Queen: Marginality in an Out-of-the-way Place.* Princeton, N.J.: Princeton University Press.
van de Walle, Etienne and Andrew Foster
   1990 *Fertility Decline in Africa: Assessments and Prospects.* World Bank Technical Paper no. 125. African Technical Department Series. Washington D.C.: The World Bank.
Vaughan, Megan
   1991 *Curing Their Ills: Colonial Power and African Illness.* Stanford, CA: Stanford University Press.
Wagner, Gunter
   1949 *The Bantu of Western Kenya, with special reference to the Vugusu and Logoli*, Vol. I. London: Oxford University Press.
   1956 *The Bantu of Western Kenya. Economic Life*, Vol. II. London: Oxford. New York: Oxford University Press.
Wallerstein, Immanuel
   1974 *The Modern World-system, I: Capitalist Agriculture and the Origins of the European World-economy in the Sixteenth Century.* New York, N.Y.: Academic Press.
Ward, Kathryn
   1984 *Women in the World-system: Its Impact on Status and Fertility.* N.Y.: Praeger.
   1985 The Social Consequences of the World Economic System: The Economic Status of Women and Fertility. *Review* 7(4):561-593.
   1993 Reconceptualizing World System Theory to Include Women. In *Theory on Gender/ Feminism of Theory*, P. England, ed. Pp. 43-68. N.Y.: A. de Gruyter.

Watkins, Susan Cotts
1991 *From Provinces into Nation: Demographic Integration in Western Europe, 1870-1960.* Princeton, N.J.: Princeton University Press.

8

Producing Agrarian Transformation at the Indonesian Periphery

Tania Murray Li

Analysis of cultural hegemony has to begin with a precise analysis of social formation; and this, according to Wolf's prescription (1982:266), has to begin at those historical moments when people enter processes of primary accumulation, when the definitions, negotiations, and structurally determined applications of terms of ownership, property rights, and appropriation change. This is where modes of production are born and die, where they begin and terminate their articulations, where cultural hegemonies struggle for dominance and where they collapse and reform (Rebel 1989:351).

World systems theory has been concerned to locate local economies within regional and global systems. This paper has the same objective, but in place of world system's emphasis on patterns of trade and the dominance of centres, focuses instead on the processes, practices, and cultural articulations through which new relations of production are generated. It investigates the intersection of local and global histories with a view to discerning the role of human agency in their creation and transformation as part of a single, if uneven, historical process (Roseberry 1989).

For much of the world "those historical moments" referred to by Rebel, although often protracted, occurred centuries ago, and reconstructing the cultural hegemonies at play is an exercise in the "historical imagination" (Comaroff and Comaroff 1992). Capitalist development being highly uneven, however, some regions are only now experiencing the separation of the direct producer from the means of production which establishes the conditions for systematic appropriation. Such regions provide an opportunity to analyze the *processes* of agrarian differentiation (White 1989), and the complex and contested cultural and material terms upon which this differentiation occurs. Instead of the sweeping and indiscriminate penetration of capitalist relations of production among unsuspecting tribes and peasantries often conveyed by globalizing accounts, the human agency involved in *creating* those relations of production at local and regional levels comes more clearly into view. Capitalist development can no longer be viewed as a "transition" to "a single teleological end," and the analyst is forced to grapple with the current conjuncture as "something new," with its own, indeterminate future (Roseberry 1989:166-167).

A study of an upland region on the peripheries of Sulawesi, Indonesia, offers some special insight into questions of culture and power in the context of economic transformation. This chapter examines the way in which the content of "tradition" (Williams 1977), including the meaning and definition of key terms (G. Smith 1989), is renegotiated in response to changing material conditions, in this case, the introduction into a swidden farm system of commercial tree crops for world markets. As relationships of gender, kinship and community are transformed there is "struggle over cultural meanings as much as over material goods and . . . struggles over meaning have significant material consequences" (C. Smith 1984:219).

This study focuses upon the Tinombo region of Central Sulawesi, Indonesia, inhabited by people known as the Lauje, numbering around 30,000. About 20,000 Lauje are swidden farmers living in the mountains, and 10,000 are labourers, small entrepreneurs and fishers living on the narrow coastal plain. Access to the mountains is by means of rough foot trails, seldom traversed by government officials, and the coastal area has been connected to the provincial capital by dry-season road only since 1980.

Although remote, the region in no sense represents a "natural," homogenous or unchanging economy. The Lauje sold cinnamon to regional traders as early as the seventeenth century, until stopped by the enforcement of Dutch monopoly on the spice trade (Nourse 1989:87). Early this century, as the Dutch exerted stronger (though indirect) control over the area, many Lauje were forced down from the hills to the coast to plant coconut trees, becoming the ancestors of the present coastal, Muslim population. A further group became differentiated socially when they retreated to the inner hills to avoid Dutch and Japanese conscriptions. They now constitute the more "primitiv(ized)" pole, continuing to mix more hunting and the collection and sale of forest products with swiddening in their livelihood strategies.[1]

The middle hill people, who will be the focus of this analysis, have produced tobacco for sale in local markets since at least the 1920s, and shallots and garlic since the 1950s. These crops have been integrated into the swidden cycle along with staple foods, and do not disturb the unity of labour and means of production. All farmers have had access to land, and neither land tenure arrangements nor the organization of labour act as mechanisms for the appropriation of surplus between classes. Even within nuclear family households, the assumption that every woman, man and child is entitled to the product of their own labour is carried through to a remarkable extent. Married women often have their own food and cash crop gardens; children of both sexes are encouraged to farm independently at a very young age, keeping any "surplus" to themselves; and old people farm to support themselves until physically incapable of doing so.

In mode of production terms, the middle hill Lauje are clearly not capitalist, since they do not meet the key criterion of free labour (Wolf 1982). They produce commodities for the market, but they have so far been able to access key means of production and meet their principal subsistence needs outside market relations, making their degree of involvement non-intense (Bernstein 1977). The unity of labour and land in the middle hills is now being broken by the introduction of commercial tree crops such as cocoa, cloves and cashew, which privatize and effectively enclose land previously accessible to a wider group for food and short term cash crop production. The shift in land use opens a new *possibility* for some to enhance their land rights while others become dispossessed. High population densities (40-80 per square kilometre) and the sparsity of hillside land for further expansion increase the possibility that some form of differentiation will occur. Moreover, the incentive for individuals to accumulate is present in the form of re-oriented consumer tastes, increasingly driven by lowland and urban standards.

The emergence of new economic opportunities and consumer demands do not mechanically define or determine new relations of production. Processes of agrarian differentiation involve actors in "far-reaching transformations of their states of being—of their relationships with things, persons, and self . . . [and their] images and ideals of what constitutes goodness—in people, in relationships and in conditions of life" (Ortner 1984:152). In other words, morality is at the core of such transformations (Hefner 1990). So, too, are the politics of identity and difference, as groups sharing newly-relevant characteristics, rights and responsibilities become defined and distinguished.

In this region, the presence of a *relatively* egalitarian social organization, both in terms of class and gender, puts some pressure on familiar terms such as domination and appropriation, forcing a more careful reading of the diffuse and subtle modes of operation of power. More work is needed to identify struggles over the creation of meaning when no obvious "other" is in place, and it is not quite clear what or who among one's kin and neighbours should be resisted. The rapid pace of change reveals, more clearly than usual, the complex and contested cultural ground upon which new relations of production, including relations of gender, kinship and community, are created. Attention can be paid to the *processes* of agrarian transformations which, analyzed *post facto* on the basis of measurable indicators (privatization of land, displacement of labour, growing inequalities of class and gender) may appear to have been simply "unfolding" according to a predetermined scheme (White 1989).

To investigate such mechanisms, terms are needed for the analysis of the production, in the course of everyday life and work, of those forms of meaningful practice that *become* the basis for the assertion of new claims as relations of production are transformed. Useful in this context is Williams's (1977) discussion of the process through which certain elements from the continuum of a population's history become "selected" as "tradition" and deployed by (emerging) dominant groups to silence alternative selections potentially articulated by others. Williams's concept effectively captures the struggles over meaning that take place not only as reflections of pre-constituted material and social power but in the context of its generation and transformation.

The notion of cultural capital, used by Bourdieu (1977) to refer to forms of socially recognized credentials which can be *transferred* and *transformed* into material capital, can also be deployed here. It suggests a mechanism through which cultural capital developed in one sphere (perhaps ritual expertise, oratory, or genealogical knowledge) which does not, in its present form, confer economic advantage can *become* a source of power through which new claims are exerted. The convertibility of distinct forms of capital still needs to be investigated: the process cannot be assumed to be automatic nor the results guaranteed. Selecting from tradition is part of the process through which existing cultural capital becomes conferred with significant new meanings.

Finally, terms are needed to identify specific forms of dissent and resistance. Williams (1977) notion of selective tradition, building on

Gramsci, asserts that all cultural processes are pervaded by relations of power and resistance. Subordinate views and alternative versions of tradition always persist, though often muted, and the potential remains for them to re-emerge. This they may do on an ad-hoc basis, at the level of individualized grumblings, submerged in the flow of everyday relationships, discourse and practice. On occasion, they emerge in more generalized forms with greater subversive potential. Wertheim's concept of counterpoint, as reviewed by Risseeuw (1988), provides a measure of the extent to which struggles over meaning are articulated and recognized in public arena, taking on a clear oppositional form.

Where the material basis for a developed counterpoint organized around class, gender, ethnic or other identities is present but the counterpoint fails to emerge, this too must be explained. As demonstrated by Risseeuw, tradition plays a complex role. While it cannot be viewed solely as a vehicle for elite manipulation, selections may take place in a manner that is so gradual, so piecemeal, so mundane, that no counterpoint acknowledging tradition as a site of struggle ever emerges.[2]

In the Tinombo hills, the introduction of long term commercial tree crops has made access to land the most hotly contested issue. An examination of struggles over land will reveal the struggles over meaning through which individuals become repositioned in relation to the community, gender relations are redefined, and the mountain people become an ethnic "community" in relation to state agendas. These are the processes through which relations of production are re-constituted, and local and global histories are made.

Redefining Individual and Community

An indigenous labour theory of value forms the core of Lauje property relations. What a person has worked for belongs to them. A pioneer has permanent rights to the land he cleared from primary forest. If he chooses to sell it to another, he sets the price in terms of the value of the labour expended: it is the price of his exhaustion, and the food used to sustain him while he worked. Although land pioneering is treated as the paradigmatic case of ownership rights established through personal effort, pioneering, like all other forms of labour, is in fact mediated by particular social relations of production which permit an individual to put him or herself to work. It is these social relations of production, which locate the individual in relation to the community that are now being renegotiated.

Land pioneers have been most successful in translating the property rights derived from initial land clearing into the undisputed right to plant commercial trees and claim fully private ownership. This has been accomplished without debate, and presented as a continuation of traditional practice. In fact, it is a new development, which selects some elements from tradition and submerges others. Under the swidden cultivation system (still practised, although on reduced areas of land) pioneers' rights are limited in two respects. A land pioneer is expected to freely loan land to kin and neighbours needing a place to farm while useful products (vines, bamboo) growing naturally on fallow land, without the expenditure of human effort, can be harvested by anyone. The same labour theory of property can be seen at play in these limitations on pioneers' rights. If a person is willing to work to secure their own livelihood, of course they need access to land; no rent should be extracted because the farmer has earned the full returns to his labour. Likewise, a person who invests labour in gathering in the fallows deserves to own the fruits.

Today, the fact that commercial tree planting excludes other land users, who previously could make claims on fallow land for subsistence purposes, is recognized as a pragmatic fact. It has not become an issue raised for debate or negotiation: no counterpoint has emerged defending the position of borrowers, and arguing that their subsistence needs amount to rights to land access. The previously acknowledged "pressure to loan land" has been effectively reconceptualized through increased emphasis on pioneers rights, and requests to borrow are regularly refused. Landowners, it is said, only loaned their land because they were not using it themselves. Now that they wish to plant trees there, it is no longer available to others.

How could primary accumulation, and the creation of a potentially landless class, take place without objection? From what source do pioneers derive the power to make *their* selection from tradition so forceful that it dominates without force or even debate, as a simple matter of commonsense? An explanation may be sought in the deployment of cultural capital, gained within the swidden production system, to new ends. Cultural capital is acquired by pioneers through the recognition bestowed upon their superior physical strength and ritual knowledge. Not everyone can be a successful pioneer. Pioneers also acquire cultural capital through their "social centrality."[3] A man who clears a large area of primary forest attracts both his sons and daughters, with their spouses, to live nearby to form a kin-based cluster for mutual cooperation and security in which he is the central figure. A man who does not clear land finds his children moving off to seek better prospects elsewhere, as pioneers or additions to the cluster formed on the in-law's territory. Loaning land to younger kin and neighbours contributes to social centrality. So, too, does superior knowledge about land, kinship and other matters in the locality. Like direct material control over land, these forms of cultural capital have not hitherto provided a means for the appropriation of labour or monopolization of land but they are now taking on this significance in the debate—or non-debate—over land enclosure.

In areas of the middle hills farmed for several generations, the original land pioneers, and even those who assisted them, have long since died. In these circumstances, struggles over land must be articulated through a different set of cultural terms, focusing upon notions of inheritance rather than labour investment. When land was used only for shifting cultivation, the notion of inheritance was not culturally elaborated—an Indonesian term is borrowed, since there is no indigenous word. Land continued to be the possession of the ancestors who first cleared it, and the younger generations effectively borrowed it from them—directly by asking for or being allocated land to farm by the pioneer, and indirectly, by asking permission from living seniors when the pioneer was no longer alive. This latter step was not rigidly observed, since senior kin who had not themselves invested labour in the initial clearing of the land were consulted more for their information than their right to control or allocate land cleared by another. Regardless of particular lines of descent, then, all the younger generation effectively worked on "borrowed" land.

To legitimate exclusive rights to land for commercial tree planting, people must now trace their descent from the original pioneer who cleared that particular plot, and thereby distinguish themselves and their rights from outsiders who were "merely borrowing." Two meanings have shifted here. The principle of inheritance based on descent has become more significant; and the practice of borrowing, once the mode in which most people accessed land from seniors, living or dead, now more clearly distinguishes a particular category of people, non descendants. The social distinction accomplished, it is widely agreed that borrowers are not entitled to plant trees. Thus, they are excluded both from the possibilities of subsistence production and from the long term investments in commercial trees in which so many are placing their hopes.

Cultural capital in the form of social centrality and greater access to information has come to play a new role with material consequences, including the possibility of laying claim to greater areas of land for commercial tree farming, and successfully making those claims count over those of others less well placed. People who, until now, have always gone to a senior kinsman to borrow land for short term farming needs lack information about the details of their relationship to the pioneer who first cleared it, and therefore are in a weak position to make strong claims and exclude others. They also lack information with which to contest the physical demarcation of the landscape by permanent boundaries which, it is claimed, are the very same boundaries marked out by the pioneering ancestors generations ago.

It is among kin, potential co-inheritors, that there are the most active current struggles over land. Siblings and cousins of the same generation, equally distant from the pioneers, have identical claims through inheritance, yet the use of the land by some of them inevitably excludes others. Those who have remained in the area may have better information than those who have been living elsewhere, and some individuals have greater social power to press claims. Most significant in asserting exclusive land rights vis-à-vis close kin, however, has been a revised version of the "tradition" stressing the investment of labour in the formation of property rights. Enclosures that exclude co-inheritors are defended on the grounds that the person who works hardest and plants trees first acquires the land: others should simply follow the example. This kind of claim is made through "direct action." If a person has not actually done the work of clearing and planting the land claimed, but has merely been talking, others then may still feel free to step in. Households without access to adult male labour, or to adults of either sex capable of advancing claims among kin, lose out when land enclosure takes place through this process. The result is often rancour, bitterness, or covert sabotage, as kin signal their dissent in principle or in practice to the fact of their exclusion from land they might have been able to make their own.

The result of these struggles over meaning is that the privatization of land has been highly uneven, but *not* random. There has been no formal public discussion of the principles for the distribution of land rights, and no orthodoxy proclaimed. When questioned most individuals have an opinion, but a deeper debate has not been articulated. There is no counterpoint on class which recognizes the unequal positions that people are coming to occupy in relation to land, names the processes through which this is occurring, and highlights its implications for livelihoods as well as community traditions and the collective imaginary. Timing seems to be a crucial issue: the emergence of new economic classes, landowners and landless labourers, occurs piecemeal, one field and one season at a time, and class identities, if they form at all, may arise too late to alter the terms.

Already, in some areas of the hills it has become difficult to borrow land for short term food and cash crop production, and inequities in the initial distribution of land and trees are compounded through the "simple reproduction squeeze" (Bernstein 1977). Some households with only small areas of land, unable to wait for young trees to yield and without additional plots to use for food production, have found themselves forced to sell land and move on.[4] A few make up production shortfalls on inadequate land by wage labouring for their neighbours. In the meantime, sporadic disputes arise, some tree seedlings are burnt or uprooted, cocoa pods are stolen, and the act blamed on kin or neighbours jealous of success but too lazy to work.

Gendering Relations of Production

Interdependence between women and men constituted through the sexual division of labour renders ambiguous the idea that a married person could be a fully individuated subject in relation to property. This ambiguity opens a space for negotiation within households on a daily basis and as forms of labour and property are transformed over time.[5]

Under swidden conditions, husband, wife and unmarried children form a unit of commensalism, co-residence, and cooperation in some (but not all) aspects of staple food production. They do not form a unit of ownership, nor do they consider all of their production activities to be part of a joint endeavour. As in other upland areas in Southeast Asia, men are responsible for land preparation where tree cutting is needed; women clear lighter brush and second year swiddens. The cleared farm plot is usually divided into separate sections for husband, wife, and children so each can plant their own cash crops (shallots, garlic, groundnuts). Family members help each other with the work on their separate crops in various reciprocal labour arrangements, and sometimes on the basis that the proceeds will be shared. Staples may also be grown on separate plots, with the rationale that it makes each person take responsibility for weeding, but more often staples are grown in one plot and women and children weed more diligently. In the middle hills men hunt rarely. When they have no shallot harvest, rattan collection or occasional labouring on the coast provide men's sources of ready cash. Women sell vegetables from the swiddens at the weekly coastal market, and a few make rattan baskets or mats for sale.

Although women and men have equal access to land for their swidden farming activities, there are some distinctions in their mode of access which are beginning to have new significance in the context of tree planting. First of all, women do not clear primary forest land, and therefore never establish the fullest set of rights to land that pioneers enjoy. Their labour growing food-crops in the current gardens, clearing brush and cooking for the pioneer and his helpers apparently does not "count" in terms of the cultural or material capital acquired from the pioneering process. Men also gain cultural capital from being the *initiators* of the production cycle, both in pioneering conditions and secondary forest. Women are the acknowledged experts in all subsequent phases of the agricultural cycle, but the prestige potentially gained from this knowledge is diminished by the cultural centrality of men's clearing work. Women who have no husband, father or son to clear land for them must ask other male kin for assistance, and commonly request the use of a section of a cleared garden in return for weeding.

As noted above, few of the original pioneers are alive to plant trees on their own land in the middle hills, so it is not their inability to pioneer which disadvantages women in the current struggles over land. There is general agreement that inheritance is gender neutral, but women are still losing out. One factor, again, is access to information about land matters. It is men who negotiate the use of swidden land, as elders and borrowers, even when the links to the land are traced through women. Now that links to pioneers through descent have to be rather vigorously asserted, women have less information with which to press their own claims, or assist their husbands in pursuing claims on their behalf.

Women's ability to press claims of any sort is generally less than men's, since they tend to have less of the cultural capital that gives individuals advantage in disputes, whether these are disputes over strictly private or more general issues. Women are present at all group gatherings—weddings, funerals, healings, dispute settlements, labour exchange, but they are secondary political actors. Their role is to provide labour and organization, and, most crucially, to constitute the audience that gives legitimacy to the process or event. However they are seldom able to "hold the floor" in terms of focusing audience attention on themselves or their concerns.[6] Islam, slowly gaining adherence in the hills, potentially increases their peripherality in relation to the public face of community events.

The sexual division of labour and ideas related to it also disadvantage women at the level of "direct action" in the planting of trees. Clearing land on which to plant trees is still men's work; it is difficult for women to act unilaterally. If a husband is not diligent in clearing land, a woman's inheritance claims are not activated, whatever her nominal right to an equal share with her male siblings and cousins. The sexual division of labour at the level of the household affects women's claims in a further respect. When a man invests labour in clearing his wife's inherited land for trees, he establishes his right to half the resulting property. Women's labour investment, planting and tending seedlings, is also considered to earn them a half share in the trees as joint conjugal property. Although the principle of joint ownership is not in dispute, some women feel that their rights to joint property have become less than secure. Trees are immovable, long term investments, and women leaving after a divorce feel uncertain of their ability to collect. More widespread and serious is the problem of gambling. Both men and women gamble, but there are many tales of men gambling away joint conjugal property while there are none, so far, of women doing the same.[7]

The cultural capital and social power of men vis-à-vis women has increased with the introduction of commercial tree crops. Using arguments based on the relative value of the different types of labour invested, some men claim that women cannot become sole owners of cocoa or other trees, since they are not capable of transplanting the heavy seedlings, nor hoeing the hard earth. Women "don't know how do work," work now redefined as heavy, men's work. Women "only weed the grass," apparently an insignificant contribution (although one for which women are paid as labourers on other people's farms). Women are also said to lack knowledge about tree crops, a view strongly reinforced by local officials and agricultural extensionists, who direct their attention entirely towards men as farmers and as owners of trees, disregarding women's labour and the ownership rights that derive from it under the conjugal contract.

In the context of these insecurities, a few women have engaged in direct, independent action to plant trees and lay individual claim to them. They acquire land by various means, including purchase (using their profits from shallots) and pay for commoditized male labour to undertake the heavy work, avoiding any "assistance" from the husband which could result in future claims on the property. Women fully understand the implications of the "tradition" that labour investments secure property rights, and the reality that, for women, this tradition is double-edged. Women's interpretation insists upon the gender neutrality of labour investments: whenever they nurture conjugal trees, they develop claims. Likewise, if women have the initiative, energy and financial resources to acquire trees on their own, they may have sole rights. At the same time, the tradition of gender neutrality makes it more difficult for women to establish a generalized counterpoint on gender which highlights systematic inequities in the way that land and trees are becoming divided. They have not articulated a collective identity as women, which enables them to engage with men in a debate over the normative issues involved in agrarian change. The style in which they are renegotiating gendered relations of production is low profile, household based, and involves direct action more than talk.

Reworking State Agendas

The state is a significant player in the process of redefining key terms in the uplands. The laws, regulations, plans and programs of the state that enter the local scene in the guise of "development" interact with already contested domains of power and meaning. The state influences, often unknowingly, the relationships between individual and community, women and men. Listening selectively, the state determines which of many distinct voices and positions becomes authoritative on the local scene. The state controls a powerful array of discursive and coercive mechanisms which enable it to "state" or assert its own agendas, rendering some local debates irrelevant. But the various agents and agencies of the state encompass diverse projects and understandings, just as "communities" do. The intersection of multiple strands in local and national discourse and practice produces complex fields of power, the contours of which are not easily controlled by state manipulation.

State laws assert that the land tenure systems of traditional communities are to be recognized and upheld so long as they are in keeping with the national interest.[8] Three questions then arise: what are the characteristics of a "community"; who defines its "tradition"; and what is the "national interest"? Exploring these questions reveals the particular ways in which national agendas, global markets, and local practices intersect and become part of a single historical process.

Defining "the community" in the Lauje area presents a problem. Lauje settlement in the hills is highly dispersed. People build their houses on the swidden fields scattered across the mountainside, so they can guard the crops from marauding wild pigs. Households are attached to certain places through land rights and through kin ties, but they do not form visibly bounded communities. Movement occurs with each new swidden cycle, and with changing allegiances and priorities. Ironically, and contrary to the hopes of village officials, even the "progressive" farmers who have planted trees have not settled in concentrated neighbourhoods, because they must now leave their trees unattended and search for new spaces in which to grow short term food and cash crops.

Leadership, predictably, is weak. There are ritual specialists of various kinds, some claiming to have been appointed by the village head, and there are designated hamlet (RT) heads, but none of these individuals sees it as their responsibility to articulate a sense of local community. Those that achieve standing in their local area do so on the basis of the kinds of social centrality described earlier: prowess as pioneers, knowledge of the landscape and its history, and the ability to attract their descendants and other kin to remain close by. To the extent that neighbourhoods have become defined, this has been largely in response to state requirements that RT leaders keep household lists, and be ready to mobilize "the community" to undertake labour duties or pay taxes. Most recently, "the neighbourhood" has been the unit adopted by state officials promoting tree planting and other initiatives. Hill farmers have found it necessary to declare their allegiance to such and such a neighbourhood in order to benefit from these schemes. Even so, officials are frustrated by the degree of flux between one list-making exercise and the next, indicating both continued mobility and people's reluctance to be *identified* by an official system from which they anticipate, on balance, more drain on their resources than benefit.

Just as "community" is difficult to pin down, so too is Lauje "tradition" which, as demonstrated earlier, is an important and ongoing political issue *within* the local scene. When the state becomes involved in attempts to catalogue tradition, the desire to locate an authoritative source able to represent "the community" or "the culture" leads to simplifications inevitably ridden with power. Articulate spokesmen, rendered more powerful by state support, overlook ambiguities in the meaning of indigenous terms and practices. Subordinate traditions become more deeply submerged and inarticulate.

The Indonesian state recognizes three potential parties to land tenure: individual, community and state. In practice, it has tended to elide communal tenure with state ownership, stating that land held in common should be available for state projects which contribute to the common good (Dove 1987). If uplanders, unaware of the risks present in this elision, emphasise the communal nature of their tenure system, describing how the land was inherited from their common ancestors and is now used by the descendants in rotation, the land could be re-appropriated by the state. If, on the other hand, they stress their individual claims to specific plots and seek title, they displace the struggle for land from their own neighbourhood and cultural terrain to the bureaucratic processes of the state, with outcomes even less certain. Critical space for waging local struggles is lost through the finality of state interventions.

The district government, through the land office, has initiated efforts to clarify land tenure in the Tinombo hills. This has occurred at the request of the Estate Crops Unit who were unwilling to provide tree seedlings to hillside farmers with uncertain status. A Canadian Institutional strengthening project focused on Bappeda levels l and ll (see Babcock 1994) has been working with hill farmers *in situ* and attempting to clarify their rights. Despite good intentions and many directives, women have lost out in the land registration process, their rights subsumed under those of their husbands in ways that leave them newly vulnerable and dependent. The dispossession of women has taken place, again, without protest. Both women and men assume the registration of individually or mutually owned land and trees under men's names to be a matter of bureaucratic convenience that does not alter the *real* separate or joint rights that they themselves acknowledge. They have had no previous experience with land documentation, nor with any paper trails sufficiently powerful to subvert human purposes and commitments. For their part, officials responsible for land documentation are responding to their own assumptions that men are the principal farmers, particularly in relation to tree-crops, and to the fact that it is men who interact with male outsiders and present information to them.

Other losers have been men and women who depend mostly on borrowed land. Pioneers and those among their descendants able to demonstrate clear lines of descent have been permitted to register fallow land, in recognition of the "tradition" of land inheritance. This is a departure from the *status quo* before state intervention, which required people to operationalize their claims by making a new labour investment and planting trees on the fallow plot in order to effectively exclude competing claimants. An unintended consequence of state intervention has therefore been to create new mechanisms and opportunities for local land grabbing, undermining the position of those who, silent, or articulate but unable to create a constituency, have been struggling to retain access to hillside land and with it their livelihoods.

State programs designed to assist hillside farmers in their efforts to establish commercial tree gardens have also had the effect of increasing class differentiation. Free seedlings and inputs have, disproportionately, found their way into the hands of richer, more powerful male farmers, increasing the ability of this group to enclose land to the exclusion of women, borrowers, and others poorly placed to make effective claims on the state. Distribution of inputs and technical training has been organized by means of all-male Farmers Groups. Officials have given instructions that the poorest are to be included in these groups, but the formulation of lists of member-recipients inevitably reflects local politics. In the early stages of the program, Farmers Groups, which were imagined by the promoting agency to be cooperative, on-the-ground "communities" of poor hill farmers, usually had none of those characteristics. The neighbourhood focus has improved the frequency with which inputs reached the hills, but there are still many inequities in distribution. The state has not been responsible for creating social classes unilaterally, but it has contributed to their formation through its bureaucratic procedures which interact with local class-structuring processes already underway (cf. Hart 1989).

National goals for upland populations focus on bringing them into the national mainstream: producing for the market (preferably for export), boosting GNP, generating tax revenue, communicating in the national language, adhering to a recognized world religion, living in a "civilized" manner in proper houses and settlements accessible by road, and supporting the New Order government through votes and participation in state-sponsored organizations and activities.[9] The promotion of commercial tree farming in the Tinombo hills is an initiative intended to help redress the region's development deficit. There is general agreement among hillsiders, coastal dwellers, and officials at all levels of government that commercial tree farming is a good thing. The merits of integration into the world market have not been an issue of debate. However, state objectives become less clear, and regional class struggles more evident, when it comes to operationalizing the commercial tree program, and defining who exactly should plant trees where. It was demonstrated earlier that this issue forms the hub of local class struggles. Regional class dynamics revolve around the same question.

From the perspective of provincial-level officials, large scale programs that boost production quickly and make the landscape appear organized, developed and modern have much attraction (Dove 1993). Giving land licenses or titles and production support to major entrepreneurs, usually city based and politically linked, is the simplest mechanism, already adopted in many parts of Indonesia, where indigenous farmers have become a landless labouring class.[10] That large scale outside capital has *not*, so far, played a major role in the Tinombo hills can be attributed in part to the inaccessibility of the area. It is smaller scale entrepreneurs living in the villages along the narrow coastal plain, who have been quick to recognize the new profits to be gained from commercial tree farming in the mountainous hinterlands they previously regarded as waste. This group has been actively seeking government support for its initiatives, using the language of poverty alleviation, production and local "development".

The coastal elites see themselves as deserving candidates. They are poor, at least by urban standards (if not in comparison to poor coastal wage workers or hill farmers). Moreover, they claim to be the group with the initiative to succeed in tree farming, in contrast to the ignorant, backward, destructive hill people. It is coastal people who can transform the "empty" hillside land (empty = wasted, unproductive, abandoned and or illegally used and abused by hill farmers). It is coastal people who can bring development and civilization to the uplands, and tax revenues to the government.

Coastal elites have not been successful in selling their model for the commercial tree program to provincial officials. As noted earlier the latter, to their credit, have been making novel and ambitious attempts to recognize indigenous tenure and to channel inputs directly to the hillside farmers, instead of insisting on their resettlement. In practice, the government's new initiatives have been subverted by the local class and

Producing Economic Transformation 141

gender struggles within the hills described earlier and by the obstruction of officials and elites pursuing other goals.

While large scale displacement of middle hill populations by coastal or urban elites operating through particular definitions of "the national interest" has thus far been avoided, displacement on a smaller scale is nevertheless taking place. It is occurring in conjunction with the cultural and economic transformations within the hills described earlier, and is thus more subtle and pervasive than any government interventions (for or against particular class interests) could possibly engineer.

The key factor is the commoditization of land. Prior to the advent of commercial tree farming, only pioneers regularly sold land, because only they had exclusive individualized rights to it. Today, individuals who have been successful in claiming and asserting exclusive rights to hillside land through planting trees on it, are at liberty to sell it to a third party. Hill farmers facing debts or other crises regularly sell land with trees to outsiders, moving on to repeat the conversion process on another plot. For those able to maintain their tree plots until they come into production, price fluctuations on the world market and crop disease bring new hazards. Over time, in piecemeal fashion, one plot at a time, those with greater access to capital (in this case, coastal and urban elites), are taking control of the land and farming it as absentee owners relying on local labour, now dispossessed.

Far from being "penetrated" by capitalism or, less abstractly, forced by governments or agribusiness to abandon subsistence production, the hill population has participated in the transformation process. Why, then, if their communities and livelihoods are being displaced, has no counterpoint emerged among hill farmers on the merits of producing commercial tree crops for world markets? In part, this question can be answered with reference to the class and gender dynamics explored earlier. Each hill farmer hopes to be a beneficiary of the transformation process, and the systematic structuring processes that make success for particular groups unlikely have yet to be identified through a counterpoint discourse leading to awareness and organization.

In part, the question of why there is ready acceptance of commercial crops can be answered by examining the motivation behind acceptance, by identifying what it is in their previous form of life that hill farmers are seeking to change. On the production side, the list would include their dependence on annual crops, subject to the vagaries of weather and pests; the declining yields caused by overuse and long term land degradation;

and the hard, dirty labour involved in the annual production cycle. Through having commercial tree crops, they imagine themselves sitting at home, hiring labourers to pick the cocoa pods and carry them down to market. Their production goals are therefore linked to their consumption goals: to *become* part of the national mainstream, at least in terms of housing, dress, diet and education, and no longer to be despised by coastal dwellers for their backward living conditions.

What is missing from this picture is a sense of the imagined community—how hill people anticipate relating to one another in the new era, when the relations of production that previously shaped their interactions have been transformed. No nostalgia for "the good old days when people cared about each other" or when "everyone had a place to farm and didn't need to work for others" is in evidence. It may emerge as the material inequalities of the new order become more apparent and intractable. It is yet to be seen whether the result will be individual discontentment, or a developed counterpoint and collective action, drawing on alternative interpretations of tradition in order to create a different future. The emerging patterns are indeed "something new," created but not fully imagined, predicted, or planned by any of those party to this history.

Notes

1. See Nourse 1989 and Li 1991 for accounts of the historical origins of cultural and economic diversity in the region. Nourse describes an elaborate system of ranks and responsibilities among coastal based Lauje aristocrats intermarried with Mandar and other Muslim non-Lauje elites. The power of these aristocrats, and that of the district and village officials appointed by the Dutch and Indonesian states, has always been limited by the independence of mountain farmers who maintain control of their own means of production. Patterns of exchange between the coastal and upland areas are significant to the regional political economy, but are not explored in this paper.

2. See Tsing 1993 for a fascinating account of some *unfamiliar* forms through which questions of identity, politics and difference are articulated in the Meratus Mountains.

3. Anna Tsing's work (1984) on Meratus in Kalimantan has been the point of departure for many of my ideas on political process in Lauje society, in particular on the question of the constitution of social centrality in these scattered, individualistic mountain conditions where leadership is an amorphous process of attracting provisional followers.

4. The opportunity costs of taking land out of swidden production for cash crops are high in this area, due to the population density. For contrasting cases in which commercial tree crops complement swidden production see Dove 1993.
5. See Whitehead 1985 for a discussion of the consequences of the division of labour for property rights. See Li (n.d.) for a fuller discussion of these issues in the Lauje context.
6. See Tsing 1990 for a fuller discussion of this phenomenon in the Meratus area of upland Kalimantan.
7. Reasons cited include mothers' relationships to their children, versions of the "doctrine of maternal altruism" (Whitehead 1981), and women's relative powerlessness in relation to men discussed earlier. More specifically in relation to gambling, women state that they are afraid of being beaten, while men risk only a scolding. Although direct observation is not possible, one could speculate on the dynamics of the gambling scene itself: would a woman's bet of conjugal property be accepted by other players as quickly as a man's?
8. On Indonesian land law and indigenous rights see Dove 1987; Lynch and Talbott 1988; MacAndrews 1986; Ruwiastuti and Blowfield 1991; Ter Haar 1948; Hooker 1978; Zerner 1990; Moniaga 1993; Seymour and Rutherford 1993.
9. See Dove (1985) for an account of central government and Javanese perceptions of Indonesia's outer islands and their deficiencies.
10. See Dove 1985 and 1987.

References

Babcock, Tim
    1994 Local and National Land Tenure Systems in Central Sulawesi, Indonesia: Two Worldviews and Systems Contend. Paper presented at Canadian Council for Southeast Asian Studies 21st Annual Conference, University of Alberta October 1993.
Bernstein, Henry
    1977 Notes on Capital and Peasantry. *Review of African Political Economy* 10:60-73.
Bourdieu, Pierre
    1977 *Outline of a Theory of Practice*. Cambridge: Cambridge University Press.
Comaroff, John and Jean Comaroff
    1992 *Ethnography and the Historical Imagination*. Boulder: Westview Press.
Dove, Michael
    1985 *The Agroecological Mythology of the Javanese and the Political Economy of Indonesia*. East-West Environment and Policy Institute Reprint, 84. Honolulu: East-West Center.

1987 The Perception of Peasant Land Rights in Indonesian Development: Causes and Implications. In *Land, Trees, and Tenure*. John B. Raintree, ed. Pp. 265-272. Nairobi and Madison: ICRAF and Land Tenure Center.
1993 Smallholder Rubber and Swidden Agriculture in Borneo: A Sustainable Adaptation to the Ecology and Economy of the Tropical Forest. *Economic Botany* 47(2):136-147.

Hart, Gillian
1989 Agrarian Change in the Context of State Patronage. In *Agrarian Transformations: Local Processes and the State in Southeast Asia*. Gillian Hart et al., eds. Pp. 31-49. Berkeley: University of California Press.

Hefner, Robert
1990 *The Political Economy of Mountain Java: An Interpretive History*. Berkeley: University of California Press.

Hooker, M. B.
1978 *Adat Law in Modern Indonesia*. Kuala Lumpur: Oxford University Press.

Li, Tania Murray
n.d. Working Separately but Eating Together: Personhood, Property and Power in Conjugal Relations. Draft in the files of the author.
1991 *Culture, Ecology and Livelihood in the Tinombo Region of Central Sulawesi*. Halifax: Dalhousie University School for Resource and Environmental Studies.

Lynch, Owen and Kirk Talbott
1988 Legal Responses to the Philippine Deforestation Crisis. *Journal of International Law and Politics* 20(3):679-713.

MacAndrews, Colin
1986 *Land Policy in Modern Indonesia*. Boston: Oelgeschlager, Gunn, and Hain.

Moniaga, Sandra
1993 Toward Community-Based Forestry and Recognition of Adat Property Rights in the Outer Islands of Indonesia. In *Legal Frameworks for Forest Management in Asia*. Jefferson Fox, ed. Pp. 131-150. Honolulu: East-West Center.

Nourse, Jennifer
1989 *We are the Womb of the World: Birth Spirits and the Lauje of Central Sulawesi*. Ph.D. diss., University of Virginia.

Ortner, Sherry
1984 Theory in Anthropology since the Sixties. *Comparative Studies of Society and History* 26(2):126-166.

Rebel, Herman
1989 Cultural Hegemony and Class Experience: A Critical Reading of Recent Ethnological-Historical Approaches (Part Two). *American Ethnologist* 16(2):350-365.
Risseeuw, Carla
1988 *The Fish Don't Talk about the Water: Gender Transformation, Power and Resistance among Women in Sri Lanka.* Leiden: E. J. Brill.
Roseberry, William
1989 *Anthropologies and Histories: Essays in Culture, History, and Political Economy.* New Brunswick: Rutgers University Press.
Ruwiastuti, Maria and Mick Blowfield
1991 *Penguasaan Tanah di Daerah TTM - IAD.* Sulawesi Regional Development Project. University of Guelph.
Seymour, Frances J. and Danilyn Rutherford
1993 Contractual Agreements for Community-Based Social Forestry Programs in Asia. In *Legal Frameworks for Forest Management in Asia.* Jefferson Fox, ed. Pp. 173-188. Honolulu: East-West Center.
Smith, Carol
1984 Forms of Production in Practice: Fresh Approaches to Simple Commodity Production. *Journal of Peasant Studies* 11(4):201-221.
Smith, Gavin
1989 *Livelihood and Resistance: Peasants and the Politics of Land in Peru.* Berkeley: University of California Press.
Ter Haar, B.
1948 *Adat Law in Indonesia* New York: Institute of Pacific Relations.
Tsing, Anna Lowenhaupt
1984 *Politics and Culture in the Meratus Mountains.* Ph. D. diss., Stanford University.
1990 Gender and Performance in Meratus Dispute Settlement. In *Power and Difference: Gender in Island Southeast Asia.* Jane Monig Atkinson and Shelly Errington, eds. Pp. 95-126. Stanford: Stanford University Press.
1993 *In the Realm of the Diamond Queen.* Princeton: Princeton University Press.
White, Benjamin
1989 Problems in the Empirical Analysis of Agrarian Differentiation. In *Agrarian Transformations: Local Processes and the State in Southeast Asia.* Gillian Hart et al., eds. Pp. 15-30. Berkeley and Los Angeles: University of California Press.
Whitehead, Ann
1981 "I'm Hungry Mum": The Politics of Domestic Budgeting. In *Of Marriage and the Market.* Kate Young et al., eds. Pp. 93-116. London: CSE Books

1985 Effects of Technological Change on Rural Women: A Review of Analysis and Concepts. In *Technology and Rural Women: Conceptual and Empirical Issues*. I. Ahmed, ed. Pp. 27-64. London: George Allen and Unwin.

Williams, Raymond
  1977 *Marxism and Literature*. Oxford: Oxford University Press.

Wolf, Eric
  1982 *Europe and the People without History*. Berkeley: University of California Press.

Zerner, Charles
  1990 *Community Rights, Customary Law, and the Law of Timber Concessions in Indonesia's Forests: Legal Options and Alternative in Designing the Commons*. Forestry Studies Report UTF/INS/065. Jakarta, Indonesia: Food and Agricultural Organization (FAO).

9

The Invisible Peasant[1]

Donald W. Attwood

Our ideas about country people often obscure the remarkable variety of things they do and the strategies and abilities they employ in doing them. Our constructs render much of village life invisible.

There are several ways of outlining the magnitude of this problem. One is to remind ourselves that, until recently, half the peasant population was invisible, due to its gender. As a result, the interplay between household production and reproduction was not well conceptualized or investigated.[2]

Another way to uncover what is normally invisible in peasant life is to discuss commercialization, a topic that has been heavily mythologized by intellectuals around the world. Peasants are generally thought to be ignorant, defensive, exploited, and resistant to new markets and technologies. Often they are portrayed as helpless victims rather than active agents, and thus exoticized as people without commercial traditions or motivations. As Richard Wilk mentions in Chapter 6, incorporation into the modern world economy is thought to rupture their lives.

These ideas may be valid in certain cases for specific reasons, but they should be questioned as universal principles of analysis. Based on old assumptions, they have been shaped in contemporary discourse by several currents: by romantic nostalgia for the "moral economy" of the premodern world; by the postmodern aesthetic and its tendency to exoticize "the other"; and by the long-standing influence of Marx and Lenin.[3] This paper focuses mainly on the latter.

In volume I, chapter 27, of *Das Kapital* (1867), Marx explained how small peasants were victimized by capitalist development in England and Scotland. His main objective was to show how the forceful expropriation of common lands drove peasants out of villages and into the nascent urban proletariat. Nothing was said here about the ability of small peasants to survive otherwise, absent expropriation; but this subject was brought up in volume III, where Marx discussed various causes of the downfall of "the self-managing peasant." In addition to "usurpation by big landowners of the common lands," he also mentioned "competition, either of the plantation system or large-scale capitalist agriculture" (1971:807). Finally, he noted that:

> Improvements in agriculture, which on the one hand cause a fall in agricultural prices and, on the other, require greater outlays and more extensive material conditions of production, also contribute towards this [downfall], as in England during the first half of the 18th century (1971:807).

Marx made it clear, then, that small peasants were not expected to contribute to economic development:

> Small landed property presupposes that the overwhelming majority of the population is rural, and that not social, but isolated labour predominates; and that, therefore, under such conditions wealth and development of reproduction, both of its material and spiritual prerequisites, are out of the question, and thereby also the prerequisites for rational cultivation (1971:813).

These brief comments, refracted through Lenin's later work on the Russian peasantry, seem to have set the tone in our own period for most theories of peasants and commercialization.

In *The Development of Capitalism in Russia,* originally published in 1899, Lenin analyzed the "differentiation of the peasantry" in an economy already geared to commodity production. The commodity economy generates contradictions in the form of competition and land grabbing, leading to "the concentration of production in the hands of a minority, [and] the forcing of the majority into the ranks of the proletariat" (1956:175).[4] In essence, when peasants are confronted with a commodity economy, they find themselves inexorably transformed, by competition among themselves, into one of two categories: either large-scale commercial farmers or dispossessed proletarians. "Middle peasants," that is, smallholders cultivating mainly with family labor, tend to disappear.[5]

Underlying Lenin's analysis, which I have called "the standard theory of commercialization" since it became almost universally accepted in peasant studies during the 1970s and 1980s, was the assumption that the old "peasant economy" was outside of, or disconnected from, the economy of markets and commodities. This assumption also underlies most of the macro-theories of world capitalist development, including modernization, dependency, and world-system theories. Macro-theorists consistently tend to underestimate the complexity and sophistication of premodern or non-European systems of household production.

This underestimation helps to support the view that peasants are doomed to extinction. For example, in discussions of contemporary Latin American capitalism, "One group of writers projects the eventual or actual disappearance of peasants within capitalist society" (Roseberry 1989:175). Even theorists with a broad knowledge of regional and historical variation have asserted or implied that peasants are doomed by the modern expansion of markets. Barrington Moore once asked: "Just what does modernization mean for the peasantry beyond the simple and brutal fact that sooner or later they are its victims?" (1966:467); and Eric Wolf asserted that it is "the middle peasant who is relatively the most vulnerable to economic changes wrought by commercialism, while his social relations remain encased within the traditional design" (1969:292). Lenin's hypothesis cast a long shadow over peasant studies.

Fortunately, a number of economic anthropologists have challenged this hypothesis. One recent contribution is Robert Netting's *Smallholders, Householders* (1993), and much of what follows here may be taken as an extension and reinforcement of Netting's basic argument. Netting vigorously refutes the notion that smallholders must be on the defensive in relation to markets. He observes that "smallholders are seldom solely subsistence cultivators" (1993:15), offering numerous examples of production for consumption combined with production for the market. Despite smallholders' presumed disadvantages in coping with markets, Netting insists that we must "explain why capitalist landlords were often unable to dispossess an existing smallholder peasantry" (1993:20).

Our tendency to underestimate Asian peasants, in particular, is related to what Jack Goody calls our tendency to overestimate the "uniqueness of the West" (1990:xix). Goody points out that we not only tend to "orientalize" Asian societies, we also tend to "primitivize" them. Specifically, kinship models derived from lineage-based societies in Africa have been applied to Asia, with the result that Asian kinship systems have been seen "as more `primitive' than they really were and therefore as more of an obstacle in the onward march of `modernization' than was actually the case, thus reinforcing the ethnocentric notions of

Marx and Weber about the place of oriental societies in world history" (Goody 1990:xi).

As with reproduction, so with production. We have tended to portray Asian peasant economies as more primitive than they really were. The stereotypical peasant embodied in our concepts and theories scarcely corresponds with the lived experience of Asian villagers who have been producing market commodities—including food, fibres, and cottage-industry products—for many hundreds, if not thousands, of years.

In some parts of Asia, peasants have produced goods for trade on regional and international markets since long before the rise of European imperialism. Of course, commodity production has varied from region to region and period to period with the ebb and flow of markets and empires. In some remote corners of Asia, markets beyond the local cluster of villages may have scarcely existed.[6] In other regions, particularly where rich farm lands were located close to water transport, much of village life was intensely focused on the production and marketing of commodities.

For example, David Ludden's *Peasant History in South India* (1985), portrays a millennium of peasant activity in a district at the southern tip of India. As he notes, "The view we inherit today assumes that Europe became the vanguard civilization leading the way in social change during modern times," yet his book describes "a regional peasant culture that produced its own distinct style of agrarian capitalism" during the period from 900 to 1900 A.D. (1985:14). Hence, Ludden concludes that,

> Dramatic changes after 1800 appear in this region to result more significantly from a very long-term process of local creativity and peasant learning, within an expanding world of interaction, than from exogenous shocks visited upon isolated villagers by the imperialist British during the industrial revolution. . . . Peasants and imperialists alike participated actively in producing Eurasian capitalism (1985:14).

Instead of rupture, this heuristic approach stresses continuity across temporal and cultural boundaries. Unlike Chayanov (1966), Polanyi (1957), and Scott (1976), for example, this approach does not necessarily assign villagers living in remote times or places to distinct economic and moral universes.

The Invisible Peasant 151

Continuity in South China

The continuity of peasant enterprise in one area of South China is described by Philip Huang in *The Peasant Family and Rural Development in the Yangzi Delta, 1350-1988*.[7] For six centuries, delta villagers have been heavily engaged in the production of marketed commodities, including rice, cotton cloth, and silk thread. As this list suggests, commodity production occurred not only in the fields but also in the household. The rearing of silk worms and the preparation of silk thread and cotton cloth were done mainly by peasant women. All the silk thread and as much as seven-eighths of the cotton cloth was destined for the market (Huang 1990:46).

Yangzi delta peasants not only had centuries of experience with commodity markets, they were also enmeshed in factor markets: land was for sale or rent, labor was for hire, and capital could be borrowed at interest. Huang is careful to point out, however, that these factor markets were imperfect. Take the market in land:

> Land was conceived as consisting of both subsoil and topsoil, and the property rights in the subsoil came to be traded more and more freely, in response both to the wish of urban elites to invest in land, and the need of impoverished peasants to sell it. . . . Topsoil ownership, by contrast, showed extraordinary stability over time . . . It was topsoil ownership that carried the traditional constraints—of extended rights of redemption in any conditional sale, and of the customary prior right of purchase by kin and neighbors in an outright sale (Huang 1990:107-08).

Likewise, the labor market was imperfect, since women, though heavily engaged in commodity production, rarely worked for wages (Huang 1990:65-66).

Despite their intense, though incomplete, involvement in factor and commodity markets, the delta peasantry showed remarkable continuity in terms of their organization of production and rights in land. Peasant households remained the principal units of rural commodity production, despite efforts to establish systems of "managerial farming"—that is, large-scale farming with hired labor. Before the Communist revolution, peasant households consistently drove the managerial farms out of business by under-selling them. They could do so because much of their commodity output, such as silk thread and cotton cloth, was produced with simple tools by unpaid female labor.[8] Managerial farms, on the other hand, could only hire male laborers at relatively high seasonal wages (Huang 1990:63-68).[9]

Huang's conclusion is that the old Leninist model of commercialization has no general applicability. Instead of being dispossessed, the peasants held onto their lands and drove the larger-scale, labor-hiring farms out of business. Commercialization did not arrive with Europeans, nor did it drive peasants off their farms and into the landless proletariat.

But if the Yangzi delta peasants failed to support the pessimism of the Leninists, they also failed to confirm the optimism of neo-classical economists who believe that active commodity markets ought to propel a rural economy into economic development and self-transformation. Such a transformation might occur via the accumulation of capital, adoption of improved technologies, and organization of more efficient production units by peasants, resulting overall in the increased productivity of labor.

According to Huang, however, no such transformation occurred in the delta prior to 1980. Instead, the delta peasantry participated in *involutionary commercialization,* with no significant increase in labor productivity over the course of six centuries. As Huang sees it, the main factor holding down the productivity of labor, despite notable increases in total output, was population pressure (Huang 1990:10-13,77).[10]

Huang's readers may thus be left with that old familiar feeling: peasants can grow commercial crops, but they're still stuck in the mud. As everybody from Marx to Stalin to Mao has insisted, only a big, external force can push them along the road toward economic transformation. In a similar vein, Huang (1990:252-65) argues that the rapid transformation of the delta economy in the post-Mao period results less from the internal dynamism of the peasant household and more from the prior effects of collective industrialization.

However, Huang notes that the Yangzi delta is a special case, given its proximity to the vast urban market of Shanghai. As he mentions, there has been vigorous debate in China over the applicability of a different case, known as the "Wenzhou model," as a path toward rural transformation. Historically more isolated from external commerce than the Yangzi delta, the Wenzhou district became an economic "miracle" in the 1980s, due to an efflorescence of household enterprises (Huang 1990:261-63; Nolan & Dong 1990; Simon 1993). While this miracle may or may not be replicated in other districts, it demonstrates that peasant economies can become self-transforming under certain conditions. As Huang himself comments:

> Given suitable market conditions and a sufficient surplus, the small-scale family production unit, to be sure, can be a unit for accumulation and capitalization, no less than the successful mom-and-pop business in the United States. "Petty commodity production," *pace* Marx, can become capitalist production even as it continues to rely on the household unit (1990:262).

Continuity and Transformation in South Gujarat

This possibility also became a reality in India. Consider the southern coastal districts of Gujarat in western India. An English doctor named John Fryer, in the service of the East India Company, visited the countryside between Surat and Broach in 1679. As paraphrased by K.N. Chaudhuri, Fryer observed that:

> The flat plains around Surat were among the most intensively cultivated and commercialized regions in Gujarat. Broach itself led the weaving and processing of cotton cloth, which was carried on in all the neighbouring villages and small towns. . . . Here in India the way was clogged and jammed with 'cafilas' [caravans] of oxen and camels. Teams of bullocks in pairs of eight, twelve, and sixteen, were yoked to heavy waggons loaded with merchandise. . . . Large, sea-going vessels were brought right up to the town [of Broach] by skilled pilots with cargo of corn and salt. The locally grown wheat and cotton contributed in no small measure to the industrial and commercial prosperity of the area, so evident in this period of Mughal rule in Gujarat. Only the previous September, Fryer observed with professional humour, the annual Red Sea Fleet had returned from the hajj voyage laden with 'Religion and Pestilence' . . . [But] the Fleet also brought back five million rupees' worth of treasure in gold and silver. The river of precious metals . . . continued to inject vast financial liquidity to the agrarian-based and at the same time highly commercialized economies of both India and China (Chaudhuri 1990:137-38).

Fryer's observations were made possible by the trading activities of the East India Company. However, his reference to the Red Sea Fleet indicates that the English were participating in a trade much older and larger than the portion which flowed directly between India and Europe. There is no reason to assume that the bustling commercial activity in the villages and towns of south Gujarat had been triggered solely by the comparatively recent arrival of European traders.[11]

What is most striking about Fryer's account of 17th-century Gujarat is that the description corresponds in every respect with what one observes in the same region today. Irrigated fields are filled with market crops, such as sugarcane, tobacco, cotton, bananas, groundnuts, chicory, and fodder for dairy cattle; the town markets overflow with their produce, and the back roads are crammed with buses and trucks—concrete evidence of the intense exchange of commodities between city, town and village.

Thus there is evidence of long-term continuity, but in contrast to the Yangzi delta, there is also evidence of regional self-transformation over the last hundred years. By 1861, one cotton spinning mill was operating in the city of Ahmedabad; by 1914 there were 49 mills in this city, which had emerged as "the second-largest cotton mill centre in India," next to Bombay (Morris 1983:575). These mills stimulated cotton cultivation in the surrounding districts, but the villagers did more than simply increase their output of cash crops. Between the two world wars, they established a number of cooperatives, owned and operated by farmers, for ginning and marketing their cotton. Some of these ventures are still doing well today (Shah 1992).

In 1939, dairy farmers in Surat district established a milk cooperative which provided (and still provides) fresh, high-quality products to city dwellers at low cost (George 1995). Immediately after independence (which came in 1947), the dairy farmers of Kheda district established a processing and marketing cooperative which successfully sold dairy products to the distant metropolis of Bombay. Today, the Amul cooperative is known worldwide as a large-scale, high-tech dairy plant producing an array of quality products, including powdered milk, ice cream, chocolate, and cheese (Baviskar 1988; George 1988; Patel 1988).

Cotton and dairy co-ops serve as examples of how the region's farmers have invested in new agro-industrial enterprises, building on technical and organizational experiments. A rich variety of other innovations could be cited to document the dynamism and prosperity of this region.

The Patidars, a prosperous caste in south and central Gujarat, are famous as commercial farmers, as the organizers of Amul and other cooperative enterprises, and as private entrepreneurs in business and industry. Though all Patidars trace their roots to village farming families, many have migrated during the last century or so to East Africa, Britain, and North America, where they have become successful businessmen.

The Invisible Peasant 155

Strange how these "peasants" could travel to distant shores and set themselves up so readily in non-agricultural enterprises. Yet not so strange, when you consider that their families have been intensely involved in commodity production and trade for a thousand years or more.

As in South China, we have here a case of long-term continuity, since a commercial peasantry has flourished in this region for centuries. We also find, over the last hundred years or so, a process of *self-transformation*. That is, the commercial peasantry has invested in modern farm technology, large-scale agro-industries, and a variety of other enterprises, both urban and rural.

However, as we saw in the case of the Yangzi delta, continuity does not necessarily lead to self-transformation. Indeed, continuity itself is not guaranteed. For example, we may contrast Gujarat, on the west coast of India, with Bengal on the east. Bengal now ranks among the poorest regions in South Asia but was once renowned for its commercial peasant production:

> The economic impoverishment which had overtaken Bengal during our century would have been unbelievable in the seventeenth and eighteenth centuries when all the contemporary historians united in extolling Bengal's overflowing agricultural wealth founded on its export of rice and fine cotton cloth (Chaudhuri 1990:236).

In the late eighteenth century, Bengal suffered severe economic shocks and depopulation, at least partly due to European misrule. But why, over the next two centuries, this region failed to regain its earlier vitality is, to me, a real puzzle.

Non-Continuity and Transformation in Maharashtra

I mention this puzzle because self-transformation does not necessarily require centuries of prior continuity. This may be illustrated by turning back to western India, specifically to the inland plateau region of Maharashtra. Compared with south Gujarat and the Yangzi delta, prior to 1800 this region was hardly commercialized at all.

There were two reasons for this state of affairs, both stemming from topography. First, the coastal mountains bordering Maharashtra on the west cast a heavy rain shadow over the inland plateau, producing a semi-arid and drought-ridden climate. Second, this coastal range, and the

Satpura mountains to the north, limited access to the coast. With its semi-arid climate and landlocked position, western Maharashtra could not nurture much commercial agriculture, at least not before the advent of modern roads, railroads, and irrigation works.

What it could, and did, nurture was mobility and warfare. Peasants were often uprooted by famine and conflict; and they were willingly set in motion by local rajas, princes, and other officials whose business it was to raise both taxes and armies as the occasion demanded. These rulers, who became known as Marathas, campaigned almost continuously during the seventeenth and eighteenth centuries; sooner or later, they invaded nearly every region of India. According to Stewart Gordon (1993), the Maratha armies were peasant armies. Villagers joined up in the dry season and returned home to plant their crops in the monsoon.

When the British conquered western India in 1818, they put a stop to all this. The Pax Britannica encouraged bureaucratic and commercial instead of military enterprise. The argument can be made, and has been made, that illiterate peasants were ill-equipped to take advantage of these new opportunities. However, conditions changed dramatically after the British began constructing large-scale irrigation canals toward the end of the 19th century. These canals were initially planned as famine-protection works, but villagers soon learned to exploit them in pursuit of commercial opportunities, particularly with the cultivation of sugarcane.

In *Raising Cane* (1992), I have offered a detailed history of sugar production in this region, so here I skip lightly over the middle passages of this story, coming directly to the situation as it stands today. Those portions of western Maharashtra which have been irrigated during the last hundred years have become prosperous zones of commercial agriculture.

Two questions may be asked in comparing this case with those already mentioned. First, what was the effect of rapid commercialization on the organization of crop production and the distribution of land? Second, was this a case of *involuntary* or *transformative* commercialization?

The first question has received detailed attention in *Raising Cane*. In a nutshell, the peasant household, supplemented to varying degrees with hired labor, is still the basic unit of production. And the pattern of land distribution has not changed very much over the last hundred years. To the extent that it has changed, the old high-status, non-cultivating castes have given up a significant share of the land they used to own, and the "middle peasant castes" (Marathas, Dhangars and Malis) have gained

The Invisible Peasant 157

more land. In other words, once the land became irrigated and acquired great commercial value, it came increasingly into the hands of those who possessed the skills and experience to cultivate it directly. The middle peasantry was strengthened rather than weakened by the rapid growth of commercial farming.

Regarding the second question, two kinds of evidence persuade me that a transformation has occurred and that it was driven largely by the innovative efforts of the new commercial peasantry. First, I collected family histories from a sample of villagers, supplemented by personal and family histories of various leaders and innovators in the research area (in eastern Pune district). Starting as far back as the period between 1900 and 1920, and in some cases even earlier, these family histories offer frequent examples of innovation, expansion, adoption of new technologies, accumulation, and diversification in their economic strategies and resources. In some striking cases, landless migrants of middle-caste status moved from unirrigated to canal villages, where they learned to cultivate sugarcane as wage laborers, then began to rent land and grow cane for themselves, and finally began to buy land and grow wealthy by village standards.[12]

I also collected data on the history of local institutions, particularly cooperative sugar factories, which have become the prime intermediaries between village producers and the national economy. I will not attempt to summarize here their origins and causes of success, since these matters are discussed at length in *Raising Cane.* Instead, let me briefly mention their achievements as of about 1990. At that time, there were just over 100 cooperative factories in Maharashtra. Their annual production was on the order of 2.7 million (metric) tonnes of sugar, amounting to about 30 percent of India's white (or industrial) sugar output. Since India is one of the world's largest producers of cane sugar, these cooperative factories have clearly played a significant role in the country's industrial growth.

Roughly 100,000 workers are employed regularly inside these factories, and another half million, at least, are employed as seasonal harvest laborers. These cooperatives are owned by more than 700,000 cane growers, the majority of whom are small and middle farmers, and each shareholder has one vote. Boards of directors are elected from among the farmer-shareholders, and these boards have complete authority over the management of their factories.

Their technology is equivalent to that which would be found in modern sugar factories anywhere. By any standard, the co-ops in

Maharashtra are more efficient than most private sugar factories in India. They are also considerably more efficient than the state-managed sugar factories found in some regions.

In order to increase their competitiveness, many sugar co-ops have diversified into by-products, including alcohol and other chemicals from molasses and paper from cane fibre. Many have also contributed to local infrastructure by building and repairing roads and helping to finance small and medium-scale irrigation schemes. In addition, many have invested in the human capital of their communities by financing the construction of schools, colleges, polytechnic institutes, health clinics, and hospitals. Whatever the needs of their local areas, the sugar co-ops serve as focal points for organization and investment.

However one cares to measure, these sugar co-ops—representing the organized, voluntary efforts of the commercial peasantry—have transformed the economy of the region. Similar transformations have also occurred in the nearby state of Gujarat; but as we have seen, a prosperous commercial peasantry was already established there centuries earlier. In the case of Maharashtra, the rise and transformation of the commercial peasantry has all taken place within the last hundred years or so.

Questions and Comparisons

When students read *Raising Cane,* they invariably ask why Maharashtra is so different from other regions of the developing world. This is a good question, but I would like to turn it around by asking whether similar, self-generated transformations could have occurred, or are occurring, elsewhere. This question more or less defines my current research agenda. I can only offer some preliminary comments in the hope that they will stimulate debate.

If we assume that similar self-transformations were possible elsewhere, then they were blocked in many instances by forces which are not hard to identify.

First, harking back to Huang's work and other studies of agriculture in China and the former Soviet Union, it is evident that forced collectivization was an obstacle to peasant enterprise and innovation.[13]

Second, in many former colonies in Africa and the Americas, where indigenous peoples were driven off the better lands by epidemics and armed conquest, they clearly had limited opportunities in commercial agriculture. In a number of these colonies, indigenous cultivators were discouraged or prohibited from growing cash crops, with export-crop production reserved for European settlers.

Third, some post-colonial governments have offered preferential tax breaks, land claims, cheap credit, and other subsidies to large-scale ranchers and plantation owners, thus effectively blocking smallholders from competing in the same markets.

Fourth, even in regions like West Africa, where most of the land has remained in the hands of indigenous farmers, the latter have often been hindered by post-colonial policies favoring export marketing boards, food price controls, subsidized food imports, and skewed infrastructural investment—in short, by powerful urban bias (Bates 1981; Hart 1982; Herbst 1993).

Fifth, these conditions were all exacerbated by the general absence of democratic rights: small rural producers, despite their numbers, generally lacked the means to persuade national leaders to heed their interests.

Given the prevalence of these and other obstacles, it is no wonder that peasants are not widely known for their ability to generate economic development. But this is not simply due to *their* usual lack of opportunity; it is also due to *our* systematic blindness to their abilities, motives, strategies, and resources.

One manifestation of this deep-rooted intellectual bias may be found in Keith Hart's (1982) *The Political Economy of West African Agriculture,* a work which I admire in many ways. Hart argues that, even assuming more favorable macro-economic conditions, smallholder cash cropping is not a sufficient basis for agricultural development, because "it does not establish a long-run dynamic of economic development through labor specialization, capital investment, and productive innovation in the sphere of technology and organization" (1982:157). Hart strongly favors the encouragement of large-scale farms, which might be controlled by governments, international corporations, or local capitalists (1982:160-61).

Why this insistence that only large-scale farming contains the seeds of development? Hart has convinced himself, partly on the basis of his reading of classical political economy, that smallholder cash cropping is inherently stagnant. For example, he respectfully quotes the passage, cited above, where Marx discusses the inherent limitations of production based on "small landed property" (Hart 1982:19). Curiously, Hart is well aware of the dynamic history of west African cocoa farming, as studied by Polly Hill (1963, 1970) and others; yet this case apparently has little effect on his basic assumptions.

Other evidence, published after Hart's book, suggests that he saw only what he expected when looking at West African peasants. According to Janet MacGaffey,

> . . . in Nigeria the official assessment of the stagnation and decline of agriculture conceals a major and dynamic change in the development of Nigerian capitalism: the dramatic expansion of commercial agriculture to supply the domestic food market . . . [Beckman] refers to this phenomenon as 'the new food frontier,' and stresses that the backbone of such expansion has been peasant small-holder production. It is small peasant farmers who provide the bulk of the food for the non-agricultural population (MacGaffey 1991:30, citing Beckman 1988:36).

Hart is also selective in his use of evidence from other parts of the world. He draws comparisons between West African and Asian peasants, yet he fails to note the implications of the "green revolution" achieved by small farmers in many regions of Asia.[14] To suggest, as Hart does, that smallholder cash cropping cannot lead to "labor specialization, capital investment, and productive innovation in the sphere of technology and organization" (1982:157) is directly contrary to the evidence cited above.

However, you don't need to be a African expert to misread or ignore the evidence on peasant dynamism in Asia: there are plenty of Asian experts to do that. The most pertinent example here is Jan Breman's (1985) *Of Peasants, Migrants and Paupers,* which is concerned with Surat district in Gujarat, the same area described by Fryer in 1679. Because Breman's study concentrates on migration, pauperization, and class polarization, he chooses to focus exclusively on two classes: "the dominant landowners" and "the landless proletariat." Thus he ignores the activities of small farmers almost entirely. As he says in an introductory chapter, the smaller landowners

> . . . are not the principal actors in the social dynamic which has arisen, and for this reason they will be largely left out of consideration in the remainder of this study. . . . I regard the term 'peasants' as still being appropriate to this class because of their hesitant and defensive reaction to the situation which has come into being. Without much hope of improvement, they try as far as possible to protect themselves from the negative consequences of this process of change, and on the whole they have been reasonably successful in this (Breman 1985:60).

The Invisible Peasant 161

The stereotype of the "hesitant and defensive" small peasant gives Breman his justification for ignoring them:

> As distinct from this wide intermediate layer I am devoting attention to the classes who have been either the entrepreneurs of rural transformation in Surat District or, on a large scale, the main victims of it. Both these strata form the exclusive focus of my research (Breman 1985:60).

This is certainly an effective method for making the majority of peasants invisible, and Breman employs another device to the same end. He lumps middle-size farmers (those owning between 5 and 15 acres) in with "the dominant landowners" (1985:61-66). Thus the confusing middle categories are eliminated, and we are left with a simple model of class polarization.[15]

In another time, this might have appeared as a useful and original research strategy; but one cannot help feeling that now it is designed to keep the old Leninist model chugging along as well as may be. So what if we ignore the majority of farmers, who are smallholders? So what if we assume, without further investigation, that their reactions to change are defensive and hesitant, rather than entrepreneurial? So what if we decide that anyone with more than 5 acres is a "dominant landowner"?

When one inquires into the family histories of successful entrepreneurs in rural Maharashtra, they turn out to come from a wide variety of backgrounds, including some whose fathers or grandfathers were migrant landless laborers (Attwood 1992). Many others come from the middle strata which Breman chooses to ignore. He has assumed that there is only one possible dynamic at work, the Leninist one, and others are not worthy of investigation.

Conclusions

Our standard terminologies, conceptual frameworks, causal theories, and sacred texts prevent us from seeing how peasants really cope with markets. We might see more of what has been rendered invisible by rethinking the terms we use.

Polly Hill is not alone in asking us to consider "why country people are not peasants" (1986:8). Since the late 1970s, much debate has centered on redefining them as "simple" or "petty" commodity producers (e.g., Friedmann 1980; Bernstein 1986). One virtue of this debate is that it discards some of the old Leninist doctrine. Theorists concerned with simple or petty commodity producers often recognize that they have endured for long periods and that, thanks to the low cost of family labor, they can survive in competition against large capitalist firms.

Moreover, some of these authors have attacked the assumption that small rural producers simply react to conditions imposed by external markets. Villagers are now seen as actors constructing local economies not only through market transactions but also through reciprocal relations among kin and neighbors, community traditions, voluntary associations, and various forms of political resistance (e.g., Long, et al. 1986; Smith 1991).

Yet I dislike the new phrases for several reasons, including their awkward length. "Petty" carries derogatory connotations in English; and "simple" is not always a fair description of the people or their products. Finally, the stress on commodity production over-corrects the old view in which peasants were seen essentially as subsistence producers. Small rural producers tend to engage in *both* subsistence and commodity production, and this is what makes them difficult to categorize.

Small and middle peasants are like mythical beasts: they combine the attributes of what are commonly thought to be different types of economic men. Like "laborers," they often work extremely hard for low returns, like "capitalists," they own land and other productive assets, like "managers," they sometimes hire and supervise labor, like "entrepreneurs," they make complex decisions in the face of many uncertainties. In the South Asian context, Lloyd and Susanne Rudolph (1987) have invented a phrase capturing the paradoxical nature of these creatures, calling them "bullock capitalists." These are villagers who "use and pay for capital and participate in markets" but who rely more on family than hired labor and are thus not fully capitalists (Rudolph and Rudolph 1987:53).

Since "the economic circumstances of bullock capitalists unite the interests of capital, management, and labor," they do not fit readily into the categories of western social science: "Their 'categorical invisibility' in agrarian class theory is due precisely to their anomalous standing" (Rudolph and Rudolph 1987:53, 341). Though invisible in terms of theory, "Bullock capitalists are advantageously placed by their objective circumstances to become the hegemonic agrarian class" in India, constituting, as they do, at least one-third of rural households and controlling half the agricultural land (Rudolph and Rudolph 1987:52, 336). It tells us something about how social theories are formed and

The Invisible Peasant 163

maintained that this invisible category consists not of people on the margins of village life but those at the very center.

Outside South Asia, the bullock is not always the draft animal of choice, so I use a less colorful phrase, "commercial peasants," to describe small rural producers engaged with commodity markets. This phrase captures some of the paradox inherent in "bullock capitalist."

However, the choice of terms matters only in a negative sense: we need to avoid terms that conceal what villagers do. A more positive and substantive goal is to engage in comparative research on their strategies of production and reproduction as they seek to overcome various obstacles in specific regional and historical settings.

The long-term historical role of the small producer is not simply to remain invisible, to suffer and disappear. Scott Cook (1986:84-85) mentions the significance of small-scale enterprise in the early history of British industrialization, and Huang (1990:263) points out that, "In England and, to a lesser extent, continental Europe, industrialization proceeded from the bottom up, from village handicraft home industry to small-town handicraft manufacturing to big city machine manufacturing." We need not assume that other regions must reiterate the English historical sequence in order to argue that peasant enterprises could contribute to economic transformation, if only they were allowed to do so.

However, opportunities to verify this hypothesis have been overlooked due to our tendency to think in dualistic terms. As Binford and Cook (1991:78-82) have noted, "peasants" and other small-scale commodity producers, have usually been seen as essentially different from "capitalists". Hence researchers tend "to ignore the mutually reinforcing and compatible elements in simple commodity and capitalist forms, [and] the extent to which capital accumulation may occur in the simple commodity form" (Cook 1986:83).[16]

The idea of small household producers surviving and even prospering within the context of the modern world economy is not as preposterous as we tend to assume, though eminent classical and modern theorists have repeatedly argued that the expansion of markets poses a mortal threat to peasant livelihoods. That hypothesis may be true under some circumstances, but the preponderance of evidence shows that far more potent threats stem from military conquest, forced expropriation, forced collectivization, and despotic or unstable government. In other words, the threats to peasant livelihoods stem primarily from the centers of political and military power, not from the marketplace.[17]

In calling attention to "the invisible peasant," then, I mean to suggest that the political oppression and economic marginalization of peasants has been assisted by our tendency, as intellectuals, not to see peasants as what they are. By ignoring their demonstrated abilities and potential as entrepreneurs, we lend support to those political forces which see peasants as backward, ignorant, stubbornly traditional, or too poor and oppressed to change their ways. Thus peasants are either seen as obstacles to colonial and national development, to be neglected and pushed out of the way, or as objects of megalomaniacal schemes of social engineering.

Notes

1. Earlier versions of this paper were presented to the annual meetings of the Society for Economic Anthropology (April 1993) and the American Anthropological Association (November 1993). Many thanks to B.S. Baviskar, Laurel Bossen, Stanley Engerman, John Galaty, Thomas Hall, Homa Hoodfar, Vasant Kaiwar, Robert Netting, Blair Rutherford, A.M. Shah, Scott Simon, Richard Wilk, and Eric Worby for their comments and suggestions.

2. In the 1920s, Chayanov (1966) framed his "theory of peasant economy," around one type of interaction between production and reproduction, but the implications were largely ignored until the 1970s and 1980s. Now we have a spate of case studies on the subject, but the effort to build analytic models of local and regional variation is still in its infancy. Jack Goody has led the way with macro-comparisons between Africa and Eurasia and micro-comparisons within Eurasia (Goody 1976; 1990).

3. Here I am paraphrasing from personall communications by Stanley Engerman and Vasant Kaiwar.

4. Chayanov suggested that Lenin had misread the *zemstvo* statistics and that the Russian peasantry was not disappearing through class polarization (see Chayanov 1966; Shanin 1972). Meanwhile, other Marxists concerned with "the agrarian question" sought to explain the curious tenacity of small farmers in western Europe (see Kautsky 1902; Gay 1962:198-204).

5. On the whole, Marx and Lenin thought this a good thing. "In modern society it is impossible to exist without selling, and anything that retards the development of commodity production merely results in a worsening of the conditions of the producers," wrote Lenin, immediately after arguing that commodity production causes the differentiation of the peasantry (1956:156-57). Later theorists have assumed this latter hypothesis to be true, *prima facie*, but unlike Lenin, have deplored the expected outcome.

The Invisible Peasant 165

6. However, even in some relatively inaccessible areas, such as the high mountain passes between South Asia and Tibet, trade caravans moved back and forth with great regularity. The long-standing survival strategies of Tibetan peoples living in the high Himalayas and beyond cannot be understood without reference to their efforts to combine subsistence farming, livestock herding, and long-distance trading activities, often within a single household (e.g., Fisher 1990:55-58).

7. Huang's study has also been discussed by Bossen (1992), Feuerwerker (1992), and Netting (1993).

8. Peasant handicraft production also put urban cotton weavers at a competitive disadvantage: "Not one large-scale, wage labor-based cotton weaving workshop emerged in the Ming and Qing" (Huang 1990:86). On the other hand, because silk weaving "was relatively capital-intensive, requiring a fairly complex loom operated by at least two or three skilled workers," peasant household production stopped at the stage of reeling the silk thread (Huang 1990:80).

9. As Bossen (1992) points out, Huang does not really explain how women were segregated from the wage labor market.

10. In comparing Huang's pessimism with a more optimistic view of the Chinese past taken by Myers (1991), Feuerwerker (1992) raises questions about the theoretical and empirical plausibility of both outlooks. It would take us too far afield to comment on this debate, but it should be noted that all participants "agree that the Chinese economy and society in the late-Ming and early-Qing dynasties were remarkably dynamic, rather than backward and stagnant" (Feuerwerker 1992:757-58). The long-term continuity of the commercial peasantry is taken for granted in this debate.

11. K.N. Chaudhuri's (1990) book, *Asia Before Europe*, from which this description of Fryer's journey has been lifted, demonstrates the variety and complexity of commercial agrarian systems, some dating back to the seventh century, in various regions of what he calls the "four Indian ocean civilizations," Islam, India, Southeast Asia, and China.

12. Land was available to be rented or purchased for two main reasons: first, due to the effects of what I call the "irrigation frontier," and second, due to the depression of the 1930s, which ruined large landowners who were not careful managers.

13. See Nolan and Dong (1990: ch.2) for a penetrating analysis of the reasons why collective agriculture was likely to fail.

14. Hart cannot be faulted for failing to notice the dynamism of commercial peasant and household enterprises in China, since the explosive growth in this sector began as he was completing his book.

15. Breman says that landless agricultural laborers amount to nearly 55 percent of the agricultural population of Surat district (1985:66-67). He also says that "more than half the farming population" (that is, the population of landowners) consists of small and marginal farmers with less than 5 acres, and "about a third of the farming population" consists of middle and large farmers

with more than 5 acres (1985:49, 52, 61). As a rough guess, at least half the total farming population (on both sides of the 5-acre divide) corresponds with my category of commercial peasants: small and middle farmers cultivating cash crops mainly with family labor.

16. Interesting as it is, *Conversations in Columbia* (1990), by Gudeman and Rivera, tends to perpetuate this dichotomy between what the authors call "house" and "corporation."

17. Marx (*Capital*, vol.I, ch.27) certainly had no difficulty in identifying expropriation by force as a major cause of peasant impoverishment.

References

Attwood, D.W.
   1992 *Raising Cane: The Political Economy of Sugar in Western India.* Boulder: Westview Press.

Bates, Robert H.
   1981 *Markets and States in Tropical Africa.* Berkeley: University of California Press.

Baviskar, B.S.
   1988 Dairy Co-operatives and Rural Development in Gujarat. In *Who Shares? Co-operatives and Rural Development.* D.W. Attwood and B.S. Baviskar, eds. Delhi: Oxford University Press.

Beckman, Bjorn
   1988 Peasants and Democratic Struggles in Nigeria. *Review of African Political Economy* 41:30-44.

Bernstein, H.
   1986 Capitalism and Petty Commodity Production. In *Rethinking Petty Commodity Production*, special issue of *Social Analysis*, A.M. Scott, ed.

Binford, Leigh and Scott Cook
   1991 Petty Production in Third World Capitalism Today. In *Marxist Approaches in Economic Anthropology*, A. Littlefield and H. Gates, eds. Society for Economic Anthropology Monograph, 9. Lanham: University Press of America.

Bossen, Laurel
   1992 The Household Economy in Rural China: Is the Involution Over? Paper Presented at the annual meeting of the Society for Economic Anthropology, University of California at Irvine.

Breman, Jan
   1985 *Of Peasants, Migrants and Paupers: Rural Labour Circulation and Capitalist Production in West India.* Delhi: Oxford University Press.

Chaudhuri, K.N.
  1990 *Asia Before Europe: Economy and Civilisation of the Indian Ocean from the Rise of Islam to 1750.* Cambridge: Cambridge University Press.
Chayanov, A.V.
  1966 [1925] *The Theory of Peasant Economy,* D. Thorner, B. Kerblay and R. E. F. Smith, eds. Homewood, Illinois: R. D. Irwin.
Cook, Scott
  1986 The "Managerial" vs. the "Labor" Function, Capital Accumulation, and the Dynamics of Simple Commodity Production in Rural Oaxaca, Mexico. In *Entrepreneurship and Social Change,* S. M. Greenfield and A. Strickon, eds. Society for Economic Anthropology Monograph, 2. Lanham: University Press of America.
Feuerwerker, Albert
  1992 Questions About China's Early Modern Economic History That I Wish I Could Answer. *Journal of Asian Studies* 51(4):757-69.
Fisher, J.F.
  1990 *Sherpas: Reflections on Change in Himalayan Nepal.* Berkeley: University of California Press.
Friedmann, H.
  1980 Household Production and the National Economy: Concepts for the Analysis of Agrarian Formations. *Journal of Peasant Studies* 7(2):158-84.
Gay, Peter
  1962 *The Dilemma of Democratic Socialism.* New York: Collier.
George, Shanti
  1988 Co-operatives and Indian Dairy Policy: More Anand than Pattern. In *Who Shares? Co-operatives and Rural Development.* D. W. Attwood and B. S. Baviskar, eds. Delhi: Oxford University Press.
  1995 Beyond Anand: Comparing the Kheda and Choryasi Dairy Cooperatives. In *Finding the Middle Path: The Political Economy of Cooperation in Rural India.* B. S. Baviskar and D. W. Attwood, et al., eds. Boulder: Westview Press (forthcoming).
Goody, Jack
  1976 *Production and Reproduction: A Comparative Study of the Domestic Domain.* Cambridge: Cambridge University Press.
  1990 *The Oriental, the Ancient, and the Primitive: Systems of Marriage and the Family in the Pre-industrial Societies of Eurasia.* Cambridge: Cambridge University Press.
Gordon, Stewart
  1993 *The Marathas, 1600-1803.* New York: Cambridge University Press.
Gudeman, Stephen and Alberto Rivera
  1990 *Conversations in Columbia: The Domestic Economy in Life and Text.* Cambridge: Cambridge University Press.

Hart, Keith
　1982　*The Political Economy of West African Agriculture.* Cambridge: Cambridge University Press.
Herbst, Jeffrey
　1993　*The Politics of Reform in Ghana, 1982-1991.* Berkeley: University of California Press.
Hill, Polly
　1963　*Migrant Cocoa Farmers of Southern Ghana.* Cambridge: Cambridge University Press.
　1970　*Studies in Rural Capitalism in West Africa.* Cambridge: Cambridge University Press.
　1986　*Development Economics on Trial.* Cambridge: Cambridge University Press.
Huang, P. C. C.
　1990　*The Peasant Family and Rural Development in the Yangzi Delta, 1350-1988.* Stanford: Stanford University Press.
Kautsky, K.
　1902　*Die Agrarfrage.* Stuttgart: Dietz.
Lenin, V.I.
　1956 [1899]　*The Development of Capitalism in Russia.* Moscow: Progress.
Long, N., et al.
　1986　*The Commoditization Debate: Labour Process, Strategy and Social Network.* Wageningen, Netherlands: Agricultural University.
Ludden, David
　1985　*Peasant History in South India.* Princeton: Princeton University Press.
MacGaffey, Janet
　1991　*The Real Economy of Zaire: The Contribution of Smuggling & Other Unofficial Activities to National Wealth.* Philadelphia: University of Pennsylvania Press.
Marx, Karl
　1967 [1867]　*Capital: A Critique of Political Economy,* Vol. I. New York: International Publishers.
　1971 [1894]　*Capital: A Critique of Political Economy,* Vol.III. Moscow: Progress Publishers.
Moore, Barrington, Jr.
　1966　*Social Origins of Dictatorship and Democracy: Lord & Peasant in the Making of the Modern World.* Boston: Beacon Press.
Morris, Morris D.
　1983　The Growth of Large-Scale Industry to 1947. In *The Cambridge Economic History of India, Volume 2.* D. Kumar and M. Desai, eds. Cambridge: Cambridge University Press.
Myers, Ramon H.
　1991　How Did the Modern Chinese Economy Develop?—A Review Article. *Journal of Asian Studies* 50(3):604-28.

Netting, Robert McC.
1993 *Smallholders, Householders: Farm Families and the Ecology of Intensive, Sustainable Agriculture*. Stanford: Stanford University Press.
Nolan, Peter and Dong Fureng
1990 *Market Forces in China: Competition and Small Business—The Wenzhou Debate*. London: Zed Books.
Patel, A.S.
1988 Co-operative Dairying and Rural Development: A Case Study of AMUL. In *Who Shares? Co-operatives and Rural Development*, D. W. Attwood and B. S. Baviskar, eds. Delhi: Oxford University Press.
Polanyi, Karl
1957 *The Great Transformation: The Political and Economic Origins of Our Time*. Boston: Beacon Press.
Roseberry, William
1989 *Anthropologies and Histories: Essays in Culture, History, and Political Economy*. New Brunswick: Rutgers University Press.
Rudolph, Lloyd I. and Susanne H. Rudolph
1987 *In Pursuit of Lakshmi: The Political Economy of the Indian State*. Chicago: University of Chicago Press.
Scott, James C.
1976 *The Moral Economy of the Peasant: Rebellion and Subsistence in Southeast Asia*. New Haven: Yale University Press.
Shah, Tushaar, et al.
1992 *Design for Democracy: Building Energetic Farmer Organizations*. Institute of Rural Management, Anand (India). (Ms.)
Shanin, Teodor
1972 *The Awkward Class: Political Sociology of Peasantry in a Developing Society, Russia 1910-1925*. London: Oxford University Press.
Simon, Scott
1993 Commentaries on Huang (1990), Netting (1993), and Nolan and Dong (1990), presented in seminars at McGill University.
Smith, Gavin
1991 *Livelihood and Resistance: Peasants and the Politics of Land in Peru*. Berkeley: University of California Press.
Wolf, Eric R.
1969 *Peasant Wars of the Twentieth Century*. New York: Harper & Row.

10

Historical Perspectives on Long Term Change: *Compadrazgo* Choice Patterns in Rural Paraguay[1]

Christina Bolke Turner

This article examines how *compadrazgo* (ritual fictive kinship) choice patterns in a spontaneous frontier community relate to the socioeconomic history of the area. The socioeconomic history of Ñu Pyajhu Guazú is intricately intertwined with events on the national and international level. The local actors have, with varying degrees of success, been actively responding to the impact of extralocal forces in the community and to themselves. Individuals in Ñu Pyajhu Guazú are intent upon "maximizing" their choices economically and socially. The history of Ñu Pyajhu Guazú makes this clear on an economic level. An analysis of *compadrazgo* choice patterns indicates this to be true socially, as well. This analysis indicates that although families in Ñu Pyajhu Guazú, located in the hinterland of eastern Paraguay, might have been expected to be making vertical fictive kin ties outside of the community, they are not. The reason for this unusual pattern is linked with the history of the frontier zone and the uncertainties that are inherent in the lives of the people who inhabit the area—socially, politically, economically, and environmentally. These basic uncertainties have lead to a type of behavior that has been termed "risk-adverse" in peasant economies, and I argue the same principles are also involved in *compadrazgo* choice practices. My data indicate that the same uncertainties that influence agricultural production choices also influence social fictive kinship choices in Ñu Pyajhu Guazú.

Changes in *compadrazgo* practices have been tied to changes in the social and economic structure of different ethnic groups and peoples throughout Latin America (Foster 1969; Mintz and Wolf 1950; Paul 1942; Van den Berghe, R. and G. Van den Berghe 1966). In Latin American countries, *compadrazgo* ties are of primary importance in social relations and are legitimized through the medium of Catholic church rituals. In Paraguay, the specific rituals used to bond fictive kinship ties are baptism, confirmation, and marriage.

My initial research concentrated on the secular motivations of *compadrazgo*, the extension and intensification of fictive kin ties both within and outside the community, and how they were being manipulated due to economic and structural changes that have been taking place in Ñu Pyajhu Guazú. While my research site was unique in the literature, my hypothesis followed the standard work in the field and I believed the outcome would support previous researchers' findings. That is, that fictive kinship choice preferences are highly adaptable to a fluid social environment. With stronger integration into the capitalist market and changing social and economic options, there should be a change from horizontal, extensive fictive kin choices to vertical, more intensive ritual kin choices.[2]

Ñu Pyajhu Guazú, in the department of Caazapá (Figure 10.1), was founded around 1914 by subsistence farmers seeking virgin land. While contact with the outside world has always been maintained, the distance of the community from any urban areas and the lack of infrastructure have kept Ñu Pyajhu Guazú extremely isolated for most of its history. Around 1975 the community built a dirt road and bridge that directly linked the area with the town of Caazapá, the nearest urban area (35 kilometers). Many changes were made possible in Ñu Pyajhu Guazú with the construction of the road, even though it was only slightly better than an ox cart trail. Heavy vehicles could travel the road and the community had its first mechanized transportation linking it to markets and goods.

The decade of the 1980s brought about substantial transformations. The amount of land available in the immediate area reached its limits in the late 1970s, outsiders have taken a new interest in the community, and various development projects have been instituted. Cash cropping not only became possible, it became a necessity for most families (see Hanks 1992). This, along with an improved transportation infrastructure, has allowed increased contact and integration with the greater Paraguayan society. Because of the new social institutions, improved infrastructure, and development projects recently implemented, previous theory would predict that there would be changes in *compadrazgo* choice patterns, from a horizontal within-the-community pattern to a vertical outside-the-community pattern.

I gathered *compadrazgo* data from every household (106 data sets) within the study area (Figure 10.2). These data clearly indicate that there

Historical Perspectives on Long Term Change 173

have been only minor changes in fictive kin choice patterns over the last fifty years and there has been no statistically significant shifting from horizontal choices to vertical choices (Table 10.1). In Ñu Pyajhu Guazú, of the 801 *compadrazgo* ties that were requested by couples, only 14 (by seven couples), or 1.7 percent, were made vertically outside the community.[3] Of these vertical choices, two couples were relatively young with smaller families. These two couples manipulated the "rules" of fictive kin choice by asking two unrelated single people to stand as godparents. They also hedged their choice by having one godparent that resides in the community and one an elite from outside the community. The remaining couples that made vertical *compadrazgo* choices are all well-established with large families. These couples all own land, are relatively well-off and have made these choices only after extensive ritual kin ties had been made within the community. Only one couple (number 7) made any vertical ties before 1980 and the choice was an intensive tie with a single individual (asked the same couple three times). This couple lives on the fringe of Ñu Pyajhu Guazú and an attempt was being made to tie themselves to their *patrón* in Caazapá. In other words, there is probably an incipient movement towards contracting advantageous vertical *compadrazgo* ties outside the community. The question, given what we know about fictive kin choice patterns, is why more vertical ties are not being made.

I discovered that the people of Ñu Pyajhu Guazú have long been attempting to join in on national "progress," but that they have been regularly, and deliberately, obstructed in this ambition by the vested interests of outsiders. Rather than development projects, and outside agencies, attempting to help the community, I found for the most part that their efforts were an impediment to development. I also found that the four main categories of uncertainty confronting peasant farmers that Frank Ellis (1989:100) identifies were also prevalent in Ñu Pyajhu Guazú's history. These are:

(a) natural hazards or yield uncertainty;
(b) market fluctuations or price uncertainty;
(c) uncertainty deriving from social relations in the rural economy;
(d) uncertainty of state actions and wars.

174 *Economic Analysis Beyond the Local System*

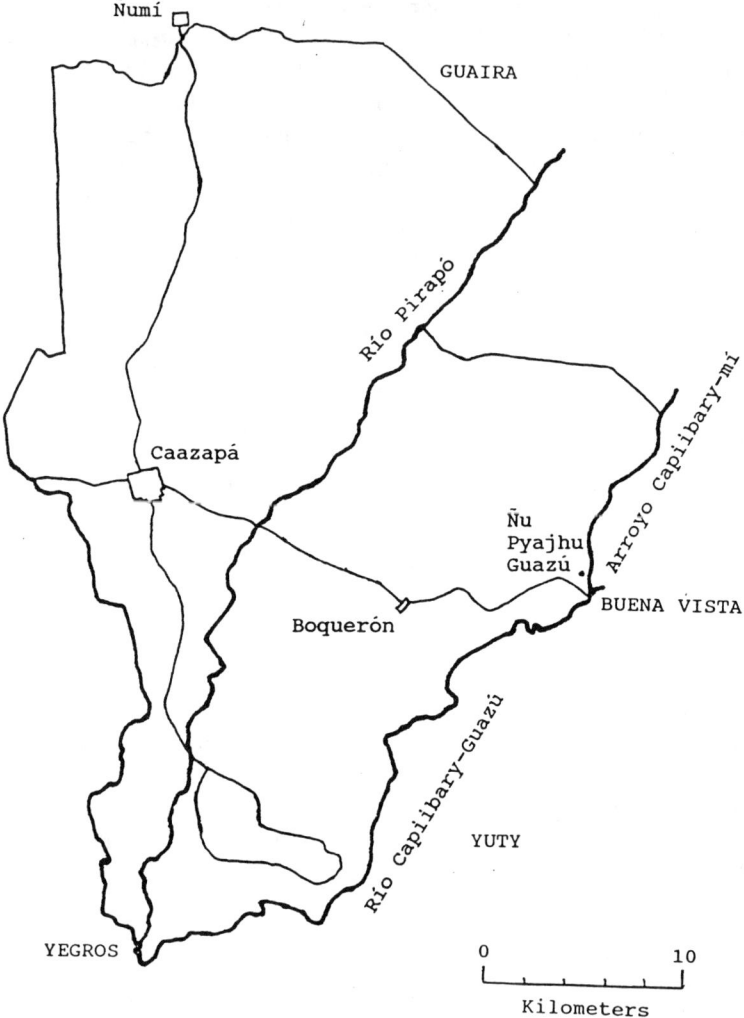

Figure 10.1: The District of Caazapá.

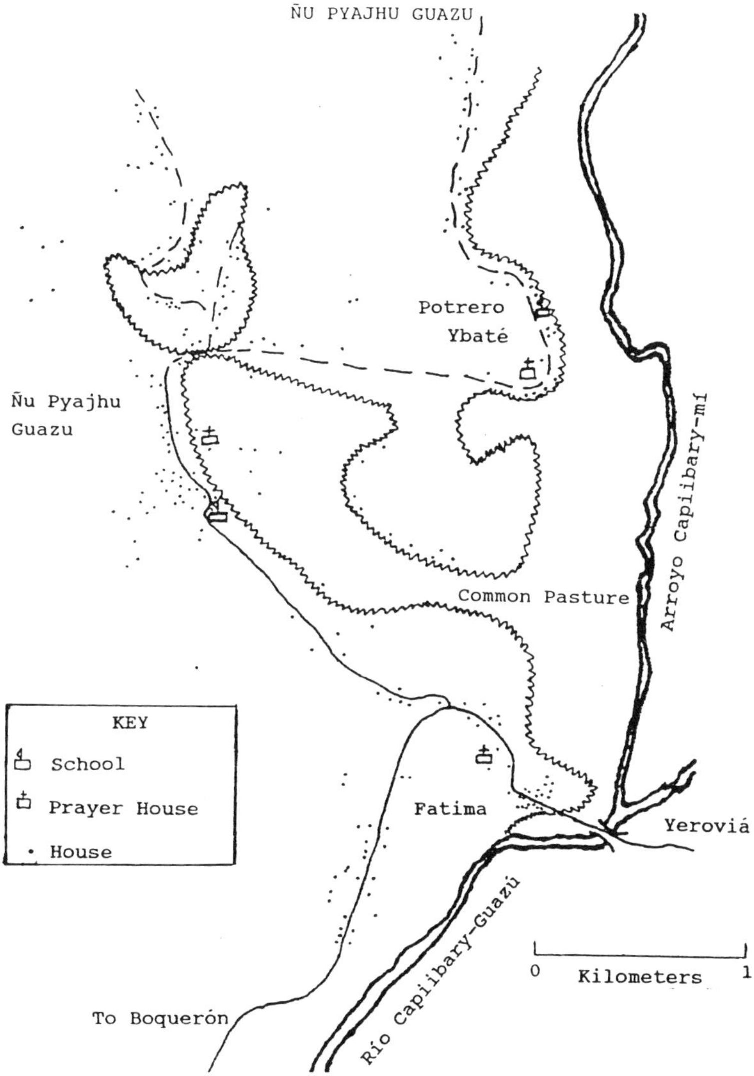

Figure 10.2: Ñu Pyajhu Guazu (adapted from Turner 1993:29).

Couple Number	Vertical Ties Made		Couple Makes the Request*		Requested of the Couple**		All Ties of the Couple	
	A	B	A	B	A	B	A	B
1	2	3	10	15	16	27	28	45
2	4	4	18	22	14	26	35	52
3	.5†	1	3	3	3	4	7	8
4	1	1	11	16	13	14	25	31
5	1	1	20	23	16	32	37	56
6	.5†	1	5	6	1	1	7	8
7	1	3	14	23	11	15	26	41
Totals	10	14	81	106	74	120	166	243

A = Number of *compadres*. B = Number of godchildren.
* All fictive kin ties that the couple has requested of others.
** All fictive kin ties that have been requested of the couple.
† Half of the tie was vertical, the other half being horizontal: two unrelated single individuals standing as godparents together.

Table 10.1: Vertical *Compadrazgo* Ties in Ñu Pyaijhu Guazú.

Furthermore, my data indicate that the same types of uncertainties that are influencing agricultural production choices are also influencing social fictive kinship choices in Ñu Pyajhu Guazú. The peasant farmers of the community can be identified as "risk-adverse" peasants who wish to "maximize their profits" both socially and economically but are wary of doing so because of the uncertainties involved in their existence.

Despite their isolation, the people of Ñu Pyajhu Guazú have always participated in the national market economy and have continually attempted to improve and diversify their cash crop production, develop access to markets and goods, and improve their position in the capitalist system. From the earliest settlement of the zone, cash cropping has been intermixed with subsistence. However, this has proven difficult, and has led to further identifiable areas of risk that have, on one hand contributed to the solidarity of the community, and, on the other, contributed to continued risk adverse economic and social decisions. In the following sections I have attempted to isolate the subsistence farmers' risk factors into Ellis's specified categories, although they are not mutually exclusive.

Natural Hazards or Yield Uncertainty

People who settle in the wilderness are always susceptible to the vicissitudes of natural hazards and lack of infrastructure. This certainly has been true in Ñu Pyajhu Guazú, which was settled around 1914. Even after a direct route was constructed in the early 1970s, the road closed frequently due to rain and commonly for extended periods. The worst year was 1983 when the road was closed for nine months and the only way to reach town was by skiff. More common were two month closures during the rainy season (May through September). Obviously, too much rain can affect crop yield. In Ñu Pyajhu Guazú the more serious result was the inability to grow non-storable diversified market crops and to have access to the market at dependable and propitious times.

Droughts also occur frequently during the dry season and this has had a significant effect on crop yields because there is no irrigation system nor any means of constructing one. In 1942-1943, Ñu Pyajhu Guazú suffered the most severe drought in its history. The six month desiccation left people with almost nothing to eat and even without seeds to begin again. Afterwards, just as plants were starting to bloom, there was an attack of locusts that "covered the sun." The locusts ate everything in sight. The one remaining staple, manioc, was ruined (the stalks are used

178 Economic Analysis Beyond the Local System

for replanting). The people couldn't even eat eggs because the few that were laid "tasted like locusts." This was the most severe and extended natural disaster that occurred, but periods of drought or flooding are common in Ñu Pyajhu Guazú's history.

Another natural hazard that has had a significant effect upon the people of Ñu Pyajhu Guazú is poor health conditions and the lack of medical care. The community has been afflicted with disease, illness, parasites, and accidents. In Paraguay the entire family contributes to both subsistence and cash crop farming. It is impossible to calculate production and manpower losses resulting from high infant mortality, high mortality rate, high costs of poor health, and lack of energy from intestinal worms, anemia, and chronic giardia. The lack of medical care is so acute that in 1984-1986, a Peace Corps health education volunteer vaccinated almost the entire community against common childhood diseases and tetanus.

A significant example of this vicissitude occurred in the late 1960s when polio swept the district of Caazapá, affecting 43 people. Only three people survived the illness, and one is crippled. Three people from Ñu Pyajhu Guazú itself contracted polio and one survived. She was only six months old at the time. The price of her survival was the economic penury of her family for two harvest seasons and the loss of past payments they had been making to purchase title for their land. The family was informed that because of the lapse in payments, they would have to renew their payments from the beginning.

Market Fluctuations or Price Uncertainty

Cotton is the cash crop for most Paraguayan peasants. Cotton always has a market, it is storable for extended periods, it requires no special equipment, and is not as physically taxing as growing alternative market crops. There are two other cash crop possibilities in Ñu Pyajhu Guazú, bitter orange extract (used for perfume) and tobacco. However, the market values vary greatly for these crops, production is much more difficult, and some years there are no buyers in Caazapá. This prevents peasant producers from attempting diversification because of the risks involved. Any perishable crop is out of the question because of poor road conditions and frequent rains. Furthermore, there are no mechanized vehicles (other than a few small motorcycles) in the community and until 1990, the nearest paved road was 85 kilometers away.

The producers in Ñu Pyajhu Guazú are almost completely dependent upon the *acopiadores*, or middlemen. They buy at the absolute lowest price possible, trading on peoples' cash necessities. There are no grain silos or cotton gins in the entire department of Caazapá. There is no means of reaching the ginners without the trucks of the middlemen who pick the cotton up at the homestead and transport it to the ginners. Many years, the peasants of Ñu Pyajhu Guazú have lost money on their crops, especially if family labor costs are included in the equation (B. Turner 1993:193).[4]

The lack of infrastructure and cash crop options has not stopped the producers from attempting diversification, seeking alternative sources of income, or trying to by-pass the buyers in Caazapá. However, every attempt to date has ended in the loss of the crop, the loss of the profit, and, in some cases, the loss of personal freedom (that is, imprisonment). The possible examples to illustrate this point are numerous and all of them involve the intersection of all four of the risk factors (see, for example, C. Turner 1994). In the interests of brevity, one example should suffice.

In 1985 the peasants in Ñu Pyajhu Guazú were offered a special, guaranteed (on paper) contract to produce tomatoes for a Paraguayan cannery. The offer was mediated through a Caazapá-based agricultural extension agent (who is also a political lieutenant of the Colorado Party) and the peasants were assured that the company would send its own trucks for transport and that it would buy all of the tomatoes, even if the roads closed and the produce rotted in the interim. Part of the contract stipulated that the necessary fertilizer and pesticides would be provided by the company and deducted from the profits, which the company representative also guaranteed would be substantial. A number of families decided to take the chance because of the guarantees, the predicted profits, and the direct market access. That year there was a two day frost that killed many of the young tomato plants. The ones that were saved were either planted in low-lying protected pockets of land or were saved by families staying up two nights carrying water from their wells to the fields in order to prevent the plants from freezing. The crisis passed with serious attrition, but the surviving plants produced a good crop. Just as the tomatoes began to ripen, the rains started. Only one truck load of tomatoes had been shipped. Before the road was passable again, all of the crop had rotted. No one had eaten the tomatoes because of the guarantee. However, the contract was not honored. One man made a profit of approximately $15 (which he had to travel to Asunción to collect), a handful of people broke even, and the remainder lost money on the price of the pesticide and fertilizer which the company insisted that they pay for (not everyone did however). Two years later, this same company tried to interest the peasants in growing carrots in order to pay off the outstanding debts, but found no takers.

As for their default crop, world market prices always fluctuate and it is impossible to predict what a year's cotton price will be. The national government sets the basic minimum buying price, but does not defend it at the farm gate. The cotton gins and the local buyers all take a slice off the buying price before it reaches the producer. Several times the people of Ñu Pyajhu Guazú have attempted to circumvent the local buyers and sell their goods directly to the ginners or to ask the Agricultural Minister to uphold the price. All such attempts have failed, some disastrously (B. Turner 1993:193).

The *acopiadores* have usually contracted with a cotton gin for a certain amount of cotton and later in the season the producer price can sometimes go up. However, because of the poor road conditions and real need for the cash, the producers find it difficult to hold out for a better price. There is a real danger that the rainy season will start, the road will close, and the hold-out will be unable to sell his or her cotton that year.

The producers are also, at times, forced to wait several months to receive payment. As an example, in 1990 the Paraguayan currency, the guaraní, appreciated against the U.S. dollar during the cotton harvest. The middlemen were loathe to lose the difference in price at the cotton gin. Some of them delayed nine months before selling their stock and paying the producers.

It is not unknown for an *acopiador* to fail to pay the peasants at all. Some producers have attempted to maximize their profits by selling to an unknown or new middleman who offered a better price in order to capture a share of an established middleman's producers. If the maverick middleman loses his bid to enter the market, or is dishonest (repeating the process in different communities every year), then the peasant producers lose too. Of course, this only happens once with a particular middleman, but there is no effective recourse for the vendor, due to the workings of the economic system and *ley mbareté* (rule of the strongest, in this case the importance of social/political connections).

Uncertainty Deriving from Social Relations in the Rural Economy

The history of Ñu Pyajhu Guazú is replete with difficulties and hardships created and perpetuated by individuals external to the community. Outsiders became aware of the squatters in the 1930s. In the early years, bandits called *gauchos* roamed the countryside "requesting" food or whatever was available. Before 1942, *gauchos* operated freely throughout Caazapá, running in groups of two to 20 or 40 men. They were common in the area because it was a *desierto* (wilderness) and there was no one to prevent them. They knew that the police in Caazapá were too few and too far to do anything. The *gauchos* were known for asking to borrow something at a homestead. Local residents report that if an item was lent to them, they would eventually return it. But if it was denied to them, they would kill the homestead owner and take it anyway.

Two Caazapá *caudillos* (bosses), Leonardo Garcete and Miguel Pangracia, swindled many occupants by selling them lots which they did not own. They arranged the financing by agreeing to accept tobacco production as payment in lieu of cash.[5] A few years later, some residents were again sold fraudulent lots. A certain Navarro and Buendia, saying they were representing the Argentine absentee owners, sold land to residents of Ñu Pyajhu Guazú but without giving title.[6]

When Ñu Pyajhu Guazú gained legitimacy as a state colony in 1940, the inhabitants were no longer squatters but "occupants" with property rights and options. Over the years, people in Ñu Pyajhu Guazú have attempted to gain title to their land through the land granting agency, the Institute for Rural Welfare (Instituto de Bienestar Rural or IBR) and its predecessor agency, the Institute of Agrarian Reform (Instituto de Reforma Agrária or IRA). This has proved difficult, not only in Ñu Pyajhu Guazú, but on a national scale. The price of the land has always been reasonable, but receiving the title has been expensive and frequently fruitless. The land was almost never surveyed well and sometimes homesteads have been paid for more than once because the title was "lost."

For Ñu Pyajhu Guazú, the local IBR office is in Caazapá. Until two years ago, the IBR agent would not process title claims without a bribe. This generally included the gift of an animal such as a pig or sheep. As one man said, "first he ate our money. And then we had to `feed' his wife too." At least three men in Ñu Pyajhu Guazú paid for their land in full, including the proper bribes, and still did not receive their "lost" titles.

Because of these irregularities, most people in Ñu Pyajhu Guazú gave up on their attempts to officially own the land, finding it cheaper and easier to remain legal occupants.

Even individual attempts to circumvent local authority have ended detrimentally. One year, the acknowledged best farmer in Ñu Pyajhu Guazú made a deal with a cooperative in Guairá (a neighboring department) to produce an unusual and expensive strain of tobacco that is extremely difficult to grow. He was successful, and sold the tobacco at a (relatively) tremendous profit. Soon afterwards, he was arrested by Caazapá (local department and district) authorities on trumped up charges of stealing his neighbor's cows. Since this farmer was a Liberal (the opposition political party) and had no political connections, and because he had always avoided tying himself to a *patrón*, he had no other option than to buy his way out. "I was the wrong color and couldn't make myself strong."[7] He was forced to "make a contribution" of fencing wire, which was arranged by one of his *compadres* in Ñu Pyajhu Guazú, and lost a year's profit. He told me that he is no longer interested in increasing his disposable income. As a result of his experience, he feels that it is a waste of time and effort and can only lead to problems. He prefers to focus his energy on subsistence production with only enough cash crop production to pay for his family's yearly cash necessities, such as for salt, sugar, and *yerba* (Paraguayan tea).

There is a long history of Catholic priests' unethical interference in Ñu Pyajhu Guazú reaching back to the 1950s. The Catholic church hierarchy was formerly tied to the national government in Paraguay; until recently the president suggested who would fill the role of archbishop. In Caazapá, the priests are from local families tied to the local elites. They contribute to the siphoning of the peasants' wealth and undermining the peasants' attempts at autonomy, with the collusion of the civil authorities. (This is a common pattern in Paraguay but is by no means true of every priest.)

In the mid-1950s, a priest from Caazapá, Pa'i (Father) Wilfrido Rivas started a cooperative, Cooperativa Pio XII. He had recently bought property on the outskirts of Ñu Pyajhu Guazú in order to start a *yerba* plantation. He paid a caretaker to work it for him using canned goods as payment, canned goods that had been sent by Caritas Paraguayas, a Catholic charity organization, for disbursement among the poor. Around 1965, the *pa'i* organized some of the residents of Boquerón (about seven kilometers from Ñu Pyajhu Guazú) to build a road directly to Caazapá

Historical Perspectives on Long Term Change 183

"so that they could come to church." It is possible that Pa'i Rivas was more interested in improved infrastructure to profit himself through the cooperative, than in people's ability to go to church in Caazapá. Although the road did not extend to Ñu Pyajhu Guazú, it did make the transportation of goods to Caazapá easier and a few subsistence farmers in the community joined the cooperative with hopes of improving their situation.

According to former co-op members, Pa'i Rivas sold their products, kept the money, and then announced that the co-op was in debt. 'We weren't in debt, but he lied, taking advantage of the ignorant peasants' (C. Turner 1994:261).

In another case, Pa'i Rivas asked for a church contribution of cattle for his ranch. When the church leader (*jefe del grupo*)[8] from Ñu Pyajhu Guazú arrived with the cattle, he observed the *pa'i* and Roque Sarubbi, the Colorado political boss from Caazapá who owns land throughout the department, supervising the branding. After the failure of the cooperative, Pa'i Rivas bought another *estancia* and he asked men from Ñu Pyajhu Guazú to be "good Christians" by fencing the "church's" ranch land.

In 1976, another Caazapá priest called Pa'i Zaracho reanimated the cooperative. He convinced the people of Ñu Pyajhu Guazú that they would have some control over the operation and that huge profits could be made by exporting their cotton crop directly to Switzerland and circumventing the local buyers and cotton gins. For two harvests, Pa'i Zaracho and his cronies skimmed the profits and pocketed development aid money intended for the cooperative's membership. The members from Ñu Pyajhu Guazú managed to seize control of the co-op and to achieve some legal recourse in recouping their losses. Before they could do so, however, two waves of arrests were made throughout the community. The crimes were unspecified, but several cooperative members were jailed for being "communists" (C. Turner 1994:263). The membership of Pio XII was advised by the head of the General Direction of Cooperatives to liquidate the cooperative, which they did (Dirección General de Cooperativismo 1990).

Shortly after the cooperative's second failure, Pa'i Zaracho attempted to organize a system whereby every church member in Ñu Pyajhu Guazú was to donate a certain percentage of their cotton production and egg production (already extremely minimal) to the church. As one man commented, "they are all 'capitalized' (meaning corrupt in this sense). We know we can't trust them, but they are the priests, and we need them."

Uncertainty of State Actions and Wars

International political and economic events after 1920 helped to greatly expand state rule-making capacities. The cotton boom integrated peasant producers more firmly into the capitalist economy and allowed for the expansion of the internal market. In the 1940s, the government sought to implement a new form of social and economic relations in the countryside. The state began purchasing surplus crops at high prices and implemented a supervised credit program (Grow 1981:72). Some aspects of the expansion of state power were beneficial to Ñu Pyajhu Guazú, such as the development of police power which greatly reduced rural banditry by rounding up the *gauchos* (B. Turner 1993:60).[9] In addition, the government set prices for cotton throughout the war years, and purchased cotton directly through the state agricultural bank (Martínez 1984:191). However, this new direction in government policy terminated during the Stroessner regime (1954-1989) when the rural middlemen were supported through credit subsidies, the encouragement of crop improvements was channeled through the town intermediaries, and there were repressions of autonomous peasant organizations.

The people of Ñu Pyajhu Guazú have regularly suffered the consequences of national events that they knew little or nothing about. Immigration accelerated slightly during the Chaco War with Bolivia (1932-35). Some men were seeking to escape war service by hiding out in the "*desierto*," where the land was still primarily forest. However, the authorities were aware of the community by this time. Many of the local men went to war under force after being rounded up by the police. The people didn't want to fight the war because they were aware of government corruption and the extreme hardships found in the Chaco. As one war veteran said, "rich people don't die on the line."

After the Revolution of 1947, there was another influx of colonists due to political persecution by the victorious Colorado Party over its Liberal Party counterparts. There was a significant in-migration of Liberal families seeking refuge from Rosario Sarandy, where the repression was much worse. These new migrants were primarily relatives of the people already settled in Ñu Pyajhu Guazú and they were hoping to be assured of a relatively safe haven. The Revolution of 1947 brought the repression of Liberals by Colorado *py nandí* (bare feet) irregulars to Ñu Pyajhu Guazú. One Liberal founding father of Ñu Pyajhu Guazú was beaten and crippled, and has spent the rest of his life virtually bedridden. "The police would beat, kill, and molest the Liberals and then the [Colorado] neighbors would beat, kill, and molest them again." No one in Ñu Pyajhu Guazú today wants to say which neighbors were involved in the "bad times," but evidently, the *py nandí kuéra* (bare footed ones) were generally not from Ñu Pyajhu Guazú itself.[10] The police would commission people to go to another community to beat people. "At that time they were killing everyone. We are lucky that we didn't die."

"After 1947 the 'blue rag'[11] became more expensive." One Liberal tried to get the harp player at a *fiesta* to play "The Dieziocho," a "Liberal" polka. The player refused, fearing the reaction of the Colorados (military police who are required to attend all social functions) who were present. The Liberal was incensed and chopped the harp stand up with his machete. The *comisário* charged him G500, a large sum at the time.

The Movimiento 14 de Mayo guerila operations in Itapúa and Caazapá were felt in Ñu Pyajhu Guazú in 1960. This was called "the killing time" when "the Argentines came." The nearby town of Gral. Eugenio A. Garay (formerly Charará) was the center of repression of Liberals and suspected guerrillas. Prisoners were tortured to force denunciations of their neighbors. According to local witnesses, some were thrown from planes over the Yvytyruzú mountains. The recently deceased Minister of the Interior, Edgar L. Ynsfrán, has been accused of directing the repression from a ranch near San Juan Nepomuceno.

Campesinos in Ñu Pyajhu Guazú were not sure what the movement was about, except that it was political and that there was an attempt on the government. They talk about the "Revolution of 60," but do not have a clear idea of what the "revolution" was about. In Ñu Pyajhu Guazú, it meant "against the Liberals," and is another example of social and political uncertainties and lack of control of political events that adversely affected Ñu Pyajhu Guazú. There were reportedly two "*comisiones garrotes*" (whipping commissions) in Ñu Pyajhu Guazú, whose Colorado members still live in the community. These two local commissions apparently restricted their activities to forced searches for books and subversive literature and denouncements to the authorities in Boquerón, one of whom was Lolo Ramírez. "He was a real torturer." Ramírez led the commissions in Boquerón and there were others in the surrounding areas. Two "*comisiones garrotes*" were formed by Colorado irregulars out of Boquerón. These two "*comisiones*" were much more dangerous for the population of Ñu Pyajhu Guazú than their own was. The "*comisiones*" would arrive in large groups of eight or so looking for guns and would "search every corner and under everything." If only two or three came, the house owner might overpower them, so they came in large and heavily armed numbers. They generally harassed Liberal families with threats and robberies. But there were more serious consequences. Three men were arrested and taken to Charará, and there was one death.

Smythe, who had his fences cut and the wire stolen at night, called this time the "little coup." "Neighbors (people from surrounding areas) turned themselves into commissions" made up of Colorado party members. "Not all of them stole, only some of them were *jodido* (in this case, sneak thieves) and took advantage of the situation." Private armies were formed by the *jefes* (big shots) in various places. "You couldn't denounce them as they might come and kill you. The `armies' were made up of *campesinos*, you didn't really know exactly who." He said they simply went back to work in the field after the "*golpe-i*" was over.

Surplus has also been siphoned from the *campesinos* through the local military elite, in conjunction with the government. Periodically, there have been police raids in Ñu Pyajhu Guazú. These are conducted at night with dogs and guns for the express purpose of finding military service shirkers. Military service is avoided in Paraguay because the conditions are so poor and the work frequently involves unpaid private labor for an officer.[12] It is easy to buy your way out of military service and those who have the money do so, receiving a *baja*, a primary form of identification in Paraguay. Those who don't have the money avoid situations where they might be asked for identification, such as traveling on buses or being caught in police raids.

The raids in Ñu Pyajhu Guazú and other areas are attempts to force people to buy *bajas*. Young boys, even if they have proof that they are underage, are taken and the proof destroyed. One young man from Ñu Pyajhu Guazú explained that they never take any money or good clothes if they are caught because their possessions would be stolen the first night. They are forced to do ridiculous exercises (such as standing on one foot for extended periods), are fed from one plate of food with one spoon being shared between two or more "recruits," and the "food is so poor I wouldn't feed it to my pigs." If the "recruits" are not "ransomed," the family loses a primary source of labor. If they do, the family loses a large

Historical Perspectives on Long Term Change 187

portion of the cotton income for that year. Another "scam" is to sell the unwilling recruit a false *baja*. In this way, he can be picked up again for military service the next year and the process repeated.

In 1986-1987 Ñu Pyajhu Guazú suffered a serious set back because of political events. Two Caazapá *caudillos*, Roque Sarubbi and Neris Dávalos, were competing for the position of Colorado *seccional* president. Most of the Colorados in Ñu Pyajhu Guazú, and even some Liberals, supported the loser, Dávalos. He had won the sympathies of Ñu Pyajhu Guazú because "Sarubbi had been there a long time, since 1965, and had not done anything." After Sarubbi won, he and his people told Ñu Pyajhu Guazú's *sub-seccional* (local representative of the Colorado party) that, "you were the one responsible and [you] let this happen." Sarubbi suspended the sub-section office in Ñu Pyajhu Guazú and it has not been reinstated to date.[13] The minor political jobs that remained (such as giving permission to butcher) were given to the one Colorado who supported Sarubbi. This man stayed with Sarubbi out of loyalty and because he feared that leaving the "*mburuvicha*," or authorities, could have been dangerous for the community. Of the 12 members of the sub-seccional, 11 went with Dávalos. He had suggested several times that the sub-section members should vote six for Sarubbi and six for Dávalos, and that way the winners would get the *cargos*. "'They would give the orders' and the losers would still be part of the *sub-seccional* and would be `treated as neighbors'" (B. Turner 1993:92).

When Dávalos lost his political battle, the residents of Ñu Pyajhu Guazú lost also. The *mixto*, an open air truck that was the only mechanized means of transport to Ñu Pyajhu Guazú, was forced to discontinue its route. The truck's owner supported Dávalos in the election and had carried *campesinos* to the polls. His truck was found in violation of "special" rules of transport that were formulated in Caazapá after the election. There was no transportation between Ñu Pyajhu Guazú and Caazapá for nine months, until a young member of the Sarubbi family took over the route with a Brazilian bus. There was a change in personnel at the Caazapá agricultural extension office, and no agents have worked in Ñu Pyajhu Guazú since, not even with the Peace Corps volunteers. Work was suspended on the new school and the health post, because Ñu Pyajhu Guazú was denied permission to hold fund-raisers (i.e., public gatherings). The former *sub-seccional*, Pasqual Araujo, recounted that the soldiers told him that they "were going to come out and beat people. We were not *tranquilo*. Susana [a Peace Corp volunteer] happened not to be here [to protect us]."[14] When the new Peace Corp volunteer did arrive, work began again on the community projects, albeit very slowly.

The history of Ñu Pyajhu Guazú substantiates that the residents have always been a part of the market economy, albeit without complete access, that they share the national ideology of individual advancement, and that they are aware of their lower class designation in the national hierarchy (C. Turner 1992). In their attempts to develop socially and economically, they have faced uncertainty from national political exigencies, from natural disasters and unpredictable weather patterns, and from variable economic markets and prices. They have been deliberately denied direct access to markets. Excess income has consistently been siphoned off by outsiders or stolen from individuals in the community.

The result has been a community that has remained in a subsistence economy for its entire history despite good land, holdings large enough for producing surplus agriculture, and recurring efforts by individuals to capitalize. Because of the continued isolation of Ñu Pyajhu Guazú, its history of political and economic repression, the vagaries of both the market and the environment, and the lack of class infrastructure within the community, the settlers found it expedient to reproduce and maintain an egalitarian, community-based social system. The uncertainties of their existence have taught the people to rely on each other and to develop social mores that require generosity, community-minded behavior, and unqualified support in times of need. This is reflected in their patterns of fictive kin choices and their hesitancy in risking ties with unproven outsiders.

Conclusion

The data on *compadrazgo* practices in Ñu Pyajhu Guazú show that the peasant population has devised a ritual kin system that promotes personal social maximization while avoiding risks. As with farming practices, individuals attempt to maximize the advantages of the ties without "gambling" on a tie that may bring no benefit. People are cautious and traditional in their choices, but manipulate the rules if it will suit their own agendas.

This pattern of *compadrazgo* choice practices corresponds with what has been termed the "risk adverse peasant," who may be attempting "profit maximization," but finds the uncertainty of future events too constraining to take a potentially unprofitable or disastrous chance.

Studies also indicate that those peasants with more economic means are more likely to take the risk of uncertainty, being less devastated by failure (Cancian 1972; Ellis 1989). While these types of peasant studies refer to agricultural practices, the same phenomenon can be discerned in the social relations of Ñu Pyajhu Guazú as demonstrated by their *compadrazgo* choice patterns. The very low percentage of true vertical fictive kin ties in Ñu Pyajhu Guazú (.3%) highlights the "risk" constraints on the population and the general lack of economic means, despite provisional ownership of land. Many of the constraints upon the community are due to national and international economic policies or market capriciousness which the local actors find difficult to control or circumvent.

After 1990, Ñu Pyajhu Guazú again began to feel a series of rapid changes. Because of a new World Bank road (still dirt, but elevated above the level of the swamp responsible for the heavy road flooding), more contact with the outside world is possible. Traffic passing on the road has increased dramatically. Ñu Pyajhu Guazú is no longer at the end of the road as the road has been extended to connect with another town center in the next district. Electricity is being brought closer to the community and it is now feasible to run lights and television sets from car batteries. Recent national events have made the land valuable at the same time that "official" land titles are finally possible to obtain. The land has also reached carrying capacity and there are new stresses on crop production and pasture lands, to the point that food production is seasonally affected by low productivity. The new scarcity of land and the opening of land colonies in distant areas is increasingly scattering consanguineous and fictive kin around the country. The new "move to democracy" has given people new expectations of accessing the market economy advantageously (although their ability to do so is doubtful). Because of the few *compadrazgo* ties with outsiders, more and more young women are working and achieving an education outside the community. For many of the same reasons, Spanish language skill is increasing, especially among the school age children. These changes are strikingly similar to Peggy Barlett's (1982:7) description of the factors leading to community social change in Paso, Costa Rica (see Hanks 1992, as well).

There are recent indications that the egalitarian fabric of the community is being rent in some respects and that there is a movement towards more individual benefits and motivations to the detriment of community solidarity. Barlett (1982:163-164) also documents a similar outcome, albeit more advanced, in Paso, as a result of increased land values, the arrival of electricity, a new all-weather road, and greater market access. In Paso, the result has been an egalitarian system going through a process of emerging internal stratification within a ten year period, but not entirely losing its community-based ethos of generosity and welfare concerns for neighbors, relatives, and fictive kin. My data indicate that an analogous process is currently in its incipient stages in Ñu Pyajhu Guazú and that recent events are contributing to a realignment of social values. The next decade in Ñu Pyajhu Guazú's history should prove to be important and enlightening with respect to the process of social and economic development in peasant societies. My prediction for the near future of Ñu Pyajhu Guazú accords with Barlett's (1982:164) own for Paso:

> As yet, interactions between the strata do not reflect the deference and distance due to outsiders. Intermarriage among the landed and landless families continues to be common, and visiting patterns among the strata are fluid. Nevertheless, the increased contact with outsiders will strengthen the awareness of stratification within the community and will continue to present a challenge to Paso's traditionally egalitarian ethos. Paso can thus be seen as an example of emerging stratification in which many egalitarian, atomistic, and cooperative patterns remain strong.

The long-term future for Ñu Pyajhu Guazú can only include further integration in the national social life and capitalist economy, with concomitant changes in the community's egalitarianism and *compadrazgo* choice patterns.

Notes

1. Research was funded by a Fulbright Institute for International Education Dissertation Research grant. I would like to thank Munro Edmonson for suggesting an ethnohistorical approach to my work, without which I would have been unable to write this article. I would also like to acknowledge my Paraguayan friends and neighbors for their infinite patience in answering my incessant questions, even when it was clear they would rather not dwell on the past. Most of all, I would like to thank Brian Turner for sharing his own field notes and for reading my work critically.

2. In the *compadrazgo* literature, the term "vertical" refers to fictive kin ties that extend beyond a community's geographic area as well as to individuals

who can be described as belonging to a higher social and economic class. "Horizontal" ties are used to describe fictive kinship ties that link together members of the same social and economic class in the same community (Mintz and Wolf 1950:342).

3. Affinal ties beyond spouse and spouses parents were not used in the analysis.

4. The subsistence farmers in Ñu Pyajhu Guazú generally do not calculate their own family labor into production costs.

5. In 1930, credit was given for tobacco production for the first time on the national level.

6. The story is that Navarro was also cheated when Buendia took off with the profits. After that, Navarro "didn't want to hear anything about `buen día'!"

7. In Paraguay, the political parties are associated with colors: Liberal is blue, Colorado is red, and Febrerista is green.

8. The residents built their own prayer house and celebrate their own services. There has never been a priest in Ñu Pyajhu Guazú and the spiritual leaders for the community are the priests in Caazapá.

9. However, there were perceived disadvantages to the community as well with the introduction of police authority.

10. The crippled man's wife told me that the man who actually beat her husband was from Buena Vista. He is dead now, having been murdered by a neighbor who went to him to get permission to butcher a cow (a politically appointed job). When permission was refused, his neighbor killed him. Not all communities in Paraguay are as cohesive as Ñu Pyajhu Guazú.

11. This refers to a type of kerchief that men of the two parties wear around their necks to identify their affiliation, i.e., a "blue rag" for Liberals and a "red rag" for Colorados.

12. A North American friend, who had married into an elite Paraguayan family, told me that when they had gone for supper at a general's house, there had been soldiers serving as waiters, one for each guest. It is a common sight in Asunción to see soldiers doing gardening and other such work at sumptuous homes. Soldiers are also used to do field work on private farms and ranches.

13. An unpaid office filled by a subsistence farmer, but it did give the community a "connection" with the town elites.

14. My husband and I were frequently credited with protecting the community, or individuals in it, from outsiders, and it is true that the presence of a North American does influence events. People in Ñu Pyajhu Guazú, at times, deliberately used us to attempt political and economic empowerment in ways that would ordinarily been viewed as too risky (see C. Turner, 1992:193-194).

References

Barlett, Peggy
    1982 *Agricultural Choice and Change, Decision Making in a Costa Rican Community*. New Brunswick: Rutgers University Press.

Cancian, Frank
    1972 *Change and Uncertainty in a Peasant Economy*. Stanford: Stanford University Press.

Dirección General de Cooperativismo
    1990 Memorias del consejo de administración. Asunción.

Ellis, Frank
    1989 Peasant Economics, Farm Households and Agrarian Development. In *Wye Studies in Agricultural and Rural Development*. New York: Cambridge University Press.

Foster, George
    1969 Godparents and Social Networks in Tzintzuntzan. *Southwestern Journal of Anthropology* 25(3):261-278.

Grow, Michael
    1981 *The Good Neighbor Policy and Authoritarianism in Paraguay, United States Economic Expansion and Great-Power Rivalry in Latin America during World War II*. Lawrence: The Regents Press of Kansas.

Hanks, Lucien
    1992 *Rice and Man*. Honolulu: University of Hawaii Press.

Martínez Cuevas, Efraín
    1984 Los eslabones del oro blanco. *La historia del algodon en el Paraguay*. Asunción: La Rural Ediciones.

Mintz, Sidney, and Eric Wolf
    1950 An Analysis of Ritual Co-Parenthood (Compadrazgo). *Southwestern Journal of Anthropology* 6:341-368.

Paul, B. D.
    1942 *Ritual Kinship, With Special Reference to Godparenthood in Middle America*. Unpublished Ph.D. diss., University of Chicago.

Turner, Brian
    1993 *Community Politics and Peasant-State Relations in Paraguay*. Lanham, Maryland: University Press of America.

Turner, Christina Bolke
    1992 *Kith and Kin Where the Jaguar Roam: Changing "Compadrazgo" Patterns in a Paraguayan Peasant Community*. Unpublished Ph.D. diss. Tulane University.
    1994 State Economic Policy and Rural Development in Paraguay. In *The Economic Anthropology of the State*. Monographs in Economic Anthropology. Elizabeth Brumfiel, ed. Pp. 241-268. Lanham, Maryland: University Press of America.

Van den Berghe, R. and G. Van den Berghe
  1966 Compadrazgo and Class in Southeastern Mexico. *American Anthropologist* 68:1236-1244.

Part III

Structural Adjustment Programs: Local Contexts for Global Policy

11

Anthropology and Structural Adjustment Programs

Deborah Winslow

For more than a decade, anthropologists have been encountering structural adjustment programs (SAPs) in the field. SAPs, the World Bank, the IMF, austerity programs, currency devaluation, and other symptoms of the world economic system of the 1980s and 1990s, all have become woven into the fabric of daily life in places where anthropologists do their research. The articles that follow in this section demonstrate that marketwomen in Ghana, Yoruba townspeople and city dwellers in Nigeria, farm workers in Egypt, and families in the communities of Mexico's Oaxaca valley, talk with interest and understanding of such arcane topics as currency reform, negative growth, foreign exchange, and national economic crisis. Part of the reality of the people we study, structural adjustment programs and related economic policies have become necessarily part of the studies we make.

However, SAPs present special problems for anthropologists. First of all, they require us not only to undertake "economic analysis beyond the local system," but also to design methods to articulate such analysis with our more traditional studies. It is no longer sufficient that we be conversant with the organization of production, consumption, and exchange at local and regional levels. We find that we also must include, and thus must understand, the macroeconomies of the nations in which we work and their relations, historical and contemporary, with international and global economic systems. The fruitfulness of doing so, of bridging yet again the micro/macro gap in anthropological studies (Roseberry 1989) through careful attention to the flows of peoples, goods, and information, as well as systemic interconnections and interpenetrations, is clearly evident in the articles here.

Second, the inclusion of macroeconomic policy considerations requires that we proceed with caution around another anthropological tradition: the single field investigation. The consequences of macroeconomic shifts do not fully reveal themselves in the short run; and local-level responses may have their origin in relationships developed long in the past. Even "before-and-after" studies can be inadequate for inquiries that inherently are concerned with ongoing economic change and transformation. All four of the authors whose papers follow have spent many years in the countries with which they are concerned, demonstrating concretely and once again the value of long-term research in anthropology (Foster et al. 1976).

Third, and this speaks to one of anthropology's strengths as a discipline, is that anthropologists are faced with defending the contingency of the local while trying to deal with universalistic patterns and relationships. Structural adjustment programs are a global phenomenon, found around the world and directed in large part by a few dominant institutions, such as the World Bank and the International Monetary Fund. Nevertheless, the actual programs developed for a particular country and the manner and contexts in which they are implemented diverge considerably. SAPs may be widespread, but they are not monolithic and their effects depend on many particulars. The studies here suggest that anthropologists, with their long tradition of attention to local detail, are particularly well placed not just to bring case studies to the discussion, but to explain the connections between the lives of real people and the economies that are being adjusted.

Fourth, and closely related to the third point, is that anthropological research on the consequences of SAPs and related policies has made it clear that not only do countries diverge in their SAP experiences, even within a single country, particular groups of people are affected differentially. In Ghana, what has been detrimental to the livelihood of urban women traders might be beneficial to rural producers of import substituting agricultural products (see Clark, this section). Economic austerity programs that lead people in one part of the Oaxaca Valley to seek work over the border in the United States, have caused people in other parts to send more adults into the local work force (see Murphy et al., this section). Policies that raise prices for consumers may increase profits for merchants (Trager, this section). The defection of construction workers in Egypt to better paying jobs in neighboring oil-rich nations may be a boon to local poorly paid agricultural workers who can move into the workers' old jobs (Toth, this section). Thus we must be careful about overgeneralizing from our specific cases. Social and geographic location—including gender, subsistence, class, locality, and other factors—distinguish people, places, and groups in terms of their relations with macroeconomic policies.

Finally, SAPs and related issues are about policy and not all of us are comfortable with the role of policy maker. We may worry that the line we tread between being useful and being co-opted is vanishingly fine; we may believe that we need a scientific detachment to provide accurate data for policy making others to use; or, on the other hand, we may feel that the "witnessing" aspect of fieldwork in all its activist guises is what gives anthropology any moral character it might have (Scheper-Hughes 1992: xii). Whatever our position, because of both the field's historical relation with colonialism and the intimacy of our mode of research, we rarely take the role of advisor for granted; it is persistently problematic.

In short, it seems that the structural adjustment programs of recent years have required of anthropologists that we not abandon the holistic and local-level orientation of our field as we deal with new challenges. Anthropological holism always has existed on multiple and interconnected levels, from household, community, and region (Redfield 1940; Skinner 1977), to the world system created by colonialism (Frank 1967; Wallerstein 1974) and the shifting connections between nations in the post-colonial world (Gupta 1992). The anthropological study of SAPs shows that these holisms are complemented but not replaced by the new globalizations of the late twentieth century.

What are Structural Adjustment Programs?

Put simply, most structural adjustment programs and policies (SAPs) are an outcome of the debt crisis of the 1980s. As such, they are historically situated in a particular set of international relationships. In the previous decade, the 1970s, a permissive lending environment, due in part to large deposits accrued by the oil boom, encouraged heavy borrowing by developing nations and loans were negotiated on generous terms. The loans financed development programs that often combined imported technologies with a local, post-colonial flavor and a high degree of state economic control. But by the 1980s, with an oil glut, declining oil revenues, and worldwide recession, debtor nations, even oil rich ones like Nigeria and Mexico, found it increasingly difficult to continue to pay debt service. When they tried to renegotiate old loans and contract for new ones, they found donors and lenders in a less liberal mood, demanding higher interest rates and insisting on new conditions for any continued largesse. This was particularly so after August 1982, when Mexico became the first major debtor nation to fail to make interest payments on its loans.

The conditions that lenders attached to new and revamped loan agreements involved far reaching domestic macroeconomic policy changes, technically referred to as stabilization measures and structural adjustments, although the latter may be shorthand for both. The stabilization measures, often instigated by the IMF whose mandate as an institution is short-term financing, were changes designed to ease immediate foreign exchange and balance of payments crises and stabilize prices. Currencies, whose value had usually been set high by government policy to make imports cheaper, were allowed to float (downwards) until they achieved a more internationally agreed upon level. Because overvalued exchange rates made imported goods cheap relative to domestic ones, they depressed domestic production and discouraged export development. In addition, efforts were made "to cut real government expenditure, raise revenues, restrain the growth of wages, and control money supply growth, usually through, or with the effect of, raising real interest rates" (Haggard and Kaufman 1992:10-11).

Stabilization measures were frequently unpopular with the citizenries of the affected countries. Depending on the rate and degree of implementation, the new policies often brought about the simultaneous introduction of an unfortunate combination of developments: rapid inflation and rising prices, on the one hand, joined with decreased government food subsidies, less spending on social services, tight money, low wages, and massive layoffs of government employees, on the other (all of which are illustrated in the papers on this section). Since almost by definition most people in these countries were very poor, any decline in living standards produced hardship. Comparative studies show that urban groups have been the most adversely affected because they consume more imports, their jobs depend more on imported inputs, and they were more likely to hold government jobs. Landless rural poor who have to buy food are also adversely affected, but rural residents who produce agricultural products for sale, as well as petty commodity producers and others who make or grow goods that can replace expensive or unavailable imports, may actually see their incomes rise under stabilization (Hood et al. 1988; also, Morrison and Arreaga-Rodas 1981). Overall, stabilization measures dominated economic policy reforms in the first part of the 1980s, but by the end of the decade, greater emphasis was given to the necessity of longer-term and more thoroughgoing structural change (Stallings 1992:77-87).

Structural adjustments proper are associated with the World Bank, whose focus has been longer-term projects and financing. These programs, too, intervened in the domestic economies of developing nations to change ("rationalize") the allocation of national resources and generate more goods for export sale (Haggard and Kaufman 1992:5-6). Many of the countries involved, their economies having been distorted by colonial regimes not so long ago, were heavily dependent on the export of agricultural cash crops such as tea, cotton, and cocoa, which had been the basis of colonial profit taking. The world market prices for these products being notoriously unstable, structural adjustment measures were designed in part to transform these economies into ones in which agriculture was less dominant and relatively capital-intensive industry more so (O'Brien 1991:26). Industry was promoted on many fronts. Governments were asked to "open up" or "liberalize" their economies, removing restrictive tariffs and taxes that might hinder the free flow of trade. They also were requested to downgrade the role of, or sell off, state-run industries which were thought to absorb state monies with little return and give unfair competition to private businesses. Governments also were encouraged to support industry with infrastructural investment in such areas as roads and electricity. Because resources were scarce, even with increased foreign assistance, implementing these measures usually has meant moving resources out of public welfare programs, such as education, health, and public assistance.

Overall, the direction of stabilization and structural adjustment policies has reflected the fact that in the 1980s, academic economists and development planners of varied political stripes had decreasing faith in the ability of centrally controlled economies and government-led programs to achieve economic growth and development. Mainstream academic economists and planners in the dominant aid institutions concluded that what was needed was a renewed emphasis on the free play of market forces to achieve optimal allocation of resources and that third world economic policies that interfered with the market should be abandoned. It is probably not coincidental that such strategies also served the needs of international businesses trying to pull out the of the recession of the 1980s by globalizing their companies. On the other hand, it is important to remember that it was not only the neoorthodox economists who had become suspicious of state-managed economies. Observers and planners critical of capitalism also were expressing doubts about wasteful parastatals, overly intrusive relocation schemes, and other top-down planning (e.g., Chambers 1983; Powelson and Stock 1987). There was consensus that in many developing nations the domestic economic policies being pursued in the 1960s and 1970s had failed to produce economic development and that change of some sort was critically necessary.

However, specialists differed and continue to differ on many issues. One major debate has centered on the nature of the disease, whether the causes for policy failure lay primarily with inefficient management and inappropriate policies or, instead, with the narrow economic base of post-colonial economies and the lack of money available for capital investment (O'Brien 1991). How to cure the problem also has continued to be controversial, with some arguing for market-oriented reforms while others contend that decentralizing programs and taking greater advantage of indigenous knowledge would be more effective and more equitable for the poor (e.g., Uphoff 1991). For the most part, SAPs reflect the eventual victory of the first group over the second, at least as far as policy making is concerned. As the papers in this section demonstrate, international influence, sometimes in opposition to local forces and sometimes in combination with them, is pervasive in the development of these new macroeconomic policies, even in countries like Nigeria (see Trager, this section) that ostensibly reject the dominance of the IMF and the World Bank.

Policies are not, of course, the whole story. To understand the effects of SAPs, it is necessary to consider implementation and outcomes as well as design. In every country that has adopted SAPs, political forces arrayed against them and the nature of local government bureaucracies have meant that implementation is partial at best. Actual rates of implementation are said to vary from about one-third of the program (in Kenya, for example) to about half (in Ghana) to a high of two-thirds (in Thailand and Turkey) (Haggard and Kaufman 1992:16). Even if implemented, the policies may not achieve the goals desired, with outcomes significantly affected by international conditions (such as world oil prices), the weather, and, as we will see, by many other local and not-so-local contingencies. The studies that follow here are primarily concerned with outcomes as the authors describe how the implementation of SAP policies have affected the lives of the people they study, why they have had those effects, and how people have responded to deal with them.

The Case Studies Ahead

In her paper, "Local-Global Interactions in Ghana's Structural Adjustment," Gracia Clark argues that SAPs have had significant negative consequences in Ghana because they have endangered an adaptive and critical flexibility in the Ghanian economy at both local and national levels. Clark's experience in Ghana includes more than fifteen years familiarity with the Kamasi Central Market (Clark 1994), as well as work in both urban and rural areas of Ghana for international development agencies, including the International Labor Organization (ILO) and the British Overseas Development Authority. Clark observes that women traders, who weathered price controls and agricultural disasters in the late 1970s and early 1980s, have been unable to cope with the structural adjustments that began in 1984. The devaluation of the currency has increased prices dramatically so that traders need more capital to buy their stocks but formal credit has been tightened up and informal credit is increasingly unavailable. As high food prices keep consumers away, middle-level traders are being driven out of business or forced into dependent relations with wealthier traders.

The result, Clark argues, is detrimental to food producers, traders, and consumers alike, because middle-level traders traditionally built trade networks with rural producers and facilitated seasonal switching among commodities, maintained credit information and contacts, and settled marketplace disputes. Increasingly, market traders are either very rich or very poor, a polarization that leaves the system less flexible in mediating economic relationships at all levels. Clark suggests that a similar inflexibility has developed in the aid system itself, with the World Bank and IMF increasingly dominating the donor scene and dictating loan terms to countries with which their highly centralized programs may not be sufficiently responsive. On balance, Clark concludes, SAPs appear so detrimental to their stated goals of economic development that it may be that their real purpose is instead to serve the needs of international capital.

Arthur D. Murphy, Mary Winter, and Earl W. Morris also are able to draw on many years of familiarity with their research area. Since 1971, they have done household surveys in the Valley of Oaxaca in Mexico. In this article, "Household Adaptations in a Regional Urban System: The

Central Valley of Oaxaca, Mexico," they use data from their 1992 investigation to focus on the linkages between household economic strategies and the wider national and world economies in the wake of Mexico's economic crisis of the 1980s. They find that during the crisis, households had coped by decreasing their dependency ratios through increasing the number of household workers, often sending them to work in Oaxaca City or the United States. In the improved environment of the early 1990s (pre-NAFTA), to some extent a consequence of the 1980s structural adjustment policies, these strategies have not been abandoned; while unemployment has declined, wages and benefits are not so good as they once were and households have had to continue to deploy several workers to maintain the standard of living they desire. Overall, the Valley of Oaxaca became more integrated as workers moved from place to place to find work, regional cities increased their ties with Oaxaca City, and the power of both regional and national political centers over their respective hinterlands has increased. Murphy, Winter, and Morris suggest that such integration parallels previous historical periods when regional integration increased and decreased in concert with ties between the region and the rest of Mexico.

In her paper, "Structural Adjustments, Hometowns, and Local Development in Nigeria," Lillian Trager describes the "privatization" of local development as a consequence of SAPs. Trager's experience in Nigeria includes not only extended field research, but also two years work for the Ford Foundation in Logos. The survey data reported on in this paper were gathered in Yoruba towns and villages in the Ijesa area of southwestern Nigeria. They show that people feel they have been affected adversely by the implementation of SAPs. They have less disposable income and the cost of living is higher. Nevertheless, they maintain a strong ethic of hometown attachment and a long tradition of organizing locally to fund major community projects such as schools and town halls. The result has a been a dynamic and positive response to economic crisis as communities seek to generate for themselves resources that might once have been provided by government programs. In the process, they reach out to successful hometown people who now live elsewhere, revitalizing regional linkages and interpersonal networks.

James Toth applies Régulation Theory (e.g., Boyer 1990) to examine the pivotal role played by labor in Egypt's economic crisis, connecting the labor activities of rural workers to larger economic and political trends. Toth's extensive background in Egypt includes many years of anthropological research on labor as well as two years working for the Save the Children Foundation; currently, he lives in Cairo where he teaches at the American University. His innovative use of Régulation Theory guides him to focus on capitalist, labor, and management relations with particular attention to how these are constrained by the Egyptian context. Historically, the Egyptian government has depressed wages for rural agricultural labor, which is culturally constructed as women's work, to keep its main exports, cotton and cotton textiles, competitive in the world market. In the 1970s, when OPEC countries used their growing oil revenues to finance major construction booms, Egyptian construction workers sought jobs abroad and their vacant jobs at home were filled by unhappy agricultural workers. The resulting decline in agricultural production caused food shortages and a growing dependence on imported food, which further increased Egypt's foreign exchange debt. The situation was aggravated by IMF-mandated stabilization measures, implemented only in 1991, which eliminated Egyptian government social programs that had been used to keep labor cheap and so attract foreign capital, further worsening the exchange crisis.

Conclusion: Linkages Beyond the Local System

There is much that connects these papers. All four make it clear that national policy changes—however incompletely, imperfectly, or late may be their realization—have local consequences. People are right to worry about SAPs because life does not go on as before. In this regard, the papers here confirm the results of earlier studies. These particular people in Ghana, Mexico, Nigeria, and Egypt are precisely those whom other studies suggest will be the most affected: urban traders, wage workers in towns and cities, and agricultural laborers. Further, they experience the effects as other studies have suggested they would: through rising prices, wages that cannot keep pace, increased competition in the informal sector, and diminishing government services. Nevertheless, what the authors here make clear is that however inequitable the effects of SAPs may be, local people have responded dynamically and, except in the poorest country, Ghana, effectively to maintain or regain a reasonable standard of living. Presumably, others differently placed in these economies might have gained or lost even more (compare, for example, Cook 1993 and Winslow 1996).

These four papers also illustrate the importance of economic analysis beyond the local system. Not only do the authors find it necessary to take national policy into consideration when analyzing local economic practices, they also find that they cannot easily isolate one local piece of the economy from another. Instead, they highlight the significance of linkages and flows of people, money, and commodities between different local areas within and between regions. In Ghana, the urban economy is threatened by the fact that the middle-level traders who managed those flows of credit, goods, and information, are no longer in a position to do so. In Mexico, people have created and used extracommunity ties to augment household incomes by sending household members to live and work in other places. In Nigeria, local townspeople called on links with former townspeople now resident elsewhere to find the resources they needed to make up for cutbacks in government spending. In Egypt, the flight of construction workers rather unexpectedly created food shortages because agricultural workers chose to abandon the countryside for the now vacant construction jobs in towns and cities. Thus, all four authors use their years of incountry experience to contextualize holistically their extended case studies on many different levels.

The debate continues to rage around structural adjustment programs, much of it in very loaded terms. The earliest reports showed unequivocally that the poorest people, especially women and children, often were hurt the most and issues of equity continue to plague these attempts at major economic change (Gladwin 1991; Nelson 1992). More recently, longer-term studies suggest that imperfect though they may be, structural adjustment programs have in many cases saved countries from disaster by breaking a cycle of stagnant or negative economic growth (Sahn 1994). But the question of whether or not this is the fairest way growth can be achieved remains. Answering that question requires exactly the sort of long-term, local- and inter-level studies that follow here.

References

Boyer, Robert
    1990 *The Regulation School: A Critical Introduction.* New York: Columbia University Press.
Chambers, Robert
    1983 *Rural Development: Putting the Last First.* London: Longman.

Clark, Gracia
1994 *Onions Are My Husband: Survival and Accumulation by West African Market Women.* Chicago: University of Chicago Press.
Cook, Scott
1993 Bricks and Capitalism in the Lower Rio Grande Corridor: Issues in Theory and Analysis From Ongoing Research. Paper presented at the Thirteenth Annual Meeting of the Society for Economic Anthropology, Durham, New Hampshire, 23-24 April.
Foster, George, Thayer Scudder, Elizabeth Colson, and Robert V. Kemper, eds.
1976 *Long-Term Field Research in Social Anthropology.* New York: Academic Press.
Frank, Andre Gunder
1967 *Capitalism and Underdevelopment in Latin America.* New York: Monthly Review Press.
Gladwin, Christina H., ed.
1991 *Structural Adjustment and African Women Farmers.* Gainesville: University of Florida Press.
Gupta, Akhil
1992 The Song of the Nonaligned World: Transnational Identities and the Reinscription of Space in Late Capitalism. *Cultural Anthropology* 7 (1):63-79.
Haggard, Stephan and Robert R. Kaufman
1992 Institutions and Economic Adjustment. In *The Politics of Economic Adjustment: International Constraints, Distributive Conflicts, and the State.* Stephan Haggard and Robert R. Kaufman, eds. Pp. 3-40. Princeton: Princeton University Press.
Hood, Ron, Judith McGuire, and Martha Starr
1988 The Socioeconomic Impact of Macroeconomic Adjustment. Washington, D.C.: Agency for International Development, Bureau for Program and Policy Coordination.
Morrison, Thomas K. And Luis Arreaga-Rodas
1981 *Economic Liberalization in Developing Countries: Some Lessons from Three Case Studies—Sri Lanka, Egypt, and Sudan.* A.I.D. Discussion Paper No. 40. Washington, D.C.: Agency for International Development, Bureau for Program and Policy Coordination.
Nelson, Joan M.
1992 Poverty, Equity, and the Politics of Adjustment. In *The Politics of Economic Adjustment: International Constraints, Distributive Conflicts, and the State.* Stephan Haggard and Robert R. Kaufman, eds. Pp. 221-269. Princeton: Princeton University Press.

O'Brien, Stephen
  1991 Structural Adjustment and Structural Transformation in Sub-Saharan Africa. In *Structural Adjustment and African Women Farmers.* Christina H. Gladwin, ed. Pp. 25-45. Gainesville: University of Florida Press.
Powelson, John P. And Richard Stock
  1987 *The Peasant Betrayed: Agriculture and Land Reform in the Third World.* Boston: Oelgeschlager, Gunn, & Hain, Publishers, Inc., for the Lincoln Institute of Land Policy.
Redfield, Robert
  1940 *The Folk Culture of Yucatan.* Chicago: University of Chicago Press.
Roseberry, William
  1989 Peasants and the World. In *Economic Anthropology.* Stuart Plattner, ed. Pp. 108-126. Stanford: Stanford University Press.
Sahn, David E.
  1994 Economic Crisis and Policy Reform in Africa: An Introduction. In *Adjusting to Policy Failure in African Economies.* David E. Sahn, ed. Pp. 1-22. Ithaca: Cornell University Press.
Scheper-Hughes, Nancy
  1992 *Death Without Weeping: The Violence of Everyday Life in Brazil.* Berkeley: University of California Press.
Skinner, G. William
  1977 Cities and the Hierarchy of Local Systems. In *The City in Late Imperial China.* G. W. Skinner, ed. Pp. 275-351. Stanford: Stanford University Press.
Stallings, Barbara
  1992 International Influence on Economic Policy: Debt, Stabilization, and Structural Reform. In *The Politics of Economic Adjustment: International Constraints, Distributive Conflicts, and the State.* Stephan Haggard and Robert R. Kaufman, eds. Pp. 41-88. Princeton: Princeton University Press.
Uphoff, Norman
  1991 Fitting Projects to People. In *Putting People First: Sociological Variables in Rural Development, 2nd. Edition.* Michael M. Cernea, ed. Pp. 468-511. New York: Oxford University Press.
Wallerstein, Immanuel
  1974 *The Modern World-system: Capitalist Agriculture and the Origins of the European World-economy in the Sixteenth Century.* New York: Academic Press.
Winslow, Deborah
  1996 Pottery, Progress, and Structural Adjustments in a Sri Lankan Village. *Economic Development and Cultural Change* 45(1):33-65..

12

Local-Global Interactions in Ghana's Structural Adjustment

Gracia Clark

The policy agenda promoted by the International Monetary Fund (IMF) and the World Bank under the name of structural adjustment has been consistently presented by them as a set of economic development policies, and it is usually critiqued as such by both hostile and sympathetic analysts. But its marginal or negative contribution to most openly acknowledged development goals, such as rising living standards, provides an inadequate explanation for the rapid and continuing proliferation of structural adjustment programs, or SAPs, particularly in Sub-Saharan Africa, where their results have left much to be desired. This accelerating pace makes more sense when SAPs are analyzed instead more directly as a global policy regime with considerable success in stabilizing and regulating the modalities of international economic and political exchange through both ideological and material interventions.

Structural adjustment has also been immensely successful as a cultural system, in reproducing and propagating itself during the 1980s through policy conditionalities attached to financial assistance from the IMF and World Bank and indirectly to that from other donors. Policy makers and citizens from a growing number of countries perceive structural adjustment programs as a dominant fact of life. IMF economic stabilization programs extended short-term financial support to about thirty countries at a time throughout the eighties, and longer-term World Bank structural adjustment loans were extended to fifty-seven countries by 1988, mainly in Latin America and sub-Saharan Africa (Commonwealth 1989). They continue to exert even more influence into the 1990s, adding India to the fold (Chossudovsky 1992) and extending in principle, if not in name, to Eastern Europe and the former Soviet Union.

My own interest in structural adjustment was aroused by the prominence given to Ghana, where I do ethnographic research, in World Bank publications justifying and evaluating SAPs and answering outside critics in the mid-1980s. Ghana was praised for its thorough acceptance of the recommended policies, which required a dramatic about-face from socialist to neoclassical ideology, and for their positive results. The frequent deployment of Ghana as a noted and indisputable success story up through this year makes it a particularly telling example, which is also relatively well documented through the activities of long established Ghanaian research institutions. I had lived in Ghana throughout the 1982-3 famine and foreign exchange crisis that had driven it into the arms of the IMF. On a return visit in 1989, to check on the effects of five years of SAP there, I found urban workers, traders and farmers eating and working at much the same level as in those dark days, which a World Bank-sponsored national living standards survey had just confirmed (Clark 1991; RGSS 1989). If this was considered success, I wondered, what had been different about failure?

This paper argues that the implementation of SAPs has made a significant difference at a number of levels. Structural adjustment has consistently moved the economy of Ghana, its marketplace system (with which I am most familiar), and the development policy-making process in sub-Saharan Africa as a whole in the same direction: towards increasing rigidity, centralization, and polarization. I first look briefly at the effects of the enacted conditionalities on the Ghanaian economy, in interaction with patterns of economic control and stratification already established at the international and national levels. For national and local level impacts, I will refer to the conclusions of a collaborative study I did two years ago with Takyiwaa Manuh, of the University of Ghana, Institute for African Studies (Clark and Manuh 1991). That analysis linked historical and recent national policy and economic changes to recent trends in relations between traders in Kumasi Central Market, where I have done fieldwork for fifteen years, towards more credit dependency and fewer middle-level traders.

I then discuss the parallel effects of intensifying Bank/Fund dominance on the process of development policy decision making, establishing trends towards institutional centralization, polarization, and rigidity at that level. The Bank and IMF were arguably the most centralized already among major international development agencies, so increasing their influence undercuts gestures towards more participative agendas by the more liberal donor countries and international non-governmental organizations or NGOs. National governments must accept more rigid conditionalities than before, and also have less scope to manipulate contradictions between donors because they must show their wholehearted commitment to SAP priorities by keeping renegade donors in line.

I argue that the widening and emptying gap between rich and poor at the local, national, and international levels leads to centralization of power and specific structural rigidities that make the economic system as a whole less capable of adapting to the challenges of rapid change. The flexibility of the marketplace system in particular, faced with drought and economic crisis, depends directly on the ability of traders to switch quickly between supply sources and commodities. Under capital pressures linked to SAP, more middle-level traders are losing their financial autonomy and becoming tied through credit to single suppliers or buyers, who have often proved unreliable under fluctuating supply and demand conditions. The market's ability to adjust sensitively to shifts in supply and demand may be permanently reduced by increasing polarization that makes the poorer traders more dependent on the wealthiest few. Parallel deterioration in national and international autonomy likewise undermines both the variety of alternative economic and political channels and the realistic option of switching.

The Conditionalities

The changes achieved by SAPs are negotiated within the conceptual framework of financial transactions rather than international treaties, legitimating secrecy and delegitimating political opposition. Debtor countries receive loans from the IMF and the World Bank on the condition that they modify their national policies to conform to its guidelines. Each country seeking substantial loans from either the IMF or the World Bank negotiates with a team from these institutions a highly secret agreement specifying what policy changes will be required for initial loan approval and for the release of successive installments of funds. Loans from both sources are typically disbursed or released in stages, called "tranches," with certification of adequate progress towards these policy goals required at each stage.

Financially desperate countries depend on renewed access to these loan funds from year to year, and amicable conclusions to Bank/Fund negotiations act as a gatekeeping "seal of approval" for access to other multilateral and bilateral assistance and commercial credit. Sub-Saharan African countries, with few exceptions, have particularly weak negotiating positions because of the degree their governments depend on external assistance for revenue. Their small economies attract little interest among foreign investors and commercial lenders, compared to Latin America or Asia, giving them fewer alternatives to multilateral agencies such as the World Bank. These conditions make the implementation of structural adjustment policies different there, but in some ways more revealing, because the Bank negotiators had freer rein.

While the terms reached do vary from nation to nation, open coordination between the two closely linked institutions leads them to recommend virtually identical policies. Conditionalities in both institutions conform closely to the economic models proposed for Africa in the 1981 Berg report (World Bank 1981). The term "Bank/Fund approach" appears without further explanation in their own publications, lending further credibility to treating this as a single coherent agenda (Mills 1989). This monolithic face conceals considerable dissent within the institutions themselves, and considerable tolerance of non-compliance in specific cases such as Zaire, but the appearance of uniformity functions much like a reality in the practice of negotiations with countries without Zaire's strategic leverage. Ghana almost broke off the 1986 negotiations when a World Bank/IMF negotiating team persistently presented the draft letters of intent they had brought from Washington as the only possible program (Rothchild 1991).

World Bank statements repeatedly assert that conditionalities are tailored to specific local conditions, but national officials are equally unanimous about their standardized quality (Mills 1989). The policy changes countries have enacted immediately after accepting an initial loan show a degree of uniformity that supports the second conclusion. Rothchild's year-by-year analysis of drafts and final agreements in Ghana shows that IMF negotiators there achieved from seventy to eighty-five percent of the targets in the drafts they brought from Washington in the late 1980s (Rothchild 1991). The variation in apparent conditions affect the speed with which reforms must be implemented, and how many must be accepted, but not their content or direction. A fictionalized account of such negotiations in a small African country, while sympathetic to the basic SAP policy goals, confirms this distinction between the negotiable and non-negotiable aspects of the agreement (Klitgaard 1990). Recent acknowledgement by Bank analysts of the political difficulties raised by SAPs in many countries has led to recommendations to reconsider the sequencing and speed of reforms and build public support for them more carefully, but not to reconsider their content (Nelson 1989).

IMF loans give fiscal support for economic stabilization, so the conditions attached to them emphasize fiscal measures to reduce deficits in government budgets and the balance of payments and to resume debt payments. World Bank loans for medium-term structural adjustment aim to reorient the economy around the exports and potential exports it produces at lowest cost. The conditions attached to them aim to divert resources to the supposedly most efficient sectors producing exports or potential exports, called "tradeable" goods, and to create favorable conditions for foreign investment. The distinction between the two loan sources is blurred in practice, because of extended stabilization facilities and other modifications, but this leads to overlap rather than contradiction.

The immediate imperative for deficit reduction brings layoffs of public employees, privatization of public enterprises and removal of any food subsidies to reduce immediate government expenses. Reductions in social services, while not explicitly required by Bank/Fund experts, are seen by governments as their only realistic option for meeting budget targets. Civic unrest in response to the reforms themselves often rules out reduction in military expenditures, the other major budget category. Liberalization of trade puts an end to controls on prices, import and export licensing and foreign exchange transactions, including capital transfers. Prompt and massive devaluation of the national currency is a key aspect of "getting prices right," intended to reduce imports by making them more expensive and to promote exports through lower export prices and still lower prices for internally consumed items. Fees for health care, education and other services rise sharply under the heading of revenue enhancement. On the other hand, wages and credit levels are tightly controlled, in order to slow inflation by reducing effective demand. Infrastructure investments concentrate on rehabilitating and servicing the established export sectors, which produce the most immediate returns in foreign exchange for debt repayment. The strong line states are expected to take in holding down wages and promoting chosen exports reduces the resemblance of this policy package to the ideal of a free market. The overall direction of these policy shifts is to open the economies of adjusting nations more fully to the international economy, and to orient their national economies more thoroughly towards its needs. World Bank advisors identify which export commodities to promote using a definition of comparative advantage that selects for and intensifies weak bargaining positions. It targets those goods produced at the lowest local cost, a situation often generated by especially low wage production regimes and unfavorable local marketing arrangements for that commodity. As larger numbers of debtor countries around the world agree to abide by the same advice to expand these same exports, world agricultural commodity prices continue to fall precipitously. The effect on beverage crops of coffee, tea, and cocoa (Ghana's most important source of foreign exchange and government revenue) has been especially severe.

Neoclassical economic models forecast increased volume in demand by industrial nations and in supply by debtor nations from more realistic export prices, but so far response has not been sufficient to compensate for the lower real prices. Devaluation required by the World Bank also directly alters the relative pricing of locally produced exports and imports, so that producers can buy fewer imported inputs with their local currency proceeds. Private investment inflows have failed to materialize despite the attraction of low wages and easier repatriation of profits, due to poor infrastructure, international recession and greater interest in Eastern Europe and Asia.

Producing countries' capacities to respond to changing relative prices depends on their ability to shift commodities or patronize new buyer networks when conditions become unfavorable. Heavy de facto specialization in a few selected commodities, hardly initiated by SAPs but renewed under World Bank advice on comparative advantage, leaves Third World producers even more vulnerable to world market conditions and the fortunes or decisions of oligopolistic corporations. Commerce in many primary export commodities is so overwhelmingly dominated by a few companies that viable alternative channels may not presently exist. Export diversification efforts supported by the Bank in Africa emphasize fresh flowers, green vegetables, shrimp, and other luxury perishables for European consumers. These are highly risky crops with high transport losses, very volatile prices, and extremely centralized marketing networks, such as the Amsterdam flower auctions. Firms need large capital cushions to ride out this level of risk, and they resort extensively to contract farming and other unusually hierarchical buying arrangements that reduce local costs below the expected range of risk, thus raising comparative advantage (Mackintosh 1989).

The citizens of the "adjusting countries" are asked to swallow the bitter pill of SAP using a medical metaphor that promises a future of

Local-Global Interactions in Ghana **215**

greater economic health that will eventually benefit the sufferers themselves. This promise is not only deferred to an increasingly distant future, but undermined by the failure of the World Bank (which does the published assessments for both institutions) to demonstrate convincingly that SAPs can deliver on central development goals, such as a higher standard of living, for the groups who have paid their cost (UNICEF 1987). Real income drops of 30 percent or more in both formal and informal sectors were seen throughout sub-Saharan Africa in the 1980s (Commonwealth 1989).

The major World Bank evaluation of its African programs of the 1980s declared them a success, using restricted criteria emphasizing GNP and finance-based indicators (World Bank and UNDP 1989). Its statistical credibility as well as its logic has been seriously challenged by the United Nations Economic Commission on Africa, for example its choice to assess results before the end of the decade, after a brief and temporary fall in oil prices (UNECA 1989). Bernstein's comprehensive critique terms the Bank's projections of sure progress towards its stated goals "a fantasy," both brutal and ineffectual (Bernstein 1990).

Accumulating documentation of negative impacts on incomes and human services among the poor, especially in sub-Saharan Africa where conditions were most dramatic, pushed the World Bank to initiate a series of programs to mitigate the "social costs of adjustment" and investigate the "social dimensions of adjustment" (ADB et al. 1990). Again, Ghana was a pioneer; its poverty assessments and mitigation programs were later replicated throughout sub-Saharan Africa, but without countering the fundamental thrust of SAPs in the direction of polarization and centralization. A 1994 Accra conference for assessment of these programs across Africa acknowledged their weak performance and promised a new direction, as yet unspecified (Agarwal 1994).

Ghana

At the national level, Ghana's SAP has confirmed and intensified structural weaknesses already established in its economy through overspecialization in a limited number of exports. Renewed policy and financial emphasis on cocoa, timber, and gold, the three exports that provide eighty-five to ninety percent of Ghana's foreign exchange, has produced modest gains in export earnings, which have been largely swallowed up in debt service (Rothchild 1991). The annual GDP growth rates of five to six percent from 1985-8, when broken down, are almost entirely located in these three sectors (QDS 1989). Large-scale timber and gold operations received direct investment loans for equipment upgrades. As capital intensification, this ironically reduced the number of workers employed, at slightly higher wages, while increasing output. Road building and other basic infrastructure projects have been limited to urban areas and to trunk roads in export producing zones.

Structural adjustment aid, while paying lip service to export diversification, has been used to prevent it in practice. At the time of the first IMF loan to Ghana for the Economic Recovery Program begun in 1984, cocoa production had already been significantly undermined by decades of declining prices paid by the Cocoa Marketing Board. Aging trees were not fertilized or replaced, and sometimes not weeded or even harvested, although some of the harvest undoubtedly was also sold in neighboring countries with higher official prices. During the severe drought of 1983, bush fires or forest fires spread out of control in the moist forest zone where Ghana's cocoa is planted, burning many acres of cocoa plantations along with plantain, oil palm, and fallow land. Many planted maize the following year in response to that year's extremely high maize prices.

When compensation payments were eventually given to cocoa farmers for their lost farms, funded through World Bank loans, rumors abounded that farmers were not replanting with cocoa, but with other tree crops, especially oil palm. Palm oil had and continues to enjoy high prices from a strong local preference over industrial cooking oil, and is sold through the marketplace system, not a parastatal. Newspaper and radio editorials denounced this spontaneous diversification as unpatriotic, emphasizing that both the loans and labor assistance through the mobisquads (work groups organized among rural young men) were intended only for rehabilitating cocoa. Cocoa had the comparative advantage precisely because of its low price locally, compared to other world producers, while the high price of red palm oil relative to the colorless industrial palm oil produced in neighboring Ivory Coast ruled it out as a potential export.

While this degree of concentration on so few exports in itself represents a significant concentration of power, these industries are also among the most stratified and polarized in their internal organization. Favoring the most highly differentiated sectors of the economy, the same ones that were historically relatively advantaged, works to increase stratification in the country as a whole. Large joint ventures such as Ashanti Goldfields, acquired by Lonrho in 1988, dominate the deep shaft mines that produce the bulk of the officially exported gold. Small firms participate more actively in timber cutting, but have benefited relatively little from government support. Only ten percent of the export credits allowed for timber were used, for example, because devaluation had reduced the paper value of these firms' assets below the required collateral levels (Hutchful 1989). Both of those industries remain overwhelmingly male in ownership and in employment.

Ghanaian cocoa farming also shows a structural dominance by larger farmers and male farmers that makes it highly stratified relative to local food farming.

The vast majority of Ghana's rural households (82 percent) grow no cocoa at all; among the 18 percent who grow any, 94 percent of the cocoa income goes to 32 percent of the cocoa farmers, on the order of 6 percent of all farmers (Rothchild 1991; ILO 1988). Several detailed studies of cocoa growing areas have shown the difficulties women face in establishing cocoa farms; women cocoa farmers are many fewer and have much smaller farms than the average male cocoa farmer (Okali 1983; Mikell 1989). By global standards Ghanaian small-holders are only moderately stratified, since they form a broader base than the large plantation owners or corporations that dominate cocoa production in Brazil or Malaysia.

Expanding the exports favored by the SAP thus expands the parts of the Ghanaian economy that are most male-dominated as well as most polarized. Along with the concentration of power in the hands of wealthy farmers, not to mention mining and timber companies, comes greater dependency for their workers, farm wives, and laborers, who also lack proportionate state support. With accumulation centralized in so few hands, the economic flexibility exercised by persons with realistic options and the resources to move into them is seriously restricted.

Although food prices have risen relative to incomes, they have fallen behind relative to cocoa and non-food consumer goods (Clark and Manuh 1991). By 1987, the relative price of food to cocoa was half that of 1977, as inflation continued at around 35 percent (Sowa 1993). Food crop production has not risen consistently in response to higher prices because of farmers' resource constraints, tightened by the removal of fertilizer and credit subsidies. Sharp increases in fees charged for health clinics and other public services accessible to rural residents, such as the high "book user fees" in primary schools have reduced real access. Primary school and clinic attendance rates are both down (Sowa 1993). Imputations of higher farm incomes due to higher urban food prices do not allow for the expense of these higher input and service costs, including farm wages, or for the higher transport charges for marketed crops, linked to imported fuel prices (Sarris 1992). They also neglect to consider that Ghana's rural farmers, many quite specialized in commercial production, also buy food at these high prices. They spend half their cash incomes on food, and their income from crop sales averages less than their food purchases (Alderman 1992).

If incomes were stagnating in the rural areas, they were declining in the cities, where higher prices for food and imported consumer goods had an even sharper impact. The explicit policy of demand restraint, by holding down real wages, could only mean a poorer diet when urban households were already spending 69 percent of their incomes on food alone. Small-scale producers and traders studied by the World Bank in Kumasi, who depend on sales for local consumption, could not even turn over their existing working capital because they lacked customers to buy their current stock, due to low consumer incomes and competition from imports (Steel and Webster 1989). Only the "urban non-poor" and the service sector targeting them were doing better, due to higher salary differentials in civil service and private firms and the expansion of those few businesses with access to international finance through ties to expatriate corporations or drug traffickers (Alderman 1992).

The massive public sector layoffs which began in the first year of SAP left many workers without access to even the devalued minimum wage. Ghanaian government workers were euphemistically "redeployed" to a private sector that was also contracting, as liberalized imports drove out many marginal manufacturing firms. Capacity utilization, which had bottomed out near 10 percent, rose only to 35 percent despite the high rate of bankruptcies, when firms sold or wrote off assets (Sowa 1993). The new, profitable enterprises expected to emerge did not materialize, so the redeployees were in effect dumped into informal and self-employment under the guise of entrepreneurship. An analysis of redeployment that explicitly relies on this safety net to prevent suffering and unrest acknowledges credit as a general constraint to the informal sector, since banks were reluctant to lend to them and require capital and other conditions they can rarely meet (ILO 1989).

At the same time, restraints on credit worked to effectively prevent local producers from expanding production. Higher interest rates did reduce the demand for bank loans, since few productive enterprises offered rates of return that kept pace with the continuing inflation credit restraint was intended to check. Wage-earners' savings or loans from them, historically an important alternative source of capital to bank loans, have likewise been reduced by frozen wages, higher school and medical fees, and big layoffs in the formal sector. Workers laid off from private and public firms or never employed swelled the ranks of the self-employed, including men and women traders. The increased competition, under conditions of local demand constraint, consistently pushed down informal sector incomes and prevented reinvestment. Disinvestment, or selling off assets to meet consumption needs, was the parallel to capital flight among these lower income groups.

The effects on Ghana's poor were severe enough to trigger an innovative World Bank response, the Programme of Actions to Mitigate the Social Costs of Adjustment (PAMSCAD) program. Although used as a model for other countries, PAMSCAD was too small and too late to reverse this trend in Ghana. The first programs under PAMSCAD aimed to compensate the politically influential redeployees, by providing lump sums to establish them in informal sector production or commercial farming. Funded at $85 million in 1987, it had barely begun implementation three years later, while IMF drawings alone each year had averaged $180 million. The funding for PAMSCAD also depended on pledges from other donors, who were slow in pledging and slower in paying. A broad internal bank analysis later mentioned such co-financing as a factor that generally reduces a project's performance (Wapenhans 1992). PAMSCAD also targeted women and the rural poor, especially in the disadvantaged Northern and Upper Regions, but specifically excluded trade and primary agriculture (their major occupations) as activities not eligible for its first credit program, which advertised for applicants in the Daily Graphic in October 1988.

The Marketing Network

A similar increase in polarization and dependency was visible within Kumasi Central Market by 1989, after five years of SAP. Although it naturally takes different forms there than in farming areas, the same effects of rigidity and vulnerability can be traced to the central SAP policy elements of demand restraint and credit restraint. With shrinking consumer buying power, added competition from the unemployed, and capital pressure from inflation and devaluation, more traders had to use capital that belonged to others to stay in business. This had begun to polarize the market between the few wealthy financiers and their agents or employees, undermining the middle layer of autonomous, self-employed traders who could adapt quickly to seasonal and occasional crises through their commodity group organizations.

The strongest impact of SAP on traders comes through impoverishing the consumers they serve, workers in both the formal and informal sectors. In Ghana, as in most of West Africa, the network of urban and rural marketplaces remains the primary distributive network for local agricultural foodstuffs, craft and industrial products, and imported foods and consumer goods. Kumasi Central Market traders, interviewed in January 1990, volunteered three major comments on current conditions they considered directly linked to recent government policy changes, although they did not use the terminology of structural adjustment. The first referred to falling overall demand as "they don't buy," which they attributed to high prices caused by the drastic devaluation of the local currency. This raised the prices for imports and manufactures using imported raw materials and machinery immediately and proportionately, but also indirectly, raised prices for local foodstuffs. They said that farmers justified their higher farmgate prices by citing higher prices for imported inputs, higher prices for consumer goods like kerosene and cloth, and higher wages needed by farm workers. Sharp rises in freight rates for transport of crops to urban markets increased urban/rural price differentials without increasing traders' profit margins. Drivers responded to higher costs of spare parts and gasoline from currency devaluations and subsidy removals when recalculating these charges.

Incomes did not match these higher prices because "there is no money," a remark which referred to both low real wages and low informal sector incomes. Lower real wages and incomes, higher rents, and higher school and hospital fees made their urban customers buy less of the food and consumer goods they sold. To tighten your belt, you need first to own one, and many of Ghana's families had already sold theirs during the famine of 1982-3, if not before. Since SAPs expressly aim to restrict demand through wage and budget constraints, this must be considered a direct intended result, not an unintended side effect. Ghana's average households already spent most of their income on food (69 percent in urban areas), so demand restraint could mean nothing else but reduced consumption of food and the most inexpensive consumer goods (Alderman 1992). These are the categories of goods most central to market volume. Only secondhand clothing sales expanded remarkably, as ordinary citizens could now rarely afford cloth or new clothing.

Individual traders' volume of sales fell further as more new traders tried to earn a share of this limited volume. Layoffs of public and private sector workers not only reduced total community income, but without any unemployment or welfare programs these people flooded into the market and other informal sector venues in search of work. Competition from would-be entrepreneurs investing their hard-won civil service severance pay and the newly desperate dependents of laid-off workers were both intense for different reasons, at the top and bottom levels of trading within the market respectively. Traders complained that the flood of new entrants reduced their own incomes, but did not try to keep them out, speaking of a fundamental right to work for persons with no realistic alternative.

These labor force dynamics notably pushed more young men into market trading, as they left or never managed to enter wage work or more lucrative skilled trades, which were predominantly male. Their appearance in the local foodstuffs wholesale yards, female-dominated since the exodus of men into cocoa farming in the early twentieth century, created some novel gender tensions. Some men, in interacting with these women who were not kin, deployed the husband/wife models that required women to defer. Other men took the option to relate to fellow traders as mothers, sisters and aunts, showing respect and deference to market leaders.

Traders also used the phrase "there is no money" to initiate discussions of a severely felt capital shortage. Traders had been hard hit by capital losses from drought, interrupted trade, and confiscations during the late 1970s and early 1980s. Traders appreciated that physical harassment by soldiers and police, which had intensified just before the SAP, had stopped with the deregulation of market trade and liberalization of imports. They could not take advantage of their new security to expand trade, however, because lower sales volumes and credit restraints rooted in SAP policies made it nearly impossible to recover even to their former levels in real terms. Soaring prices continually raised capital requirements in local currency terms at a rate few traders could match. Those barely hanging on were vulnerable to bankruptcy from minor personal or business crises they could previously have weathered with relative ease.

The effects of capital shortage could be seen clearly among traders in yams, who had higher average capital requirements already for selling a relatively high-priced local staple crop, and with whom I had worked closely since 1978. Individual traders who could fill a truck in 1978 with several thousand yams could only afford to buy a few hundred at a time in 1990. When yam traders can no longer fill a truck by themselves, they can no longer charter a truck to travel to the supply areas, so they face a difficult choice. They can buy in smaller quantities in small town markets, where passenger trucks regularly go, at higher prices than buying directly from farmers. They can become dependent on one of the few remaining wealthy wholesalers, using her working capital to make up the difference and splitting the profits on those purchases with the lender, reducing their chances to work back up to independence. Others stopped going on the road, withdrawing into retailing in Kumasi Central Market stalls and settling for the lower profits from reselling yams bought from the same wealthy wholesalers. Some retailers who could no longer afford a hundred yams, the wholesale unit, had to buy from intermediaries or switch to cheaper commodities, giving up their stalls in the yam section. One yam trader who had also survived a major illness had resorted to selling fried snacks and boiling pineapple skins for a medicinal drink.

Credit restrictions under SAP both limited the overall amount of local currency credit extended by banks and raised interest rates above the rate of inflation, while devaluation reduced the value of houses and other collateral required. Farmers I interviewed in villages that had participated in an appropriate technology project said they no longer applied for loans since they did not expect their annual incomes to reach the level of the interest; demand had been effectively restrained. Few market traders ever received formal sector loans in the first place, but the more privileged family and community members who had qualified for such loans before now competed with traders for informal loans from kin and neighbors, on which traders and other informal sector workers had relied. Many of these originated in savings of wage workers, including government officials, whose demand was now being restrained and who might now be subsidizing the consumption needs rather than the investment needs of their extended families.

These dynamics pushed many middle-level traders out of business and widened the gap between rich and poor traders within a single market.

Bankrupt middle-level traders either operated from hand to mouth or became dependent on credit to operate on a more efficient scale. Larger traders surviving now placed their capital out with direct agents or employees, since this gave higher returns, instead of giving supplier credit to autonomous customers as before (Clark 1991). When I returned briefly to Kumasi in 1992, traders were concerned to point out that the renewed supplies of printed cloth in the market was a visual illusion of wealth, because it all belonged to someone else. The cloth seller, faced with rapid increases in import prices, now sold on commission and received her entire inventory from an outside supplier, who could take it back at any time. The few wealthy traders who could take advantage of this demand for dependency gained in power, mainly those who had access to sources of capital outside the marketplace system. Those newly rich secondhand clothes wholesalers whose affairs I heard rumors about, for example, had drawn on outside capital. The weakness of their competitors enabled those few traders with capital to capture a greater proportion of the shrinking overall volume of trade. They continued to make profits because they could hold subordinates and associates in more dominant relations that reserved a greater proportion of the profits for them.

These credit-dependent traders lose significant autonomy by being tied to a single supplier. They can longer depend on receiving credit from any one of a number of suppliers and buyers they know well. They can no longer switch commodities or locations, because their funding is tied to a single partner linked to one commodity or location. Seasonal and improvisational shifts that proved to be central to maintaining reliable food supplies and incomes throughout the year and in years affected by natural or political upheavals become much more difficult. When supplies were interrupted, dependent traders had to wait more passively for an improvement because they had no money to take elsewhere, searching out alternative or secondary sources of supply. Their financiers or employers had less motivation to try innovative strategies that might bring more risk or less return. With more personal wealth for maintaining their own consumption, they could afford to suspend trading until conditions improved.

The strategies of Kumasi Central Market traders and rural food producers in adapting to fluctuating supply and demand conditions during the decade just before SAP show how critical this flexibility is to weathering acute crises and stimulating long-term production. Annual seasonal shortages, for example, triggered a set of responses that were extended and combined during the longer period of drought. Consumers normally vary their diet as different grains and root crops are harvested, encouraging the diversification of farm production. Farmers diversify plantings and extend their harvests, specializing heavily in crops like tomatoes if they can hand irrigate or otherwise sell off-season supplies at high prices. They rely on a marketing network willing and able to collect small amounts frequently from dispersed farms, and to supply their families with compensatory foodstuffs from other regions in the small amounts appropriate to farm incomes. As the dry season intensifies, the total supply remaining to be sold becomes smaller and more dispersed. More traders turn to scouring the farm villages, convincing farmers to sell and bringing cash advances from anxious wholesalers and retailers remaining in Kumasi. Other traders and farmers turn to processing foodstuffs, to maintain incomes by increasing value added to a smaller volume. Still others count on switching commodities, ideally something with a seasonality opposite to their main commodity. These minor commodities benefit from not having to provide income enough for the entire year, sharing human overhead. Non-farm occupations provide a substantial proportion of cash income to rural households, including crafts sold through local markets and trading itself. These local options minimize the need for migration out of the village, stabilizing rural communities. The same markets also enable those left behind to buy food and start enterprises more effectively with the remittances sent. Because the majority of labor migrants are men, those seeking these local options include more women.

The strategies of women in Damongo, a small town in the Northern Region, show the worth of this flexibility to members of one of the designated "vulnerable groups." Women were not considered the principal farmers in their community, where men grew grains for the local dishes and also yams intended for sale to southern cities like Kumasi. Women planted vegetables on the sides of yam ridges, weeding both crops at once. The 1982 drought freed women of their usual weeding duties early, since the crops had died. They turned immediately to their established dry season activity, making shea butter (an edible fat resembling margarine) from the nuts of wild trees whose yield was affected very little by the drought. In normal years, they collected shea nuts from stands of trees within a day's walk of their homes, stockpiling nuts in the rainy season to make the butter months later, when they had more time. That year, groups of women camped out at more distant groves and made large quantities on the spot. Market networks could absorb these larger quantities to partly replace palm oil, which was in short supply because these moist forest trees bore little during the drought and many had been burned.

The only farm crop that survived that drought in Damongo was cassava, which a few men had been planting as an experiment. A few women had learned how to make gari, a toasted cassava meal, but their low quality brought a low price. They approached some local schoolteachers from the Volta Region, where gari is a staple food, to learn how to make it properly. Due to the food shortages, their high-quality product was bought eagerly by local schools and barracks. Within a year or two, they had established a thriving local industry and organized to obtain a tractor on credit for bringing cassava from the farms to their homes. They also used it for hauling the large amounts of water needed for shea butter making. Their market contacts, established for sideline occupations, continued to function under conditions of extreme shortage of supply and were willing to accept both new and more old products. These enabled the Damongo women to earn income critical to their families' survival during the drought, to obtain steady food supplies (although at high prices) from other regions, and to experiment with new products and new relations of production that expanded food security for the region as a whole in the long run.

Analysis of traders operating out of Kumasi Central Market showed that the network of commodity groups based in markets greatly facilitated the seasonal switching that kept options open and the rapid recovery from acute crises like government attacks on traders or demolition of markets. Commodity groups centered on the Kumasi wholesale yards were information centers where traders knew each other and could update their knowledge of prices, government policies, and individual creditors with little delay. Traveling traders had current membership in groups in a series of supply locations with staggered harvest times, and perhaps in secondary commodities. They could count on receiving credit when needed from any of the group members who regularly bought from travelers, and they could extend credit when needed with the confidence that the group leaders would stand ready to enforce debt collection. This enabled marginal members to shuttle between different locations or commodities on short notice, absorbing more than their fair share of economic fluctuations without loss of

226 Economic Analysis Beyond the Local System

efficiency, precisely because the more central or core members, such as wholesalers and group elders, remained in place to monitor local conditions.

The same structural elements characterized helpful responses to state-triggered crises, such as the complete currency exchange in 1979 and the episodes of violent price control enforcement in 1979 and 1982. Groups were conspicuously active in gathering and sharing information about the new events. Apart from closing the wholesale yards for a day or two when conditions got too chaotic, group leaders did not enforce any particular response. They facilitated discussions of various strategies individuals were trying to deal with the crisis, collected information from travelers about conditions in different parts of the country, and continued to enforce whatever payment or other agreements traders had negotiated on an individual basis. By providing reliable dispute settlement, the commodity group leaders helped to stabilize relations quickly under the new conditions. The same dispute settlement service already meant that traders had not needed to enter into more hierarchical dyadic relationships in order to extend or receive credit as needed. Traders who had survived many unexpected crises explained that these more rigidly defined obligations might well turn out to be useless or worse when neither side could fulfill them.

The autonomous middle-level traders are also the backbone of the market commodity organizations, so their dwindling numbers seem likely to undermine these or transform them into patronage networks for the wealthy. Very wealthy traders and very poor traders were markedly less active and not interested in Kumasi market group leadership positions before SAP. Now that the market is increasingly staffed by very rich and very poor traders, the latter swelled by many new entrants without established group loyalties, it remains to be seen whether the commodity group structure will eventually take a more rigid and exploitative form, as in some neighboring countries, or alternatively become weaker and less effective. This polarization leaves the market system with less flexibility in mediating relations between city and country, between exports, imports and local production and between formal and informal workers.

The implications of these degenerative changes in the financial autonomy of traders and their commodity group institutions are important and alarming in the context of the regional marketplace system around Kumasi. This adjustment capacity has been critical over the past fifteen years in helping the regional economy keep going through serious dislocation from a variety of human and natural causes. When the next disruption comes along, that capacity may no longer be there to absorb and compensate for it. Similar trends towards centralization and polarization at the national and international levels of economic organization, including within the various development agencies themselves, are equally alarming because they imply the formation of structural rigidities that may be equally inadequate to deal with future and present crises in those wider arenas.

The Agencies

A more centralized and authoritarian hierarchy of decision making within the arena of international development assistance has arisen both because of the increased dominance of the IMF and World Bank in their relations with other international and national agencies and because of their own internal structure of authority. The organizational and ideological rigidities of the World Bank and IMF, far from making them aberrations within the development industry, present instead, in extreme form, features which have received very widespread criticism as general problems in development practice and discourse. Top-down decision making, universal policy recommendations based on stereotypes rather than local conditions, dependence on Western models and expertise, emphasis on Gross National Product (GNP) to the neglect of social indicators, favoring exports over local consumption—few aid agencies or practitioners escape these accusations entirely.

Continued replication of projects and policies despite poor performance on proclaimed goals, sometimes despite repeated and fairly well-publicized negative evaluations, is another unfortunately commonplace phenomenon. Several ethnographic studies of development projects, programs and agencies, including the World Bank itself, remarked upon this phenomenon (Carloni 1990; Kardam 1990; Reyna 1986; Staudt 1985; Ferguson 1990). The dangers and disadvantages of top-down, rigid approaches have been argued so extensively in the debates over more participative development strategies even within the Bank itself that I will not attempt to summarize here the arguments for and against (Cernea 1985; Korten 1980). In this section I am more concerned with documenting how Bank/Fund dominance has shifted the balance farther in that same direction.

Control within the World Bank itself is held even more tightly at the top than other agencies such as UNDP or USAID. Its president takes a stronger individual role in determining overall policy directions than in the United States Agency for International Development, for example, making US nomination of the president even more significant (Sen 1993). Some of the most detailed studies of the policy-making and project design processes in various development agencies have been made by analysts interested in tracking the incorporation of concerns with women in development (Staudt 1985; Kardam 1990). Routine decisions about which projects to fund and what kinds of projects to propose involve a more restricted range of people than in other agencies, and less discretion remains at lower levels of the bureaucracy (Kardam 1990). World Bank field offices in other countries take less part in generating projects than their USAID equivalents, and have less input into negotiations with their host governments, which are handled by emissaries from the head office in Washington, DC. Only the six largest Resident Missions in the World Bank have full responsibility even for managing any projects, and the standard internal guidelines for project implementation mention only briefing the local office before departing (Wapenhans 1992). Interestingly enough, both an external political analysis and an internal investigation by the World Bank recommended addressing the problems of poor performance and formulaic approaches by giving more influence in loan negotiations and project design to regional department staff at headquarters, Country Strategy Papers, in-country resident directors, and improving country field offices (Rothchild 1991; Wapenhans 1992).

The World Bank emphasis on purely economic analyses and imitating Western models is likewise even more absolute than in most other aid agencies. Ferguson has analyzed the technocratic, economic style of reasoning that marks leaked World Bank internal memos but extends to public relations documents in only slightly more subtle forms (Ferguson 1993). People-centered development has received some attention in its research and analysis documents, perhaps as a legacy of its 1970s basic needs approach, but has not appreciably affected the direction of policy making or project design (Cernea 1985; Kardam 1990). Kardam similarly notes the unusually extreme detachment of rhetoric from implementation in the Bank for the case of gender issues. Judgments on proposed projects continue to be based primarily on financial measures, particularly the rate of cash return and rewards to staff made on the basis of cash flow rather

Local-Global Interactions in Ghana 229

than on success in socially grounded terms. This has led to distortions in the internal evaluation of projects and a de-emphasis on implementation, so that unrealistic proposals generate an excessive percentage of problem projects, even by internal standards (Wapenhans 1992).

Some structural rigidities derive more simply from the growing monopoly status of the Bank and Fund. An equivalent degree of control by any one development organization, such as the Food and Agricultural Organization, for example, would be a centralizing move in the sense that it would concentrate control over funds and policies within the leadership of that organization. Historically, the capacity of smaller international agencies, non-governmental organizations (NGOs), and liberal donor countries (such as the Netherlands and Scandinavia) to pursue divergent development agendas has created an important space for experimental, innovative, or simply different approaches, of which one might better fit specific local conditions even by accident. The gatekeeping role IMF/World Bank approval now plays means that countries who refuse their conditions no longer have access to alternative forms or sources of assistance, however meager these were. The United Nations Development Fund (UNDP) and other UN affiliates coordinate closely with the World Bank, publishing joint analyses (ADB 1990). Smaller donors now work only with countries in good standing with the IMF/World Bank, with very few exceptions such as Oxfam and the American Friends Service Committee.

This degree of policy dominance has been achieved smoothly despite, at best, ambiguous progress towards the criteria of higher incomes or better standards of living generally presented by these same agencies as the goals of development. Major critiques by UNECA (1989) and DAWN (Antrobus 1990) even argue that SAPs have reduced both immediate progress toward these goals and long-term prospects for reaching them. Setting aside the idea that promoting these goals is the primary motivation, either among donors or recipients, for adopting structural adjustment programs endorsed by the IMF and World Bank makes the strength and consolidation of international support for these programs and their remarkable degree of consistency and coherence from place to place much more comprehensible.

Looking at the actual effects of Bank/Fund conditionalities, rather than their stated intentions, reveals clear success in accomplishing two quite different major goals. The reorganization and disciplining of debtor economies has served to put their financial and human resources more conveniently at the disposal of international demand, even though the promised rewards for this adjustment have not been forthcoming. Stabilizing and liberalizing financial conditions in debtor nations has made it easier for international firms to operate within individual nations and to move farther towards globalization of the economy. Just as Ghana's SAP negotiations began in 1983, an imminent Mexican credit default threatened serious collapse in world banking and financial relations. International flows of repayment, investment, and profit now continue without interruption.

Stability in these terms was achieved by ideologically demonizing and economically starving out alternative patterns of economic integration. The apocalyptic rhetoric of structural adjustment, even in the moderate form that appears in authoritative Bank syntheses, presents a stark choice between the Bank/Fund approach and a chaotic picture of total collapse that far outbalances any doubts about current performance (World Bank and UNDP 1989). Even relatively critical assessments also accept the underlying hegemonic assumption that something very like a SAP is inevitable, if not desirable, calling basically for modifications that reduce its human cost and obvious inequities (UNICEF 1987; Commonwealth 1989). This unilineal, neoclassical vision becomes a closer approximation of reality to the extent that Bank/Fund activities themselves increasingly reconstruct the world in this image by orchestrating the allocation of resources to divert human and financial capital from activities and relations not conforming to this model.

Ironically, the rigidity and centralization accepted in the name of stabilization actually seriously undermine long-term stability by restricting the range and viability of alternative economic channels. The example of the Ghanaian marketplace system demonstrates how fiscal policies and investment priorities integral to SAPs can make it very difficult to maintain the autonomous middle-level traders who are poised for rapid adaptation to new conditions. Historical experience of drought and economic crisis there shows how this flexibility to move between a wide range of commercial options has been crucial in absorbing and compensating for such shocks. Increasing stratification and rigidity under SAPs in the key arenas of agriculture, industry, and economic policy-making indicate that parallel structural weaknesses are intensifying there.

The success of SAPs in disciplining the international economy has paradoxically reduced its structural capacity to adjust. The direct and indirect effects of these policy conditionalities attack and weaken existing or potential alternatives to its chosen patterns and priorities and reduced effective access to those that remain. This loss of structural diversity, including the skills, resources, and relationships needed to implement such alternatives promptly and successfully, seriously handicaps future responses to crises and to opportunities for innovation at the local, national, and international levels.

References

(ADB) African Development Bank, United Nations Development Program, and World Bank
    1990 *The Social Dimensions of Adjustment in Africa.* Washington, D.C.: World Bank.
Agarwal, Rita
    1994 Personal communication.
Alderman, Harold
    1992 *Incomes and Food Security in Ghana.* Cornell Food and Nutrition Policy Program, Working Paper 26. Ithaca, NY:CFNPP.
Antrobus, Peggy
    1990 *Crises and Challenges of Caribbean Women in the 1990s.* Paper presented at Development Alternatives with Women for a New Era (DAWN) conference, May 6-11. Cited by Maria Nzomo, (1992) Beyond Structural Adjustment Programs: Democracy, Gender Equity, and Development in Special reference to Kenya. In Julius Nyang'oro and Timothy Shaw, eds. Beyond Structural Adjustment in Africa. New York: Praeger.
Bernstein, Henry
    1990 Agricultural Modernization and the Era of Structural Adjustment: Observations on Sub-Saharan Africa. *Journal of Peasant Studies* 18(1):3-35.
Campbell, Bonnie K. and John Loxley, eds.
    1989 *Structural Adjustment in Africa.* London: Macmillan.
Carloni, Alice
    1990 Women in FAO Projects: Cases from Asia, the Near East and Africa. In *Women, International Development and Politics: The Bureaucratic Mire.* Kathleen Staudt, ed. Philadelphia: Temple University Press.
Cernea, Michael
    1985 *Putting People First: Sociological Variables in Rural Development.* Washington, D.C.: World Bank.
Chossudovsky, Michel
    1992 India Under IMF Rule. *The Ecologist* 22(6):271-275.

Clark, Gracia
  1991 Colleagues and Customers in Unstable Market Conditions in Kumasi, Ghana. *Ethnology* 30(1):31-48.
Clark, Gracia and Takyiwaa Manuh
  1991 Women Traders in Ghana and the Structural Adjustment Program. In *Structural Adjustment and African Women Farmers.* C. Gladwin, ed. Gainesville: University of Florida Press.
Commonwealth Secretariat
  1989 *Engendering Adjustment for the 1990s.* London: Commonwealth Secretariat.
Ferguson, James
  1990 *The Anti-politics Machine: "Development," Depoliticization and Bureaucratic Power in Lesotho.* Cambridge: Cambridge University Press.
  1993 De-moralizing Economies: African Socialism, `Scientific Capitalism' and the Moral Politics of Structural Adjustment. Paper presented at the Annual Meeting for the American Ethnological Society, Santa Fe, New Mexico.
Gladwin, Christina, ed.
  1991 *Structural Adjustment and African Women Farmers.* Gainesville: University of Florida Press.
Hutchful, Eboe
  1989 From "Revolution" to Monetarism: The Economics and Politics of the Adjustment Programme in Ghana. In *Structural Adjustment in Africa.* Bonnie Campbell and John Loxley, eds. London: Macmillan.
(ILO) International Labor Organization
  1988 *Employment Promotion in the Informal Sector in Africa.* Addio Adaba: ILO (Jobs and Skills Programme for Africa).
  1989 *From Redeployment to Sustained Employment Generation: Challenge for Ghana's Programme of Economic Recovery and Development.* Addis Adaba: ILO.
Kardam, Nuket
  1990 The Adaptability of International Development Agencies: The Response of the World Bank to Women in Development. In *Bringing Women In: Women's Issues in International Development.* Kathleen Staudt, ed. Boulder: Lynn Rienner.
Klitgaard, Robert
  1990 *Tropical Gangsters.* New York: Basic Books.
Korten, David
  1980 Commodity Organization and Rural Development: A Learning Process Approach to Rural Development. *Public Administration Review* 40(4):480-511.
Mackintosh, Maureen
  1989 *Gender, Class and Rural Transition.* London: Zed Press.

Mikell, Gwendolyn
  1989 *Cocoa and Chaos in Ghana.* New York: Paragon.
Mills, Cadman Atta
  1989 *Structural Adjustment in Sub-Saharan Africa.* Economic Development Institute Policy Seminar Report No. 18. Washington, D.C.: World Bank.
Nelson, Joan, ed.
  1989 *Fragile Coalitions.* Oxford: Transaction Books.
Okali, Christine
  1983 *Cocoa and Kinship in Ghana: The Matrilineal Akan of Ghana.* London: Kegan Paul.
(QDS) Quarterly Digest of Statistics
  1988 *Quarterly Digest of Statistics.* Accra: Republic of Ghana Statistical Service.
(RGSS) Republic of Ghana Statistical Service
  1989 *Ghana Living Standards Survey.* World Bank Social Dimension of Adjustment Project Unit, First Report. Accra: World Bank.
Reyna, Stephen
  1986 Donor Investment Preferences, Class Formation and Existential Development: Articulation of Production Relations in Burkina Faso. In *Anthropology and Rural Development in West Africa.* Michael Horowitz and Thomas Painter, eds. Boulder: Westview.
Rothchild, Donald
  1991 Ghana and Structural Adjustment. In *Ghana: The Political Economy of Recovery.* D. Rothchild, ed. Baltimore: Johns Hopkins University Press.
Sarris, Alexander
  1992 *Household Welfare During Crisis and Adjustment in Ghana.* Cornell Food and Nutrition Policy Program, Working Paper 33. Ithaca, N.Y.: CFNPP.
Sen, Gita
  1993 *Gender and Global Economic Transformation.* Talk presented at the University of Michigan and conversation with the author.
Sowa, Nii Kwaku
  1993 Ghana. In *The Impact of Structural Adjustment on the Population of Africa.* Aderanti Adepoju, ed. London: James Currey.
Staudt, Kathleen
  1985 *Women, Foreign Assistance, and Advocacy Administration.* New York: Praeger.
Steel, William F. and Leila Webster
  1989 *Small Enterprises in Ghana: Responses to Adjustment.* Industry Series Working Paper No. 33. Washington, D.C.: World Bank.

(UNECA) United Nations Economic Commission for Africa.
  1989 *African Alternative Framework Structural Adjustment Programs for Socio-Economic Recovery and Transformation.* Addis Ababa: UNECA.
(UNICEF) United Nation's International Children's Emergency Fund
  1987 *Adjustment With A Human Face.* Giovanni Cornia, Richard Jolly, and Francis Stewart, eds. Oxford: The Clarendon Press.
Wapenhans, Willi
  1992 *Report of the Portfolio Management Task Force.* Washington, D.C.: World Bank.
World Bank
  1981 *Accelerated Development in Sub-Saharan Africa: An Agenda for Action.* Washington, D.C.: World Bank.
World Bank and (UNDP) United Nations Development Program
  1989 *Africa's Adjustment and Growth in the 1980s.* Washington, D.C.: World Bank.

13

Household Adaptations in a Regional Urban System: The Central Valleys of Oaxaca, Mexico

Arthur D. Murphy
Mary Winter
Earl W. Morris

Introduction

This paper deals with the regional system in the central portion of the Valley of Oaxaca, Mexico. We are trying to understand the linkages between households within that system, how they articulate with the wider national and world economies, and the effects that changes in the world system have had on household organization. We found that households in Oaxaca City are experiencing an economic recovery through an intensification of the strategies, principally female labor, they developed during the crisis of the 1980s. Households in the regional capitals that surround the city seem to use migration as their major mode of economic adaptation.

Since 1971, we have carried out ethnographic and survey research in the city of Oaxaca, Mexico, in order to understand how households in this regional primate center have adapted to socioeconomic change.[1] Comparisons of survey data from 1977 and 1987 (Morris 1991; Murphy 1991; Murphy et al. 1990; Pacheco Vásquez et al. 1991; Rees et al. 1991; Selby 1991; Selby et al. 1990; Winter 1991; Winter et al. 1990) indicated that households adjusted through migration and placement of workers in the labor force. Household size and general demographics remained the same even though the labor market was steadily informalizing as fewer workers had access to jobs with benefits such as health insurance and end-of-year bonuses (often equivalent to one month's salary).

In 1992 we carried out a third survey of the city of Oaxaca. This time, however, we wished to gather data that would provide a better understanding of the linkages between households in the central region of

Oaxaca Valley. It has become clear to us that to understand Oaxaca City, we must look at the regional context in which it is embedded (Figure 13.1). Tlacolula, Etla and Ocotlán are the closest district capitals to Oaxaca City. Each day innumerable buses, cars, motorcycles and bicycles crowd the roads between them and Oaxaca City. To learn more about regional economic patterns in 1992, we sampled approximately one hundred households in each of these district capitals, in addition to our sample of households in Oaxaca city. We feel confident that the data from these random samples are representative of the populations of the regional cities.

Mexico's Recent Economic History

For three decades after the end of World War II, Mexico experienced one of the longest and strongest periods of sustained economic growth known in the world. The nation moved from a rural country in which most of its citizens worked the land to an urban industrial society boasting a significant industrial capacity. Much of that industrial growth during the late 1960s and 1970s was made possible by Mexico's increasing oil reserves.

With the discovery of large oil deposits off the coast of Campeche, large and small banks flocked to Mexico eager to lend it money; loans were secured by the rising price of oil and the power of OPEC to control production. The money was used to finance a political and social welfare infrastructure. Because the government subsidized basic foodstuffs, it was possible for Mexican industry to pay wages approximately one tenth of those north of the Río Grande.

Through the early 1970s, Mexico was the example for all developing countries to follow. It was seen as a stable democracy that provided opportunities for industry and basic necessities for its citizens. The Institutionalized Revolutionary Party (PRI) might be the only party, but its ability to co-opt opposition, even after the 1968 student uprisings, gave it the appearance of an open party with local support. (For example, the PRI's candidate for president in 1994 was a leader in the student uprisings of 1968).

In September of 1976, President Luís Echeverría announced the first devaluation of the Mexican peso since World War II. Through most of his administration Echeverría had continued the economic policies of Miguel Alemán and Gustavo Díaz Ordáz by resisting any devaluation of the peso. By 1976, however, the peso was so overvalued that a devaluation could no longer be avoided, but, with all that oil, no one, not even the banks, was worried. Then, in 1982, Mexico announced it would not make the interest payment on its foreign debt and the peso suffered another slide. However, the price of oil was still rising and banks were willing to help roll over the debt on the assumption that Mexico's oil would increase in value. In the fall of 1986, the price of oil collapsed, and for the first time in three decades, Mexico suffered negative economic growth. President de la Madrid announced that the purpose of his administration would be to manage the crisis.

When they agreed to re-negotiate Mexico's debt, private lenders as well as the International Monetary Fund (IMF) and World Bank required Mexico to make significant structural adjustments to its economy. Subsidies were gradually removed from basic food products and wage increases were held significantly below inflation. Perhaps most important, Mexico agreed to join the General Agreement on Tariffs and Trade (GATT), opening its doors to foreign products. This reversed the policy of economic development based on "import substitution" in place since the administration of Miguel Alemán. Alemán took office in 1952 with the expressed goal of developing Mexico's industrial base through public works, which would build the infrastructure needed for industry, and protective tariffs, which would allow national industries to develop and "substitute" their products for those imported from abroad. This all ended with the crisis. Mexican capital and industry was forced to enter a new stage of competition, one in which products from the international market would be allowed to enter under terms set by the GATT board and not by national interest.

The impact on the economy was dramatic. Factories closed, inflation rose to an annual rate of more than 150 percent, and workers began wondering how they would feed their families. For most, the traditional Mexican solution of moving back to the land was no longer viable. Society was now urban and Mexican households had to adapt to the crisis in the cities of Mexico or, as many have done, in the cities and fields north of the Río Grande.

A good deal of research by economists, political scientists, sociologists, and anthropologists has focused on the effects of the crisis on the larger cities of Mexico (Bazán 1991; Cortez and Rubalcalva 1991; González de la Rocha 1986; González de la Rocha and Escobar Latapí 1991; Sheridan Prieto 1991; Schteingart 1989; Villarreal and Castañeda

1986). In addition, much has been written on the border region between Mexico and the United States and the *maquiladora* industry that has grown up there as Mexico has tried to create new jobs for its growing population by allowing multinational corporations to take advantage of the disparity between wages in Mexico and the price for finished products in the United States (Acevedo 1990; Canclini et al. 1989; Hiernaux 1986; Nolasco 1989).

One area that has not received a great deal of attention by researchers is how the crisis has affected the moderately-sized interior cities of Mexico and their hinterlands. Prior to the 1970s, Mexico's secondary cities had not suffered from the more dramatic problems of traffic congestion and pollution found in the nation's largest centers. However, since 1970, their rate of growth has been higher than Mexico City's.

For example, in the decade of the 1970s, the nine intermediate cities studied by Selby, Murphy, and Lorenzen (1990) had a global population increase of eighty percent compared to fifty-five percent for Mexico City and forty percent for Mexico as a whole. The difference in growth rates continued during the 1980s although not as dramatically. As a result, many of these cities are just now experiencing the effects of population growth without economic growth or investment in urban infrastructure.[2]

Oaxaca City and its Region

From the very founding of the grand city of Monte Albán, at about 500 B.C., on the top of the mountain where the three arms of the Valley of Oaxaca come together, the region we now know as Oaxaca City has been the central place for the valley and its hinterland (Blanton 1978; Blanton et al. 1982; Kowalewski et al. 1989). During that long history, the degree of integration and articulation between the valley and the wider world in which it was embedded, be it Mesoamerica or the Eurocentric world system after the arrival of the Spaniards (Wolf 1982), has ranged from strong linkages to almost complete isolation (Kowalewski and Finsten 1983; Murphy and Stepick 1991a).

Historically, those periods when the region was strongly linked to the outside world were those with the greatest degree of articulation within the valley and the greatest degree of social stratification and inequality (Kowalewski 1990; Murphy and Stepick 1991a, 1991b). In periods of engagement, Oaxaca City (here used synonymously with Monte Albán) grew relative to other cities in the region. During each period of engagement, the local economy grew and became subject to the vagaries of a world system. In each case local households adjusted their patterns of organization and demography as they attempted to deal with the new context in which they found themselves (Selby, Murphy and Lorenzen 1990; Murphy and Stepick 1991b).

The paving of the Pan American highway into the valley in the late 1940s changed the valley's relationship to the outside world. It was no longer necessary to ship goods in and out of Oaxaca over an inadequate rail line built during the reign of Porfirio Díaz (Chassen 1990), or over an unpaved road that traversed some of the most rugged terrain in Mexico. Locally produced goods such as leather, pottery, matches, beer and other consumer items were gradually replaced by goods manufactured in Puebla, Mexico City, Guadalajara and Monterrey or by local subsidiaries of national and international corporations. Shoes manufactured in the north of Mexico replaced local products and Coca-Cola and Pepsi-Cola established bottling plants in Oaxaca City and began a marketing campaign that would eventually reach the farthest valleys of the surrounding mountains. The increased trade brought on by this new link to the national and international economy increased commerce and prosperity in the region. However, it also brought new political conflicts. The state's local elite, who had only marginally supported the revolution, found themselves challenged for economic and political power by interests from Mexico City. Political unrest led to several uprisings in which governors were forced out of office and individuals lost their lives (Benítez Zenteno 1982; Bustamante et al. 1984).

As the national government strengthened its position in Oaxaca it increased the type of expenditures which would help it and its party consolidate power.[3] Increased numbers of government workers in Oaxaca City caused a housing shortage and consequent building and service boom. These middle class government workers wanted housing like they had in Mexico City and since many of their wives also worked they required increased restaurant and other services to help with domestic chores. As has happened in other central places, this service "boom" resulted in a migration spurt increasing Oaxaca City's population tenfold in the four decades after the road was paved.

240 *Economic Analysis Beyond the Local System*

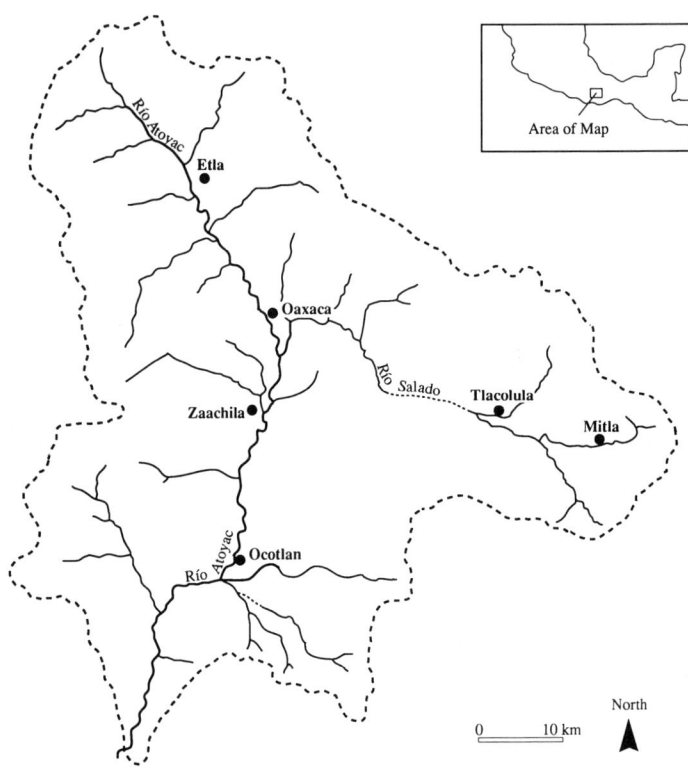

Figure 13.1: Study Locations in Oaxaca Valley.

Household Adaptations in a Regional Urban System 241

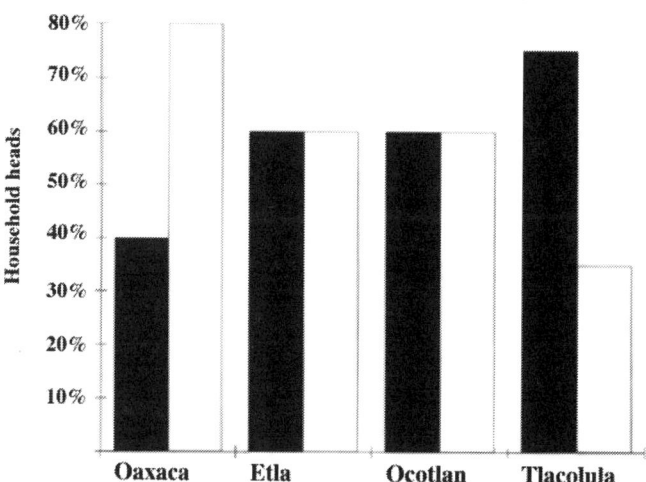

Figure 13.2: Migration.

Migration

Today fewer than fifty percent of the heads of household in Oaxaca City were born there (Figure 13.2). Most of these individuals have moved to Oaxaca from within the state. As Rees et al. (1991) point out, most have migrated from either the central valleys, where the city's influence is strongest, or from those district capitals where roads and schools were first introduced. The importance of these links cannot be underestimated. In Mexico in general, and Oaxaca in particular, the purpose of road building and schools is to bring "marginal" regions and peoples into the national discourse. "Mexicanization," linking individuals, households, villages and regions to the Mexican national system through trade and culture, has been, and continues to be, a state priority. Roads built to take forest goods out of the mountains to the Pacific and Gulf coasts also bring industrial products in the form of plastic buckets, manufactured clothing and processed foods to individuals and villages who now have a modest cash income which they can exchange for products from the same international market that purchased their primary products.

The same roads bring school teachers whose primary duty is to teach children the Spanish language and Mexican identity. In the context of Mexico's post World War II developing industrial economy, it was easy for a child with six years of education who could read, write and do basic arithmetic, to move to one of Mexico's growing industrial and tourist centers and find a job.

The same migration effects occurred in the regional capitals around Oaxaca City. In both Etla and Ocotlán, forty percent of the current heads of household were not originally from those cities. This figure does not seem remarkable for Etla, which is only twenty kilometers from Oaxaca City and sits on both rail and highway links between Oaxaca and Mexico City (Kowalewski and Saindon 1991). Ocotlán, on the other hand, is over thirty kilometers from Oaxaca City, "on the way to nowhere," unless you are traveling to Pochutla or Puerto Escondido over a road that is even more treacherous than the one from Mexico City to Oaxaca.

The striking anomaly among these three regional capitals is Tlacolula. Only twenty kilometers from Oaxaca City on the Pan American highway, Tlacolula is overwhelmingly made up of residents who were born there. Only twenty-five percent of the heads of household are migrants. This strong endogamy may account for Tlacolula's reputation as a "closed" community of people who do not like outside business or governmental interests.[4] We shall return to Tlacolula again below.

A further measure of integration through migration is the number of households in each regional capital that have a relative living in Oaxaca City. Etla, Tlacolula, and Ocotlán were some of the first cities to have paved transportation to Oaxaca City. The transportation and communication network intensified the flow of commerce in and out of Oaxaca City. Young men and women could leave for school in morning and return in the evening. The Valley of Oaxaca became more and more integrated as a single urban system where "urban/rural" dichotomy had little meaning (Uzzell 1976; Murphy and Stepick 1978). Given this long history of linkage we expect a substantial percentage of the households in each of these cities to have relatives in Oaxaca. Again, we find that Etla and Ocotlán are similar in meeting our expectations (Figure 13.2). In each case approximately sixty percent of the households have a relative living in Oaxaca City, indicating a significant tie to the central capital. Once again, Tlacolula stands apart from the other cases. There, only slightly over a third of the households reported having a relative living in Oaxaca City, further demonstrating the historic and continuing animosity between Tlacolula and any centralized government.

Migrant Workers

This does not mean that Tlacolulans do not migrate and are not tied to the world economy. The district of which Tlacolula is the capital is well known for its linkages to the wider world economy. During the days of "import substitution," when it was difficult to purchase foreign electronic and other consumer durables, Tlacolula was the home for a thriving smuggler market. Each Sunday an entire section in the middle of its weekly rotating market (Beals 1975) was devoted to goods which had entered Mexico under dubious circumstances. The weaving villages of Teotitlán del Valle (Stephen 1991) and Mitla (Parsons 1936) each have long histories of sending members to work in the United States. In particular, during the *bracero* program which lasted from World War II until the mid 1960s, many men from this region traveled to the United States to work as temporary farm laborers. These ties have continued to the present. They are so strong that in some communities in the Tlacolula wing of the valley it is considered a "rite of passage" for a young man to spend some time working "*en el otro lado*," on the other side of the border.

In addition to those who go to work in the United States, many households send workers to other parts of Mexico (Figure 13.3). This is the case for one-quarter of the households in the central valleys of Oaxaca. However, as is the case for almost every socioeconomic variable, the degree and nature of migrations varies among the cities we studied. Rates range from twenty-five percent for Oaxaca City, expected since much of Oaxaca is made up of migrants who moved there looking for a better life, to thirty percent in Etla and Tlacolula, reflecting the lack of economic activity and opportunity in these regions as well as their long standing links with the national economy.

244 *Economic Analysis Beyond the Local System*

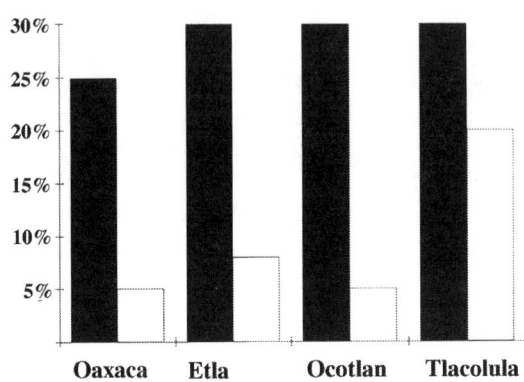

Figure 13.3: Households With Non-Resident Workers.

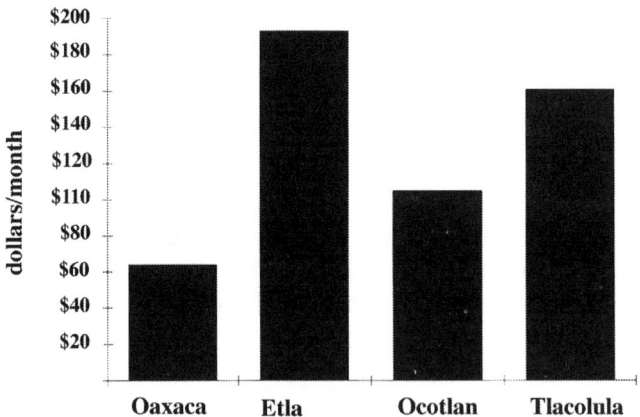

Figure 13.4: Average Remittance, for Houseolds Receiving Remittances.

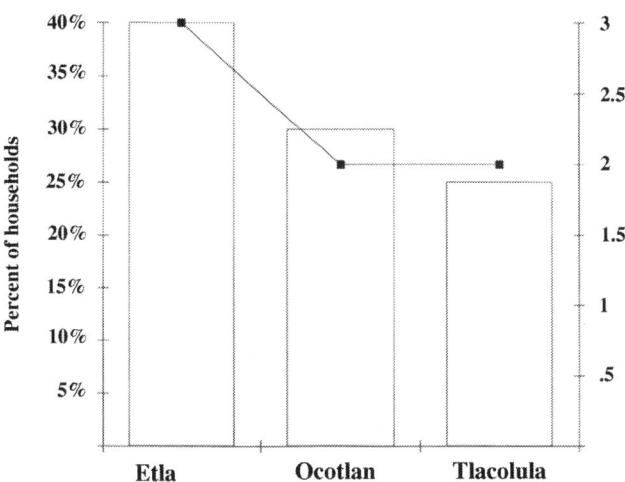

Figure 13.5: Purchases in Oaxaca City.

Remittances

The funds households receive from members not living at home are quite significant. In Tlacolula, twenty percent or so of the households receive an average of nearly U.S. $160 a month from an external member (Figure 13.4). In Ocotlán, where not as many households have migrant workers and therefore fewer households receives remittances, the figure is close to $140 dollars a month. Even in Oaxaca City where the lowest percentage of households receive remittances and the average amount is the lowest, the $80 received per month is still close to an official minimum salary of U.S. $100/month. Previous calculations (Lorenzen et al. 1989) indicate that, on average, children living at home who work contribute about one half a minimum wage to the household. In addition, they must be fed and housed. This means that, in reality, for those households that receive remittances, the external worker is worth much more than an individual at home. They return more than workers residing in the home and at the same time do not have to be housed or fed.

Thus, while the numbers of workers and the amounts they send home vary from district capital to district capital, all of these cities are clearly linked to Oaxaca City and the national and world economic system. More than twenty-five percent of the households in each district travel to Oaxaca City to make purchases and many households in Etla make the trip three times a month (Figure 13.5). The national and state governments argue that this increased commerce is largely responsible for the national economic recovery that has made Mexico the example held up by the World Bank and IMF to the rest of the world's debtor nations.

The recovery, however is not the same everywhere. It seems to be having a greater impact in the regional centers than in Oaxaca City. Twenty to thirty percent of the households in the regional centers feel they are better off economically today than they were five years ago. In the city of Oaxaca the figure is closer to eight percent. There, the vast majority of households say they have simply held their ground. Our longitudinal data allows us to see what households in Oaxaca had to do in order to hold their place in society.

Oaxaca City 1977-1992 (Appendix)

The Crisis (1977-1987)

As is well known, Mexico and much of the developing world suffered some of the effects of a severe economic crisis in the late 1970s and into the 1980s. The crisis was the combined result of over-lending and over-borrowing on the international market combined, and in the case of Mexico and other oil-producing states, with a collapse in the world price for oil. As a result, Mexico, for the first time in well over three decades, suffered several years of negative economic growth. Households, like nations and international capital, had to adjust to this new economic reality.

In the years of economic crisis, median household incomes suffered a significant decline, despite the fact that more individuals per household were in the work force. The proportion of households with two or more workers rose from slightly over thirty percent to nearly sixty percent. Most importantly for household social organization, a large number of these second workers were female heads of household who could no longer afford to stay at home taking care of the house and children. Forced to move into the informal labor market where salaries tend to be low and job security non-existent in order to supplement the household income, they had to leave the daily management of the household to older children and work two shifts, one for cash income and the other unpaid at home.

Not wanting to increase the number of biological children in the home and needing extra help quickly, some households incorporated an extended member into the home. This individual, often a relative from the home community, works in the home with the expectation that he or she, most probably she, will be able to attend school and increase her employment skills by helping the relative in the city. In most cases, it does not work out that way. The weight of taking care of the house all day makes it difficult to attend any type of educational institution.

We can see, then, that by 1987, at the height of the economic crisis in Mexico, Oaxaca's households had imploded. They had reduced their dependency ratios (the number of individuals each worker had to support) by holding household size constant and putting more people to work. Even so, they suffered a decline in real income.

The Recovery (1987-1992)

By 1992 things had begun to look better. As reflected in the national income accounts as well as IMF and World Bank reports, the economy was back on track. Incomes were back to their pre-crisis levels. Reflecting increased incomes, more households in Oaxaca City were able to afford consumer goods such as refrigerators, although the percentage of households with automobiles remained essentially unchanged (Figure 13.6).

Increased income, however, does not mean that households have been able to return to their pre-crisis style of organization. Over fifty percent of household heads work in the informal sector with no benefits, and female heads of households continue their high post-crisis levels of participation in the labor force. The numbers of workers per individual in each household remains approximately one worker for every two household members. There was a seven percent increase in the number of households with three or more workers even though household size was declining as households lost, on average, nearly half a member each.

248 Economic Analysis Beyond the Local System

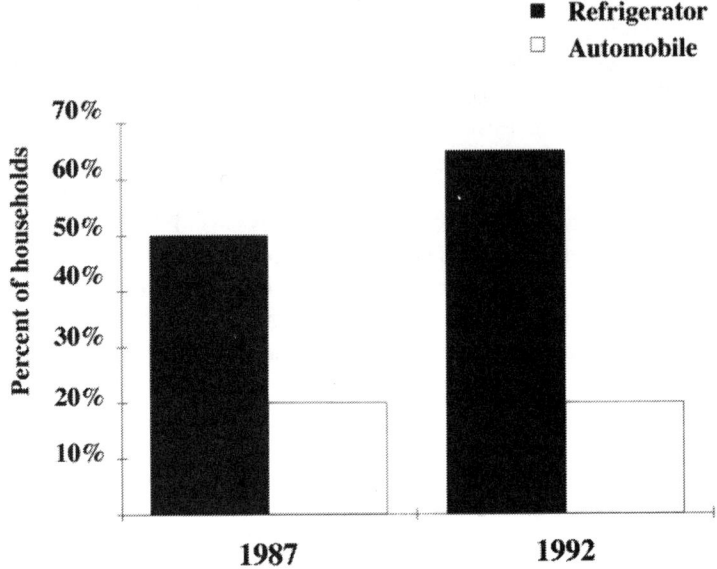

Figure 13.6: Consumer Durables

Conclusions

For two millennia prior to the arrival of the Spanish, the valley of Oaxaca was the site of a complex urban-centered system whose political and economic relations to the wider world were reflected the region's social stratification and in the daily lives of its people (Kowalewski and Finsten 1983; Kowalewski 1990; and Murphy and Stepick 1991b). With the arrival of the Spanish, Oaxaca was brought directly into a centralized system centered in Mexico City with links to the world economy through Spain. After independence in 1821, Mexico went through a series of periods of greater or lesser unification.

Today, Mexico is unified through a strong central government that attempts to control access to resources and the world economy through the apparatus of the state. The result is that once again the Oaxaca Valley is a strong regional system focused on the state capital. At the same time, we can also see that migration and other economic linkages tie regional capitals and the world system bypassing Oaxaca City altogether. This may account for the higher levels of economic optimism in the three district capitals compared to attitudes in Oaxaca City itself.

Mexico's entry into the GATT and NAFTA trade international agreements increased Oaxaca's ties to the national and world system. And, as in the past, this increased the total amount of wealth in both Mexico and Oaxaca. However, again as in the past, this wealth is increasingly concentrated among the rich and powerful and away from those in the middle and lower ends of the economic scale. Since 1984, Mexico's income distribution steadily shifted towards the top ten percent of the households to the extent that today Mexico has 24 of the 358 individuals on Forbes' list of super millionaires, while as recently as 1982 Mexico had only two on the list, one a banker and the other an industrialist. Reflecting Mexico's shifting economy, the current group consists mostly of individuals in consumer products and banking as opposed to manufacturing and heavy industry.

During this same period, less wealthy households have stabilized or increased their income by raising the number of workers per unit and the number of hours each works. In the district capitals, such workers are often migrants to other parts of Mexico or the United States. In Oaxaca City, households intensify activity within the resident domestic unit itself, increasing the number of workers (especially women) and supporting fewer members per worker.

This is why, despite Mexico's renewed prosperity, residents of Oaxaca City say they are worse off. They can remember back to the pre-crisis period when they could aspire to a refrigerator with only one male worker who probably also had access to social security benefits. Under the new regime they need two workers and even then they may not achieve the standard of living they had before.

Appendix: Comparison of Household Socioeconomic Indicators in Oaxaca City

	Survey Year		
	1977	1987	1992
Median Income*	$193	$123	$220
Number of Workers (mean)	1.4	1.9	2.1
0	6%	1%	2%
1	61%	43%	37%
2	22%	36%	34%
3+	1%	2%	27%
Female Heads Working**	25%	4%	5%
Female Household Heads in the Informal Sector†	65%	75%	7%
Household Size (mean)	5.3	5.6	5.2
Extended Households	20%	30%	30%
Worker Dependency Ratio	3.9	2.9	3.0
Male Household Heads in the Informal Sector	40%	60%	55%

*1987 dollars.
**Reported earning an income from any source
†No fringe benefits

Notes

1. Support for this research has come from the National Science Foundation; the Fulbright program; the Department of Human Development and Family Studies, the College of Home Economics and the World Food Institute at Iowa State University; the Institute of Environmental Studies at Baylor University; the Center for Applied Research in Anthropology at Georgia State University; the Department of Design, Housing and Apparel at the University of Minnesota; the Mexico Center at the Institute of Latin American Studies at the University of Texas at Austin; and the Welte Institute for Oaxacan Studies, Inc. The authors would like to thank Martha W. Rees, Pedro Pacheco, Brian Riley, Henry A. Selby and Deborah Winslow who made special contributions to this paper.

2. In this paper we use population figures for the cities studied by Selby et al. (1990) to represent secondary cities in Mexico. They are Querétaro, San Luís Potosí, Tampico, Reynosa, Mexicali, Mazatlán, Oaxaca, Villahermosa, and Merida. While perhaps not representative in a statistical sense, these cities do represent a cross section of secondary cities with respect to economic activity, size, and place in the national system of cities.

3. Despite increased economic activity and government expenditures, Oaxaca was and continues to be one of the poorest states in Mexico (Unikel 1976; Osuña Castelán 1990).

4. The "closed corporate" nature of Tlacolula was demonstrated during the time of this research. As a result of a contested election the state government took over the running of the city's affairs. As a result there were two "municipal" governments operating in Tlacolula in 1992. We found that we could not show our permission letters for the interviews for fear of offending supporters of one side or the other.

References

Acevedo, María Luisa
    1990 *Los Municipios de las Fronteras de México: El Medio Ambiente.* Mexico, D. F.: Centro de Ecodesarrollo.
Bazán, Lucía
    1991 *Vivienda Para los Obreros: Reproducción de Clase y Condiciones Urbanas.* Mexico, D. F.: Ediciones de la Casa Chata.
Beals, Ralph L.
    1975 *The Peasant Marketing System of Oaxaca.* Mexico. Berkeley: University of California Press.
Benítez Zenteno, Raúl, ed.
    1980 *Sociedad y Política en Oaxaca 1980: 15 Estudios de Caso.* Oaxaca: Instituto de Investigaciones Sociológicas, Universidad Autónoma Benito Juarez de Oaxaca.
Blanton, Richard E.
    1978 *Monte Albán: Settlement Patterns at the Ancient Zapotec Capital.* New York: Academic Press.
Blanton, Richard E., Stephen A. Kowalewski, Gary Feinman, and Jill Appel
    1982 *Monte Albán's Hinterland, Part I: The Prehispanic Settlement Patterns of the Central and Southern Parts of the Valley of Oaxaca, Mexico.* Memoirs of the Museum of Anthropology, No. 15. Ann Arbor: University of Michigan.
Bustamante, V. R., P. Cuauhtémoc González, F. J. Ruíz, C. M. Lozano, S. Millan E., and F. A. Gomezjara
    1984 *Oaxaca, una Lucha Reciente: 1960-1983.* Mexico: Ediciones Nueva Sociología.

Canclini, Néstor García, Patricia Safa and Lourdes Grobet
  1989 *Tijuana: La Casa de Toda la Gente.* Mexico, D. F.: Conaculta.
Chassen, Francie R.
  1990 *Regiones y Ferrocarriles en la Oaxaca Porfirista.* Oaxaca: Obra Negra.
Cook, Scott and Martin Diskin, eds.
  1976 *Markets in Oaxaca.* Austin: University of Texas Press.
Cortez, Fernando and Rosa María Rubalcalva
  1991 *Autoexplotación Forzada y Equidad por Emprobrecimiento.* Mexico, D. F.: Colegio de Mexico.
González de la Rocha, Mercedes
  1986 *Los Recursos de la Pobreza: Familias de Bajos Ingresos de Guadalajara.* Guadalajara: El Colegio de Jalisco.
Gonzáles de la Rocha, Mercedes and Agustín Escobar Latapí
  1991 *Social Responses to Mexico's Economic Crisis of the 1980s.* United States-Mexico Contemporary Perspectives Series, No. 1. La Jolla, California: Center for United States-Mexican Studies.
Hiernaux, Daniel
  1986 *Urbanización y Autoconstruccion de Vivienda en Tijuana.* Mexico, D. F.: Centro de Ecodesarrollo.
Kowalewski, Stephen A.
  1990 The Evolution of Complexity in the Valley of Oaxaca. *Annual Review of Anthropology* 19:29-58. Palo Alto, California: Annual Reviews, Inc.
Kowalewski, Stephen A., and Laura Finsten
  1983 The Economic Systems of Ancient Oaxaca: A Regional Perspective. *Current Anthropology* 24:413-441.
Kowalewski, Stephen A. and Jacqueline J. Saindon
  1991 The Spread of Literacy in a Latin American Peasant Society: Oaxaca, Mexico, 1890-1980. *Comparative Studies in Society and History* 34(1):110-140.
Kowalewski, Stephen A., Arthur D. Murphy and Ignacio Cabrera F.
  1984 Yu?, Be?e, and Casa: 3500 Years of Continuity in Residential Construction. *Ekistics* 51:354-359.
Kowalewski, Stephen A., Gary Feinman, Laura Finsten, Richard E. Blanton, and Linda M. Nichols
  1989 *Monte Albán's Hinterland, Part II: Prehispanic Settlement Patterns in Tlacolula, Etla, and Ocotlán, the Valley of Oaxaca, Mexico.* Museum of Anthropology, Memoirs, No. 23. Ann Arbor: Museum of Anthropology, University of Michigan.
Lorenzen, Stephen A., Arthur D. Murphy, and Henry A. Selby
  1989 Household Budgetary Strategies in Urban Mexico: Mediating the Income-Consumption Nexus. In *Problems and Issues in the Study of Consumption.* Benjamin Orlove and Henry Rutz, eds. Monographs in Economic Anthropology, No. 6. Lanham, Maryland: University Press of America and Society for Economic Anthropology.

Morris, Earl W.
1991 Household, Kin and Nonkin Sources of Assistance in Home Building: The Case of the City of Oaxaca. *Urban Anthropology* 20(1):49-66.

Murphy, Arthur D.
1991 City in Crisis: Introduction and Overview. *Urban Anthropology* 20(1):1-13.

Murphy, Arthur D. and Alex Stepick
1978 Economic and Social Integration among Urban Peasants. *Human Organization* 37(4):394-397.
1991a Oaxaca's Cycles of Conquest. *Urban Anthropology* 20(1):99-107.
1991b *Social Inequality in Oaxaca: A History of Resistance and Change.* Philadelphia: Temple University Press.

Murphy, Arthur D., Martha W. Rees, Karen French, Earl W. Morris, and Mary Winter
1990 Informal Sector and the Crisis in Oaxaca, Mexico: A Comparison of Households 1977-1987. In *Perspectives on the Informal Economy.* Estelie Smith, ed. Monographs in Economic Anthropology, No. 8. Lanham, Maryland: University Press of America and Society for Economic Anthropology.

Nolasco, Margarita
1990 *Los Municipios de las Fronteras de México: Economía y Trabajo.* México, D. F.: Centro de Ecodesarrollo.

Osuña Castelán, Germán
1990 Dinámica de la Desigualdad Regional en México 1970-1980. *Estudios Demográficos y Urbanos* 5(1):5-35.

Pacheco Vásquez, Pedro D., Earl W. Morris, Mary Winter, and Arthur D. Murphy
1991 Neighborhood Type, Housing and Housing Characteristics in Oaxaca. *Urban Anthropology* 20(1):31-48.

Parsons, Elsie Worthington Clews
1936 *Mitla: Town of the Souls.* Chicago: University of Chicago Press.

Rees, Martha W., Arthur D. Murphy, Earl W. Morris and Mary Winter
1991 Migrants To and In Oaxaca City. *Urban Anthropology* 20(1):15-29.

Schteingart, Martha
1989 *Los Productores del Espacio Habitable: Estado, Empresa Y Sociedad en la Ciudad de México.* Mexico, D. F.: El Colegio de México.

Selby, Henry A.
1991 The Oaxacan Urban Household and the Crisis. *Urban Anthropology* 20(1):87-98.

Selby, Henry A., Arthur D. Murphy, and Stephen A. Lorenzen
1990 *The Mexican Urban Household: Organizing for Self-Defense.* Austin: University of Texas Press.

Selby, Henry A., Arthur D. Murphy, Stephen A. Lorenzen, Earl W. Morris, and Mary Winter
  1990 La Familia Urbana Mexicana Frente A La Crisis. In *Estudios Sobre la Sociedad Urbana en México*. Guillermo de la Peña, Juan Manuel Durán, Agustín Escobar y Javier García de Alba, eds. Guadalajara: Universidad de Guadalajara/CIESAS.
Sheridan Prieto, Cecilia
  1991 *Espacios Domésticos: Los Trabajadores de la Reproducción*. Mexico, D. F.: Ediciones de la Casa Chata.
Stephen, Lynn
  1991 *Zapotec Women*. Austin: University of Texas Press.
Sutro, Livingston D. and Theodore E. Downing
  1988 A Step Toward a Grammar of Space: Domestic Space Use in Zapotec Villages. In *Household and Community in the Mesoamerican Past*. Richard R. Wilk and Wendy Ashmore, eds. Pp. 29-50. Albuquerque: University of New Mexico Press.
Unikel, Luis
  1976 *El Desarrollo Urbano de México*. Mexico, D. F.: El Colegio de Mexico.
Uzzell, Douglas
  1976 Ethnography of Migration: Breaking out of the Bi-Polar Myth. In *New Approaches to the Study of Migration*. David Guillet and Douglas Uzzell, eds. Houston: Rice University Press.
Villarreal, Diana R. and Víctor Castañeda
  1986 *Urbanización Y Autoconstrucción de Vivienda en Monterrey*. Mexico, D. F.: Centro de Ecodesarrollo Editorial Claves Latinoamericas.
Whalen, Michael E.
  1988 House and Household in Formative Oaxaca. In *Household and Community in the Mesoamerican Past*. Richard R. Wilk and Wendy Ashmore, eds. Pp. 249-272. Albuquerque: University of New Mexico Press.
Winter, Mary
  1991 Interhousehold Exchange of Goods and Services in the City of Oaxaca. *Urban Anthropology* 20(1):67-86.
Winter, Mary, Earl W. Morris and Arthur D. Murphy
  1990 Planning and Implementation in the Informal Sector: Evidence from Oaxaca, Mexico. *City and Society* 4(2):131-143.
Wolf, Eric R.
  1982 *Europe and the People Without History*. Berkeley: University of California Press.

14

Structural Adjustment, Hometowns, and Local Development in Nigeria[1]

Lillian Trager

(SAP) has destabilized everything. Things are getting difficult with every passing day.
Interviewee in Iwoye-Ijesa, May 1992

The masses are angry. SAP has pushed Nigeria's poor to the wall, and they are angry as hell.
Headline, Citizen *magazine, 18 May 1992*

Government cannot do everything alone.
Osun State Administrator,
Daily Times *newspaper, 25 November 1991*

Introduction

Sometime during 1992, the then President of Nigeria, General Ibrahim Babangida, was widely quoted as having said that he did not understand why the Nigerian economy had not completely collapsed. More recently, another senior official was reported to have said, ". . . The state of the Nigerian economy is still anything but promising. All the relevant macroeconomic indices portend problems, and a steady deterioration in the standard of living of the populace" (*The News* 11 October 1993). These statements followed a period of years during which Nigeria had promulgated, and presumably implemented, a set of economic reform policies known as the Structural Adjustment Program (SAP), designed to address a number of earlier economic problems. Like many other third world countries, Nigeria's Structural Adjustment Program, initiated in 1985 and 1986, followed the general plan promoted by the International Monetary Fund and the World Bank, although it was not directly mandated by them.

The reasons for this deepening crisis of the Nigerian economy have been widely discussed and debated. Likewise, there has been considerable discussion regarding the effects of the Structural Adjustment Program—who has benefited, who has been hurt, and how. Yet, relatively little consideration has been given to the effects of SAP and the broader economic crisis at local levels, on specific communities, and on specific local processes and activities.

The goal of the chapter is to examine the ways in which structural adjustment and the economic crisis in Nigeria have affected local activities in local communities. In particular, I am concerned with the effect on local-level development activities, that is, efforts by people to make some change in community life through organizations, fund raising, building projects, and so forth. The paper focuses on such efforts in one region, the Ijesa area of southwestern Nigeria.

I argue that two broad, and somewhat contradictory, trends are apparent in the effects of SAP on participation and involvement in local development efforts. On the one hand, SAP has resulted in a perception by the vast majority of people that they have less money to contribute to local development, a perception no doubt rooted in the economic realities of the past few years. On the other hand, government is spending less, and therefore the need for such contributions is greater. There is great emphasis on the need for community self-reliance, and community fund raising efforts have expanded greatly. Some key individuals, with access to considerable financial and personal resources, are making sizeable contributions which have potential for considerable impact on local development, at least in the short run. For the most part, the resources that such individuals draw on come from outside the local community, and they themselves are usually resident outside the community although deeply involved in the affairs of the locale which they consider to be "home."

Thus, while one effect of SAP has been an increased call for local participation and contributions to development, it has, at the same time, led to increasing reliance on those well-off and well-connected individuals, originally from the community but now resident elsewhere, who have access to resources and networks beyond the local community. By focusing on a set of processes broadly termed "local development," this paper asks how the global economic changes of the past few years have affected the local. It raises as well the question of what the "local" is in this context.

Journalistic and scholarly discussion of the effects of SAP in Nigeria clearly portray a society in severe economic crisis. Just how that crisis is

Structural Adjustment, Hometowns, and Local Development 257

playing out—not simply who is benefiting and who is hurt, but more significantly, what they are doing about it—is much less clear. Recent work on the response of individuals and households suggests great complexity and dynamism (Mustapha 1991). This paper suggests that at the level of communities, as well, there are also complex and dynamic processes taking place. It may well be that the answer to President Babangida's question about why the economy had not completely collapsed lies in the resiliency resulting from the wide variety of economic activities and strategies of individuals, households, and communities that respond rapidly and in a number of different ways to a continually changing and unpredictable situation.

The first part of the paper provides an overview of SAP and of the more general economic crisis in Nigeria. The paper then examines data collected during field research in Nigeria in 1991-92. Two types of data will be considered: survey data about the effects of SAP, and interview and ethnographic data about local development activities. The data derive from research in five communities—a city, two medium-sized towns, and two small towns—all in the Ijesa area of Southwestern Nigeria.

The Economic Crisis and Structural Adjustment in Nigeria

In 1987, Nigeria was ranked by the World Bank as a "middle-income" economy, with a ranking of 54th in the world; by 1989 its designation had been changed to "low-income" and by 1990 it was ranked as the 17th poorest country in the world (World Bank 1987; 1989; 1990). This low ranking has continued up to the present. The GNP per capita has declined, according to The World Bank *Development Report*, from $800 in 1987 to $340 in 1993 (World Bank 1993).

A major oil producer and a member of OPEC, Nigeria went from oil-based boom into rapid decline in the early and mid 1980s. In 1986, the military government headed by General Babangida instituted a set of economic reforms. A number of policies were promulgated, but the one that received the most attention was the devaluation of the currency. By the late 1980s, however, it was clear that the economic situation was worsening, a situation that has continued up to the present.

In this section of the chapter I provide: (1) a brief review of the economic situation prior to the introduction of the Structural Adjustment Program; (2) a description of the policies that were instituted as part of the reform efforts; and (3) a discussion of some of the dimensions of the continuing crisis as it is felt by various sectors of Nigerian society.

The Economy Prior to SAP

In the early and mid-1980s, the Nigerian economy went from oil-based boom into rapid decline. The following statement by a leading businessman in 1985 summarizes the situation at that time:

> Our economy became dominated by a single commodity—oil and . . . it provided 25% of our Gross Domestic Product, 95% of our foreign exchange earnings and 60% of Federal Government revenues in 1985. At the same time the world economy reflected a fall in oil prices and Nigeria's earnings from oil exports became less than half of what they used to be. Nigeria had a crushing debt service burden which was consuming 40-50% of the foreign exchange and part of the remainder was swallowed by imports of the agricultural products which were necessary to feed the population but which we should be capable of producing in the country (Shonekan 1985:1-2).

During the period of the oil boom, the country had become heavily dependent on imports; this was exacerbated by policies of the civilian government in the Second Republic (1979-1983) which included the importation of cheap rice and other grains. Nigerian agricultural production declined substantially and commodities that had been major exports and earners of foreign exchange, such as cocoa, became much less important. In addition, the currency was greatly overvalued; for a time in the early 1980s the exchange rate was fixed at N1 to $1.50; up until 1986, just prior to the introduction of SAP, there were very strict currency regulations and the rate was N1 to $1.00.

The Structural Adjustment Program was not the first effort to institute economic reforms; there had been earlier attempts by previous governments (Phillips 1987:1). In the late 1970s, the regime of General Obasanjo responded to a decline in oil revenues by introducing a variety of "austerity" measures, which included banning various imported consumer goods. Likewise, the civilian government of President Shagari introduced austerity measures to reduce imports in 1982. These regimes also introduced programs that were supposed to increase agricultural production: Obasanjo introduced Operation Feed the Nation, while Shagari had his Green Revolution Programme. The latter "could hardly

Structural Adjustment, Hometowns, and Local Development 259

be identified except in the form of preferential tariffs, granted panel vans and agricultural implements. The . . . regime presided over the collapse of the programme as it embarked on massive politically motivated importation of foodstuff, the most notorious of which was rice" (O. Olashore 1991:30).

By 1984, when Nigeria returned to a government under military rule, there were further cutbacks in government expenditures and additional efforts to reduce imports. Despite the considerable debt burden and the decreasing revenues available from oil, however, the Buhari regime was not able to come to an agreement with the International Monetary Fund for a loan, as it refused to fulfill IMF conditionalities of trade liberalization, removal of petroleum subsidies, and devaluation of the currency (O. Olashore 1991:51).

The Structural Adjustment Program

In June 1986, the government began its Structural Adjustment Program. What was most noteworthy at the time was the debate that preceded the announcement of the SAP policies, a wide-ranging public debate about whether the country should take a loan from the International Monetary Fund and meet the Fund's conditionalities. The newspapers and magazines at the time were filled with articles from a wide variety of viewpoints, there were public speeches and debates and, in general, it was probably a period of some of the most open debate that has been seen in the country. (For discussion of the issues leading up to the debate and of the debate itself, see, for example, articles in Olukoshi, ed. 1991; O. Olashore 1991). In the end, the decision was made not to take an IMF loan. However, many of the same policies that would have been adopted under an IMF loan became part of Nigeria's SAP program. Nigerian commentators have therefore argued that in fact the SAP program is basically a conventional IMF/World Bank mandated set of policies. For example, one academic analyst argues:

> Although Nigeria presents us with an interesting, even unique example of a state that is undergoing market reforms without actually taking an IMF loan, it would be too far fetched and too misleading to suggest that these reforms were themselves the exclusive creations of Nigerians . . . What structural adjustment represented when it was formally launched in 1986 was the total capitulation of the state to the conditionality clauses of the Fund . . . It was only after the Nigerian programme was launched that

260 Economic Analysis Beyond the Local System

various social forces in the country began to struggle to stamp their own influence on it . . . If, therefore, there is anything authentically Nigerian about the adjustment programme which the state has been implementing, it is the stamp which the reality of the domestic politics of adjustment has imposed on what is essentially an orthodox IMF economic recovery package (Olukoshi 1991a:77-78).

Even those who argue that Nigeria's SAP is unique and "her own creation" agree that the basic orientation is directed and supervised by the IMF and the World Bank (Phillips 1987:6; see also Callaghy 1993:489-491 for discussion of the role of the World Bank in developing these policies).

The policies mandated under SAP included devaluation of the currency; deregulation; reduction of administrative controls and greater reliance on market forces; trade and payments liberalization; privatization of public enterprises; removal of oil subsidies; and adoption of measures to stimulate production and broaden the supply base of the economy (Phillips 1987:2; see also O. Olashore 1991:70-87). Efforts at diversifying the productive base of the economy led to the development of several new government bodies, such as the Directorate of Food, Roads and Rural Infrastructure (DFRRI), which was established to improve flows of resources to rural areas.

However, the greatest attention has been focused on the implementation of the first of the above list of policies—devaluation of the currency, the Naira. Widely (though not universally) agreed to have been overvalued in the early 1980s, devaluation was the first and fastest of the SAP policies to be implemented, with the institution first of what was called the Second Tier Foreign Exchange Market (SFEM). By 1987, the exchange rate had gone from N1 equal to $1.00 in 1985 to N4 equal to $1.00. By March 1992, the official exchange rate was N9 to $1.00; at that time, the government decided that the official exchange rate should be essentially equal to the black market rate. This decision led rapidly to further devaluation so that by May-June 1992, the rate was about N20 to $1.00. The decline in the value of the Naira continued; by December 1993, the parallel market rate was N40 or more to $1.00. The current regime has attempted to stem that decline by once again establishing a fixed official exchange rate, announcing in the budget speech in January 1994 that the official rate is fixed at N22 to $1.00 (*NewsUpdate* 10 January 1994).

Structural Adjustment, Hometowns, and Local Development 261

Exchange rates may not seem to be central to an understanding of local economies, or of the way in which economic activities in local communities are affected by global processes. However, in the case of Nigeria, exchange rates are fundamental to an understanding both of how people's livelihoods are being affected and to an understanding of how people perceive their economic situation. It is not just the newspaper columnists and professional business commentators who have been commenting on the rapid decline of the Naira. Ordinary people—taxi drivers, market women, office workers—usually are familiar with the exchange rate, and, even in small rural communities, comments are often made to the effect that the decline in the value of the Naira has affected the economic situation. It is not that these people are dealing in foreign exchange. Rather, their comments reflect the situation that has developed during and since the oil boom: the importance of imported items and the fact that even those who work as farmers and traders buy goods that are either imported or made with imported raw materials.

The SAP policies have been variously implemented. For example, the degree to which public enterprises have been privatized has been quite variable. While petroleum prices have increased over the years, there has been a continuing debate on the complete removal of subsidies, and rioting in major cities when attempts have been made to increase the prices of fuel, most recently in fall 1993. Furthermore, all of the policies have had political implications. As Ihonvbere (1993:145) put it in a recent article, "The gains [resulting from SAP policies] are constantly eroded by the inconsistency, insincerity, corruption and inefficiency of the government." Callaghy (1993) has argued that the attempt to carry out a transition from military to civilian rule simultaneously with structural adjustment (an attempt which failed with the annulment of the June 1993 elections by President Babangida) mitigated against the successful implementation of SAP; he states that "as the return to democratic rule came closer, the economic reform effort continued to fray" (p. 494).

Recent discussions of Nigeria's economic problems have pointed to massive corruption, high expenditures by the military, and a variety of "extra-budgetary" demands from all levels of government (Callaghy 1993). An official in Babangida's transitional government was quoted as having said that by mid 1993, the extra-budgetary requests that had not been honored exceeded N40 billion. "It appears that all units, ministries, department, security agencies and the Presidency regard the approved official budget as a trivial and irrelevant document" (*The News* 11

October 1993). He also pointed out the impossibility of "objectively determining" the actual revenue accruable to government. As Callaghy (1993:493) makes clear, massive amounts of oil revenues have been siphoned off to private interests; in 1991, the *Financial Times* reported that about $3 billion of the oil windfall that Nigeria received as a result of the Gulf War was unaccounted for.

Effects of SAP

While the Structural Adjustment Program refers to a specific set of policies that were first implemented in 1986, the debate and criticism of SAP tends to reflect the response not only to those policies *per se*, but to the much wider economic crisis that began in the early 1980s and that is continuing and in fact worsening. It is often difficult to separate what is an effect of SAP, in the narrow sense of those specific policies, and what is the effect of the continuing crisis. This is true both in the published discussions of SAP and to an even greater extent, in the responses of ordinary citizens. The fieldwork discussed below took place during a period when the effects of a disastrous economic situation were felt in one way or another by almost everyone; as a result, when people were asked about the "effects of SAP," they tended, not surprisingly, to respond in terms of the effects of the overall economic situation.

While some economists supported SAP and others opposed it from the outset, the general descriptions of the current situation are remarkably similar across a broad spectrum of observers. Newspapers and magazines have been particularly graphic in their descriptions. One magazine provides a photograph of garbage pickers and the headline, "Nigerians became poorer and poorer amidst stupendous resources and wealth just because of incoherent economic policies and a badly managed structural adjustment programme" (*Tell* 13 April 1992), while another provides more details: "The total effect of SAP was to shoot up the prices of food, housing and transportation. The army of unemployed persons expanded, and social services for the poor and the middle classes all but withered away" (*Citizen* 18 May 1992). A similar analysis of the effect of SAP on prices, cost of living, and the widening "income and social gap between the various classes in Nigeria" comes from a banker, who, like many of the newspapers and magazines, points to the increase in the price of staple foods like *gari* to demonstrate the problems posed by the effects of SAP (O. Olashore 1991:163-164).

Structural Adjustment, Hometowns, and Local Development 263

Figure 14.1: SAP in Action (*National Concord*, 28 April 1992).

As *West Africa* magazine has pointed out, it is difficult to find anyone in Nigeria today who praises SAP (15-21 March 1993). Several cartoons, reproduced here, accurately reflect the public perception of SAP and of the economic situation in the country. The first (Figure 14.1) comments on a doctor's statement that three million Nigerians are hypertensive, suggesting that SAP is the cause. The second, from the period in March 1992 when the Naira was declining rapidly, shows the concern over devaluation and more generally over relying on "market forces" (Figure 14.2), while the third comments on the "relief package" that the government announced in March-April 1992, to benefit civil servants, and shows the various groups waiting to reap those benefits from the government workers (Figure 14.3).

A recent World Bank report provides a different view. In a review of structural adjustment programs in Africa, The World Bank ranks Nigeria as "fair" in its overall macroeconomic policy stance by 1990-91, and states that it is one of six African countries to have had a large improvement in macroeconomic policies (World Bank 1994:58). The report also shows Nigeria as having had growth in its Gross Domestic Product per capita, from a rate of -4.6 percent in the period 1981-1986 to a rate of 2.4 percent in the period 1987-91 (1994:135-139). The report does not argue that structural adjustment has led to development, but rather asserts that "adjustment—even incomplete adjustment—can put African countries back on the road to development" (1994:16). An important question raised is what would have happened without structural adjustment. The report argues that "often the poor would have benefited from *more* adjustment, not less" (1994:163). But the picture is complex, and as noted below, various sectors and groups have been affected differentially.

Recent and ongoing research provides insights into the ways in which SAP policies have affected specific groups and economic activities, and provides further context for considering the ways in which SAP is affecting local-level development activities. Several different approaches are utilized in this research. On the one hand, some research examines the effects of SAP on specific sectors of the economy; on the other hand, others have focused on specific groups of people. Overlapping to some extent with both these approaches, is work that considers the effects of SAP from the point of view of changing livelihood strategies.

Structural Adjustment, Hometowns, and Local Development 265

Figure 14.2: The Great Slide (*Citizen*, 6-12 April 1992).

Figure 14.3: SAP Relief '92 (*Daily Times*, 9 June 1992).

Within a year of the beginning of the Structural Adjustment Program, the first research on its effects on sectors of the Nigerian economy began to appear (Phillips and Ndekwu 1987). Articles on industry pointed out the variable effects of changes in tariffs and the devaluation, especially on industries (the vast majority) that depend on imported raw materials (Ohiorhenuan 1987). However, the banning of certain imports, such as grains, seemed likely to have the greatest effect on key industries such as bakeries and breweries (Kayode 1987). While presumably the goal was to force industries to develop local sources of raw materials, it is unclear the extent to which that was in fact possible.[2] Other studies point out that some industries that utilized local materials have benefited to some extent under SAP, but that they, like all industry, have also faced major problems, in particular the problems deriving from the currency devaluation. Overall, this research concludes that "the adjustment process in Nigeria's industries has had dramatic and, largely, negative consequences for manufacturing concerns in the country" (Olukoshi 1991b:106).

Likewise, research on agriculture emphasizes mixed but largely negative results. A 1992 study by the Central Bank of Nigeria and the Nigerian Institute of Social and Economic Research, reported in *Newswatch* July 27, 1992, points out that production of export crops like cocoa increased following the abolition of the marketing boards under SAP. Cocoa production and marketing were also affected; cocoa traders could earn more Naira from their overseas sales as a result of the devaluation.[3] There is some evidence that the development of industry based on local agricultural produce (e.g., beer made from maize), should have had positive effects on agriculture, but it is not clear to what extent it has. While other aspects of SAP programs, including new institutions to encourage rural development, should have had positive affects on agriculture, the overall impact is not clear; and rural people, like others, have been adversely affected by the rising prices of all commodities (Usoro 1987; Titilola 1987).

However, reports on the aggregate effects of SAP on agriculture mask the "multimodal" nature of Nigerian agriculture. Guyer's research in one region of southwestern Nigeria identifies four modes of agriculture— male small-scale farming; female small-scale farming; local large farmers; and corporate agribusiness. She argues that the "various modes found different aspects of the SAP configuration beneficial or threatening" and that one must examine not only specific SAP policies but also the history and context of each of these agricultural modes in order to attempt to delineate the varying impacts of SAP on Nigerian agriculture (Guyer, with Idowu 1991:263).

Similarly, research on the effects of SAP on specific groups tends to be broad, discussing the effects on women or on workers in general, rather than specific groups in specific locales or specific socioeconomic activities. According to Amale (1991:123), "those who feel the pain of structural adjustment the most are the members of the working class." First, there was considerable retrenchment, leading to greater unemployment; this was particularly the case for public employees. This retrenchment actually began much earlier, in the early 1980s, but increased later in the decade. Amale (1991:127; see also Olukoshi 1989), for example, estimates that 151,000 construction industry workers lost their jobs in 1988. Secondly, workers' standards of living were reduced substantially, as prices rose and wages remained basically unchanged; there has been no change in the minimum wage since 1981. Again, the devaluation of the Naira is seen as the major cause of the reduction in living standards for workers (Olukoshi 1989:231). However, workers have also benefited from relief packages (note the cartoon discussed above) and there have been attempts to expand employment through the National Directorate of Employment. These attempts have been particularly directed at creation of self-employment.

The retrenchment of industrial workers and public employees, together with efforts to assist them to become self-employed in small enterprises, has affected still another significant group in Nigerian society—women. Large numbers of Nigerian women work in the informal sector, and recent studies of the effects of SAP on women have suggested that there is now increased competition for the resources and opportunities provided by self-employment as retrenched workers (mainly male) with greater access to resources move into self-employment (Dennis 1991; Trager 1989). Dennis (1991:101-102) further suggests that women bear a disproportionate share of the burden of the effects of SAP, because their household responsibilities are intensified, forcing them to engage in a variety of survival strategies to ensure household survival. At the same time, there is also evidence that women have responded in a variety of creative ways, both individually and collectively, in part through the development of new organizations and associations which seek to assist women in generating access to new resources (Trager and Osinulu 1991).

Structural Adjustment, Hometowns, and Local Development 269

A recent study moves beyond the efforts to analyze the impact of structural adjustment on specific sectors and specific social groups by examining economic processes. This analysis argues that it is not women alone, or workers, who engage in a variety of survival strategies, but rather that in general there has been an expansion in "multiple modes of livelihood" (Mustapha 1991). As Mustapha points out, multiple modes of earning a living "were always a feature of the Nigerian economy;" he suggests, however, that there has been intensification and expansion in multiple modes strategies as a result of SAP. Urban workers and those in the informal sector have become more dependent on a variety of survival strategies, including, for many, part-time agriculture. In addition, middle class and professional people have added informal sector activities and farming to their income-earning strategies. And rural people have expanded their repertoire of non-farm as well as farm-based activities. Not mentioned by Mustapha, but also important, are flows of income between households and communities; remittances and child fostering are ways in which households draw on resources generated by individuals and households elsewhere.

The complexity and dynamism suggested in Mustapha's analysis make clear the difficulty of delineating the "effects of SAP" on any particular group or sector of Nigerian society. Journalistic and scholarly descriptions clearly portray a society in severe economic crisis. An annual inflation rate estimated at 70-100 percent by June 1993 has affected everyone (*The Economist* 21 August 1993). Overall living standards have declined. Yet at the same time, efforts continue to seek strategies to improve not only individual livelihoods but also community resources. The rest of this chapter explores the effects of SAP and the economic crisis on local-level development efforts, suggesting that in this area, as well, there is considerable dynamism and complexity.

**The Global and the Local:
Structural Adjustment at the Local Level**

What is the effect of structural adjustment in specific communities and regions of Nigeria? How have people responded to the worsening economic situation? And how do the responses vary from community to community and from one social stratum to another? These are complex questions, which are no less difficult to answer for specific communities and groups than for the country as a whole. In the following section of this chapter, I focus on one specific process—local development—and consider a range of ways in which that process has been affected by various aspects of structural adjustment. I suggest that it is useful to consider both peoples' perceptions of the situation as well as their actual activities.

It is clear that nearly everyone has felt the effects of the economic crisis. At the same time, the fact that that crisis has lessened the ability of government to carry out the types of development activities that used to be expected of it has also led to statements such as that quoted at the beginning of the paper, that "Government cannot do everything alone." That there are many calls for community self-reliance and activities at the local level indicate that, in many cases, those calls are being heeded, with a variety of community fund raising and local development activities. Yet, the extent to which community members are able to contribute varies greatly, leading to questions about what actually is meant by "community" and "local-level" development.

The following discussion is based on research in one area of southwestern Nigeria, Ijesaland, in eastern Yorubaland. The research has been carried out in five communities—the main city of Ilesa, two medium-sized towns, and two small towns or villages. The Ijesa, like many other Yoruba, have tended to be highly mobile, at least in the twentieth century (see Berry 1985; Aronson 1978; Trager in press). Mobility among the Ijesa has been influenced by the fact that many worked as traders, known as *osomaalo* (Peel 1983:148-159). Despite this mobility, continued maintenance of ties with the "hometown" is considered crucial; the hometown is the place where one has kinship connections, basically the place where one's father's lineage is from. It is, however, more than the place of origin; it provides a source of social identity and a web of social connections, which influence actions regardless of where a person resides. The notion of hometown, and the ties maintained with it, are central to an understanding of current dynamics of local development activities in Ijesaland.

Two types of data are used in the following analysis. Survey data are used to consider responses given to specific questions on the effects of structural adjustment, while both survey and ethnographic data are used to consider actual local development activities in which people are involved. The first type of data provides insight into peoples' perceptions, while the second helps to demonstrate some of the ways in which they have responded.

Structural Adjustment, Hometowns, and Local Development 271

The research on which this paper is based took place from October 1991 to July 1992. The survey data were collected in the five communities in May-June 1992. The survey was designed to include information on a wide variety of characteristics of current residents of the community, and focused on issues such as migration and occupational data, household membership, and participation in community organizations and activities. In addition, I included questions on the effects of SAP, and on perceived problems in the communities. A total of 281 individuals were interviewed.[4] The discussion below of survey results draws on the data collected in two of the five communities, the medium-sized towns of Osu and Ijebu-jesa, and includes 119 respondents.

The timing of the survey has significant implications for the results, as this was a period of heightened awareness of the economic situation of the country and of heightened tensions. As noted above, the devaluation of the currency has been seen as the central policy of SAP. In March 1992, after many months when the official exchange rate was around N9 to $1, the government decided that the official rate should be the same as the black market rate. Almost overnight, the exchange rate changed to N20 to $1. There was a great deal of attention to this in the press, and prices of many goods rose almost immediately. At around the same time, there was renewed discussion of the possibility of lifting the subsidy on oil, and a severe shortage of fuel (apparently due to a number of different causes, including the shutdown of refineries) led to major difficulties in the transport system.

Much of this came to a head in May, when both diesel fuel and petrol (gasoline) became unavailable in Lagos and much of the rest of the country. Lagos, dependent largely on privately-owned buses for public transport, was particularly hard hit. What transport was available had substantially increased prices. A student-organized protest in mid-May quickly became a full scale violent protest, with crowds of workers and others (described in the press as "hoodlums") attacking banks, government vehicles and private individuals. The riots continued for several days, and almost immediately, the government announced that the fuel shortage was about to end. While the violence was concentrated in Lagos, there were scattered demonstrations elsewhere, and people throughout the region were affected by the fuel shortage, as the vehicles that provide transport between cities also either increased prices or disappeared from the road. In the city of Ilesa, for example, it was nearly impossible to buy gasoline for cars and taxis for two or more weeks, and the same was true in other nearby cities. When petrol was available, one had to wait in line for several hours.

It was coincidental that the survey portion of the research was scheduled for this period; May had seemed an appropriate time for a variety of reasons. Actual interviewing took place after the most severe aspects of the fuel shortage had ended (when I myself, and my interviewers, were again able to travel around), in late May and early June. However, there was no doubt that just about everyone was well aware of what had been happening, and had in one way or another been affected by it. I relate these events in some detail as I believe they must be taken into account when considering the responses to questions asked in the survey. In addition, some of the other activities described in the next section of the paper, including some of the community fund raising activities, also took place around the same time and should be seen in this context.

Perceptions of SAP at the Local Level

Of the 119 people interviewed in the two towns of Osu and Ijebu-jesa, there were 66 women and 53 men. They range in age from 18 to over 100; the mean age is 51. Forty-five percent of the respondents report having had no education; most of the rest have had either primary or some secondary education. Nine percent have had technical college or some university education. Their occupations are typical of the range in small and medium-sized Yoruba towns: 22 percent (mainly men) are farmers; 37 percent (mainly women) are traders; 23 percent are in other informal sector occupations such as tailors and seamstresses, mechanics, carpenters; and 5 percent are in professional occupations such as teachers and civil servants; the rest include students, retired people, and others who have no occupation. Only 9 percent of the sample have lived in only one place during the course of their lives. As noted above, Ijesa Yoruba are highly mobile, and those in this sample are no exception. Sixty percent are currently living in their own hometown (either Osu or Ijebu-jesa), while the hometowns of the rest are located elsewhere.

The survey included three sets of questions about the effects of structural adjustment. One set focused on the overall effects; the second asked about the effects on travel; and the third asked about effects on contributions to the hometown. These are summarized in Table 14.1.

	Overall Way of Life*		Travel**		Involvement in Hometown†	
	% Yes	% No	% Yes	% No	% Yes	% No
All Respondents	88.1	11.9	57.7	42.3	43.1	56.9
Males	92.4	7.5	66.0	34.0	60.8	39.1
Females	84.6	15.3	50.8	49.2	28.5	71.4
Under 60 years	94.5	5.5	68.4	31.5	44.4	55.5
60 years and over	77.7	22.2	36.8	63.2	41.0	59.0

*118 respondents answered this question.
**111 respondents answered this question.
†102 respondents answered this question.

Table 14.1: Effects of SAP.

On the question of whether SAP had affected their "overall way of life," 88 percent responded "yes" while 11 percent said it had not done so. When asked to explain more specifically how it had affected them, the majority, not surprisingly, gave explanations referring to some aspect of the high cost of living: 51 percent said that the cost of living is high, that the economic situation is difficult, or that food is expensive. Others referred to more specific effects: that their children contribute less; that farm expenses have increased; that they eat less than before; that it's expensive to purchase things they need. Several referred specifically to the devaluation of the Naira and others referred to problems with their business or job.

There were also a few people, however, who said that they had not been affected by SAP. These included people who stated that they are not affected because their children are supporting them; that they are not affected because they are not government employees; or because they are farmers. One person said that he didn't know what SAP is. Only one respondent said that he or she had been affected positively by SAP, stating that he is now making more profit in his business than before structural adjustment.

There was little difference in the responses by sex; 92 percent of males and 84 percent of females said they had been affected by SAP. On the other hand, there does seem to be variation in terms of age, with 22 percent of those over sixty saying that they have not been affected by SAP. This probably reflects the fact that older people are more likely to be either dependent on others such as children for support, or to not be working and therefore less likely to be affected by changes in jobs or incomes.

The second set of questions concerned whether SAP had affected the extent to which the respondent travelled outside their town. Of those who responded to the question, 57 percent said that it had, while 42 percent said it had not. Given the events described above, it is not surprising that the majority said that their travel had been affected by the fact that it has become too expensive, with 27 percent referring specifically to high transport fares as the problem. Others indicated that they had reduced the number of times they travel, while others said that they still had to travel for business so that there hadn't been any effect. About 6 percent said that they don't travel anyway, because they are too old to travel.

There are differences in the response to this question based on sex: 66 percent of males and 50 percent of females said that SAP had affected their travel, differences which may be due to the importance of regular travel for males and females. There were also age differences: 68 percent of those under sixty say that the extent to which they travel has been affected, in comparison with 36 percent of those sixty and over.

The final set of questions dealt with the way in which SAP had affected respondents' involvement in activities in their hometown. Of those who responded, 43 percent said that it had, while 56 percent said it had not. Some people would not be involved in hometown activities in any case, regardless of the economic situation, and 16 percent said that explicitly—that they are not affected because they don't participate. But others made clear that they can't participate, or that they participate less than before, because they have less money. Some said that they have to take care of their family before they contribute to the hometown, others that they are using their money on food that they would have used for contributions; still others referred to their inability to build or complete a house in their hometown. Twelve percent stated that they had reduced their contribution, while only one person stated that contributions were increased.

Again, there are differences in terms of sex: 66 percent of males said that SAP had affected their involvement in the hometown, whereas only 28 percent of females were affected. This reflects the fact that men are, in general, more involved in hometown affairs and contributions, although there are women who do participate actively (see Trager in press). On the other hand, there is not much difference by age, with 44 percent of people under sixty and 41 percent of those sixty and over stating that their involvement has been affected.

It is clear that there is a broad negative perception of structural adjustment. Most people see themselves as having had their overall way of life affected negatively, and the effects on specific activities such as travel and hometown involvement are also largely negative. Perceptions such as these are important as they are likely to affect people's level of participation in local development activities.

Contributions to Local-Level Development

This section of the paper examines actual participation in local-level development activities. This discussion is based both on responses to several questions in the survey data and on in-depth interviews with key participants and observations of major events. The latter, ethnographic data, are particularly important for understanding what "local development" is thought to be, and for considering who the key actors are, both in setting the agenda for community development activities and for making major contributions to those activities.

Participation in hometown activities can be determined in a number of different ways. On the one hand, activities which are essentially carried out at the individual and family level constitute one type of participation. Such activities include building a house in one's hometown and sending money to family there. On the other hand, activities involving community participation constitute another type of involvement. Such activities include membership in organizations and contributions to community-wide projects. Table 14.2 shows the survey results on questions concerning both individual and community activities.[5]

Of the 113 who responded, 37, or 32 percent, report that they have built a house in their hometown; 57 percent of males and 14 percent of females have built a house, while 19 percent of those under sixty and 53 percent sixty and over have done so. This is what would be expected. There are greater expectations for men to build in their hometown, and building a house at home is often something that people do over time, as they have money to put into it. Building a house is something an individual does ideally, and the completion of a house often represents a significant measure of status and success.

	Built House in Hometown*		Member of at Least One Hometown Organization**		Contribution to Hometown Activities†	
	% Yes	% No	% Yes	% No	% Yes	% No
All respondents	32.7	67.3	50.4	49.6	40.4	59.6
Males	57.1	42.8	58.4	41.5	61.5	38.5
Females	14.0	85.9	43.9	56.0	21.1	78.9
People under 60	19.1	80.9	48.6	51.3	38.8	61.2
People Aged 60 and up	53.3	46.7	53.3	46.7	42.9	57.1

*113 respondents answered this question.
**119 respondents answered this question.
†109 respondents answered this question.

Table 14.2: Involvement in Hometown Activities.

On the other hand, membership in hometown organizations reflects an interest in community activities. There are many such organizations in all communities, ranging from social clubs to service and church organizations to mutual assistance organizations. Of the 119 respondents, 60, or 50 percent, belong to at least one hometown organization, and a number of people belong to more than one. Both men and women belong to such organizations—58 percent of all men in the survey and 44 percent of women. Likewise, people of all ages belong to these organizations, 48 percent of those under sixty and 53 percent of those sixty and over. Among the activities of these organizations are assistance to members; assistance to others in town; and "contributing to the progress of the town." In other words, for a considerable number of people, membership in organizations is not simply for one's own social benefit—although that is surely part of it—but also for the improvement of conditions in the community.

Structural Adjustment, Hometowns, and Local Development 277

Interest in community affairs is shown not only through membership in organizations but in other ways as well. I therefore asked in the survey whether respondents had contributed "to any activity" in their hometown recently. Forty percent of respondents said that they had. More men than women reported such contributions; 61 percent of males and 21 percent of females said that they had made contributions. There is not much difference by age, with 39 percent of those under sixty and 43 percent of those sixty and over reporting such contributions.

The types of projects and activities to which people contributed are revealing; Table 14.3 shows the responses for the 44 people who reported making contributions. Many reported contributions to the "development of the town" and to a "development fund" without specifying further the nature of the project. When contributions to specific projects were reported, the activities were for the most part building projects: the building of schools, hospitals, and town halls or *obas'* (kings') palaces. Building projects of this sort are the most common type of "development project" found in communities; in one of the towns under discussion, a very large town hall was built a few years ago, and there have been other building projects there as well. Other types of contributions that were specified included contributions to church activities, to the protection of the town, and to chieftaincy installations.

Development of Town	9	20.5%
Development Fund	4	9.1%
Building Projects	15	34.0%
Unspecified Monetary Contribution	9	20.5%
Other	7	15.9%
Total	44	100.0%

Table 14.3: Contributions to Hometown Activities

Of those who reported contributions, 34 percent made the contribution during the year preceding the interview, and 13 percent stated that they contribute regularly, or every year. The most commonly reported way of contributing was to donate money; 73 percent of those who contributed gave money, while the rest gave either a combination of money and labor, money and land, or labor only.

In an effort to explore further whether the economic crisis of the past few years has affected people's contributions in their hometowns, respondents were asked whether there had been any change in the way they contributed during the past five years, and if so, how. Of those who contribute, 26 or 59 percent said that there has been a change in the way they do so. Of these, half said that there was a change because the project was completed. However, a number of others indicated a change in their economic situation as the reason: seven stated that they have less money to contribute because of SAP or the economic situation, and one other said that they have less profits than before. On the other hand, three people reported that they have increased their contribution.

In sum, an examination of participation in community activities and contribution to community development indicates that a considerable number of people are involved in a variety of ways. Half of the respondents belong to organizations, while more than a third report making contributions—primarily monetary contributions—to community activities and projects. Many of the latter are specific projects, such as the building of a community facility, although more general contributions to "community development" funds are also reported. Despite the economic crisis of the past few years, and the especially difficult circumstances of the time period when the survey was taken, only a few respondents referred specifically to their economic difficulties in discussing their contributions and changes in them.

Community Fund Raising Activities and Local Development

Among the Yoruba, there is a long history of participation in local organizations and community development activities. In the early years of this century, most Yoruba towns had one or more "improvement" or "progressive" unions, usually organized by the educated elite, which sought to provide amenities for the community. For example, in the city of Ilesa, the Egbe Atunluse Ile Ijesa (Ijesa Improvement Society), which celebrated its seventieth anniversary in 1992, founded the Ilesa Grammar School, the first—and still viewed as one of the best—secondary school in the city. The type of project mentioned above—building schools, hospitals, town halls and *oba's* palaces—is typical of community development efforts (see Berry 1985 for discussion of an unsuccessful effort to build an *oba's* palace).

However, I would argue that there has been a resurgence of such efforts in recent years, in response to SAP and the economic crisis, and to some extent, a shift in orientation about the type of project most needed.

Structural Adjustment, Hometowns, and Local Development 279

New organizations have formed (see Trager 1992a; 1992b; Trager and Osinulu 1991 for discussion of new women's organizations) and new forms of community fund raising have been developed. There is a specific rhetoric that recognizes the inability of government to do those things that used to be expected of it. It is not only government officials (as in the quote at the beginning of the paper) but many others as well who argue that citizens must make their own contribution. "Privatization" under SAP has come to mean the taking over of a wide variety of governmental functions, including the provision of basic infrastructure or the recognition that if a community is going to obtain basic facilities, it probably has to raise its own funds to do so.

As a result, one finds a wide variety of "launchings" and community fund raising activities being organized in Yoruba communities today. Particularly noticeable are what I have termed community day celebrations (see Trager 1992a; 1992b; 1993), which seek to bring together all members of a community. While these celebrations take the form of ritual, and are seen as being important mechanisms of community solidarity and of bringing community members living elsewhere back to the town (see Trager 1993), these celebrations also have clearly articulated instrumental goals. The most important of these goals is fund raising for specific community projects. Thus, the speech made by the chairman of the organizing committee at the community day celebration in Ijebu-jesa stated:

> For a very long time, Ijebu-jesa people have always believed in the old adage which says "The Heavens help those who help themselves." It is for this reason that apart from what the Government, State and Local alike have been able to provide for us, we have always believed in self-development (T. Olashore 1991).

The speech then went on to enumerate past projects that had been undertaken in the town, and then listed some of the current projects being considered, and concluded by announcing that they are therefore "launching the first phase of our N25 million development fund" (T. Olashore 1991).

Unlike most of the projects of the past, which were undertaken by one community organization, such as the Egbe Atunluse in Ilesa, the current efforts are being organized by community-wide umbrella groups, which bring together a number of associations. For example, the first Ijebu-jesa Day in November 1991 was organized by the Ijebu-jesa Union

Conference, with a national executive committee of 18 members. In addition, there was a 25 member Ijebu-Jesa Day Celebration Committee. Furthermore, many of the key members of these committees are not full time residents of the community; rather, they are people who reside elsewhere and who come "home" on weekends and for holidays. The chairman of the Ijebu-jesa day committee was a lawyer who resides in the city of Ibadan, coming home to his house in Ijebu-jesa only on occasional weekends.

It is useful to consider in more detail one such community day celebration, in order to consider more closely who is involved in these activities, and how, what kind of money is raised, and some of the implications of these community-based fund raising activities. In early May 1992, the small town of Iloko had its first community day celebration, at a time when the fuel shortage was at its peak and about two weeks before the Lagos riots described above.

The activity took place on a Saturday, in the late morning and early afternoon, on the grounds of the local primary school. People began arriving at about 10 AM and the festivities began at noon. Members of local clubs came dressed in *aso ebi* (identical outfits) and bearing banners announcing the name of the organization; they were seated on benches under canopies along the two sides of the field. At the end of the field, chairs were set up under canopies and on risers. The first rows had comfortable armchairs for visiting dignitaries, including chiefs and *obas* from neighboring towns, and members of the local elite, as well as elite visitors from elsewhere in Ijesaland and from outside the area. Behind these were metal folding chairs for other, less important (or less wealthy) dignitaries. A printed program (in English) was sold for N10,[6] and there were other small amounts being raised through the sale of other items, such as paper badges and bright ribbons that could be pinned on one's clothes to indicate that one had attended the event. The proceedings included displays by the various organizations that organized the event, and a number of speeches.

However, the main event of the day was the speech by the Chairman of the Iloko Development Committee, and the collection of donations. In his speech, the Chairman described previous activities undertaken by the community and stated that "the Development Committee wishes to embark on the next stage of development which will correct the inadequacies of the existing infrastructure and enhance general quality of life of the people." He then listed projects that they plan to carry out, beginning with the drilling of boreholes for water, "to augment the water supply which at the moment is very erratic." He also announced plans to build a sports facility for the high school and the building of a town hall. He then announced the launching of the town's N10 million development fund, which was followed by donations to the fund. Each major donation was announced publicly.

Donations were made by a wide variety of people and in widely varying amounts. There were some small donations, from N50 to N250, and others in the N500-N1000 range. Several of the latter were given by *obas* from neighboring communities. Larger donations were also given, of N5000 and more. Some of these were made by public officials, and one donation of N5000 from the Federal Military Government was announced. Key individuals, both from Iloko and elsewhere, also made sizable donations. Members of one Iloko family contributed over N100,000. In addition, each of the clubs made donations, drawing on contributions made by their members, who were asked to contribute N50 each.

Altogether, several hundred thousand Naira were raised, according to one of the organizers of the event. By July, two months later, work had begun on the digging of the boreholes to improve the town's water supply. The amount of money collected, and the rapidity with which work was begun, are not necessarily typical of such fund raising activities. Rather, they reflect the ability of community members to draw on resources, largely through personal networks, and to mobilize those resources quickly, as well as to channel those resources effectively into the projects selected.

Discussion

The ability to mobilize financial and other resources for local community development purposes raises a number of questions. The following discussion focuses on three issues: 1) where does the money come from? 2) who sets the agenda for the utilization of that money? 3) what are the implications for community development activities?

As noted above, the money donated comes from a variety of sources. Some is contributed by local residents, primarily in the form of small donations to the organizations to which they belong; these organizations in turn make a contribution in the name of the group. Other money comes from better-off local residents; however, most of the better-off members of the local community are not in fact residents of that community. Rather, they are primarily people who live elsewhere (in the large cities of Ibadan and Lagos) but for whom Iloko is the hometown to which they maintain connections. They may or may not have a house in Iloko. In addition, at this particular event, considerable sums of money were contributed by people who are not either from Iloko or resident there. Rather, they are friends and acquaintances of key people from Iloko; they were invited to the celebration, and came from Lagos or other cities to attend. Hence, the success of this particular event was dependent on the ability of certain key individuals from the community to mobilize the participation and resources of others.

Since numerous communities throughout Nigeria are engaged in the same effort, the ability to mobilize such resources is crucial. Each local community is vying for resources, both those generated from its own members and those drawn from external sources. The ability to extract contributions depends largely on existing personal networks, which may vary greatly from one community to another.

Likewise, the goals of these fund raising efforts are dependent largely on what those who are contributing the major portion of the money consider to be "development." In the case of Iloko, the first priority was improved water supply, certainly a laudable goal and one that most would consider to be an example of development. But is the building of a town hall or an *oba's* palace development? Many Nigerians would argue that it is, but others would disagree.[7] The issue is not whether something should or should not be considered development, but rather with who makes that decision. Most of those involved in organizing community fund raising and community day celebrations are not full-time residents of their communities; they are members of local and national elites, whose main activities and interests lie outside the local area. However, they are largely the ones who determine the development agenda for their home communities.

What are the implications for local development? On the one hand, participation of elites gives access to resources, not only their own financial resources but also their networks, providing access to a wide variety of people and institutions throughout the country. It would be difficult for any sort of local development to take place without the participation of well-connected individuals from the community, regardless of where they reside. On the other hand, their interests are likely to differ from the interests of others in the community, the vast

Structural Adjustment, Hometowns, and Local Development 283

majority of whom have few resources and relatively limited connections. In determining the agenda for local development and for using money raised through community fund raising efforts, there is little evidence that others in the community are consulted or involved. Is access to better water everyone's priority? Is building a town hall a major item for ordinary men and women in the community? Or do they perceive other needs that are not being addressed?

Conclusion: SAP and Community Development in Nigeria

Under structural adjustment and as a result of the broader economic crisis in Nigeria, there is a clear, and well-justified, perception among the majority of people that they are worse off than they were previously, that they have less money in general, that the cost of living is higher, and hence that they have less money to spend on hometown activities, whether individual activities such as building a house, or community-wide activities such as contributing to community development. At the same time, there is widespread recognition that the government is also spending less and less for local development, including infrastructure that would ordinarily be expected to be provided by the government. In this context, there has been an increased emphasis on community self-reliance; while there have long been organizations dedicated to community improvement and development, there is now an expansion of community-wide fund raising efforts oriented to local development.

As a result, the generation of resources from both within and outside the local community has become increasingly important. Since resources are limited, especially among the people resident in small communities, there is great emphasis on contributions from those who are from the local community but resident elsewhere. Some key individuals, with access to considerable financial and personal resources, are making sizeable contributions that have potential for considerable impact on local development, at least in the short run. For the most part, the resources that such individuals draw on come from outside the local community, and they themselves are usually resident outside the community although deeply involved in the affairs of the locales which they consider to be "home."

In other words, while one effect of SAP has been an increased call for local participation and contributions to development, it has, at the same time, led to increasing reliance on those well-off and well-connected individuals, originally from the community but now resident elsewhere, who have access to resources and networks beyond the local community. These individuals feel a genuine commitment to their home areas. Their motivations are complex. Unlike migrants in other parts of the world for whom family ties are paramount (see, for example, Trager 1988), Yoruba who leave their homes are expected to maintain ties not only with kin, but also with the community. In the past, this was done largely by building a house at home and in some cases retiring there. As a Yoruba demographer pointed out to me, it is particularly important to have maintained one's place when it comes time for one's funeral; if a person who has never been home comes home only to be buried, questions will be raised (Lawrence Adeokun, personal communication). At the same time, displays that demonstrate status and wealth are important and achievement of status in one place helps to reinforce status in another (Trager in press). But while some observers have seen such activities as being only displays of wealth and conspicuous consumption, I would argue that the involvement of elite in local development activities goes beyond display. Much time and effort is spent discussing the problems of the hometown, meeting with others in the community, and contributing to development efforts. For some, the political and economic uncertainty of the present may strengthen this commitment. It may be even more important than in the past to retain a viable base in one's home community; as Eades (1994:197) points out in his study of Yoruba migrant traders in Ghana, those who have used their earnings to build houses in their hometowns as "a form of long-term security" are probably "still wise to do so." Some intend to retire at home, and some have already done so, and they want as well to see that their children have a place and commitment at home.

The effort to develop hometowns during a period of economic crisis has several further implications. First, communities, like individuals and families, have become involved in "multiple modes" of income generation. Mustapha (1991) has argued that SAP has led to household survival strategies in Nigeria that draw on a variety of sources of income. But it is not only at the household level that such processes are taking place. What seems to be happening is that communities are seeking to draw on multiple sources of income for their survival rather than depending solely on the government for the resources needed for local development, they are looking both to their own residents and to more widely based networks of people for providing the material and social resources needed by the community.

Secondly, the process that is occurring may be seen as the "privatization" of community development. Just as the government has sought under SAP to privatize various government enterprises—such as the electric company and the airlines—by selling them off to private investors, so now there is a process of "investing" in community development activities by making private contributions. Since those investments do not generally yield profit, a further question must be asked about why people are willing to contribute, why members of the elite, for example, are willing to donate substantial sums for a local development project. It is possible to argue that these donations constitute a set of social investments, especially for those who are from the local area but reside elsewhere, but also for their friends and acquaintances. Why else would people willingly travel by car for four hours to attend Iloko Day, in the midst of a fuel shortage, as many did?

Finally, the privatization of community development, and the necessity of drawing on resources from community members has the potential to lead to significant differentiation between neighboring communities. For example, if one small town has a wealthy individual, who is interested in contributing to his hometown, and who can draw not only on his own wealth but also on the resources of those in his personal network, and another nearby town does not have such a person, there may be significant differences between the two communities. One community may be able to dig boreholes for water, while the next town cannot. Where community resources are necessary for the provision of basic infrastructure, in particular, the resulting variation may be substantial.

In sum, the recognition that "government cannot do everything alone" and the call for increased participation in local community development activities has broad implications for the way in which those activities are funded, structured, and carried out. In the context of structural adjustment and a broad economic crisis, there has been a dynamic response at the level of the community, with communities seeking to generate resources for a variety of perceived needs. However, the raising of money from individuals for community development goals leads to a new set of questions concerning how access to those resources is structured, and the differential implications for different communities in a region.

Notes

1. The research on which this paper is based was carried out while I was a Visiting Professor in the Department of Sociology and Anthropology, Obafemi Awolowo University, Ile-Ife, Nigeria and was supported by National Science Foundation grant BNS-9120584 and The University of Wisconsin-Parkside Committee on Research and Creative Activity. I would like to thank Brooke Schoepf and Deborah Winslow for their comments on an earlier version of this paper, as well as participants in the PICA Institute on Development at Northwestern University in winter 1994.

2. It is interesting to note that it was only in 1993 that the government finally lifted the ban on imported cereals, and there were indications at that time of plans for the United States to export large quantities of wheat to Nigeria—so much for the development of wheat as a major crop in Nigeria.

3. One of the few groups to publicly complain about the recent revaluation of the Naira has been cocoa traders; one dealer was quoted as saying that the fixed exchange rate would kill the cocoa industry: "Farmers now get for their cocoa twice what 22 Naira to the dollar will give them and they will just abandon cocoa farms" (*NewsUpdate* 11 January 1994).

4. The research continued in May and June 1993, however the present analysis is limited to the data collected in 1991-92. The sample for the survey was selected by delineating sections of the five towns and cities, to include all types of housing and residences. In the city of Ilesa and the two medium-sized towns of Ijebu-jesa and Osu, samples were selected in several of the delineated sections (or quarters) of the town; in the two small towns, the sample was taken from the entire town. Preliminary mapping identified residences and compounds; a 10 percent sample of residence and compounds was then taken in each delineated area. Interviewers were instructed to interview one adult male or female in each of the residences or compounds selected. The survey included data not only on the individual interviewed but also on other household members and on non-resident members of the family. However, the following analysis focuses on the individual data.

5. This discussion does not include data on remittances to family; that data will be examined in a separate paper.

6. As noted above, the exchange rate at this time was about N20 to $1.00.

7. I have discussed this issue with a number of Nigerian friends, nearly all of whom argue that obas' palaces and town halls *are* important aspects of local development.

References

Amale, Steve
1991 The Impact of the Structural Adjustment Programme on Nigerian Workers. In *Crisis and Adjustment in the Nigerian Economy*. Adebayo Olukoshi, ed. Pp. 123-136. Lagos: JAD Publishers.
Aronson, Dan R.
1978 *The City is Our Farm: Seven Migrant Ijebu Yoruba Families*. Cambridge: Schenkman.
Berry, Sara S.
1985 *Fathers Work for their Sons: Accumulation, Mobility and Class Formation in an Extended Yoruba Community*. Berkeley: University of California Press.
Callaghy, Tom
1993 Political Passions and Economic Interests: Economic Reform and Political Structure in Africa. In *Hemmed In: Africa's Responses to Economic Decline*. John Ravenhill and Tom Callaghy, eds. Pp. 463-519. New York: Columbia University Press.
Citizen 18 May 1992.
Daily Times 25 November 1991.
Dennis, Carolyne
1991 Constructing a "Career" under Conditions of Economic Crisis and Structural Adjustment: The Survival Strategies of Nigerian Women. In *Women, Development and Survival in the Third World*. H. Afshar, ed. Pp. 88-106. London: Longman.
Eades, J.S.
1994 *Strangers and Traders: Yoruba Migrants, Markets and the State in Northern Ghana*. Trenton, N.J.: Africa World Press.
The Economist 21 August 1993.
Guyer, Jane I., with Olukemi Idowu
1991 Women's Agricultural Work in a Multimodal Rural Economy: Ibarapa District, Oyo State, Nigeria. In *Structural Adjustment and African Women Farmers*. Christina H. Gladwin, ed. Pp. 257-280. Gainesville: University of Florida Press, Center for African Studies University of Florida.
Ihonvbere, Julius O.
1993 Economic Crisis, Structural Adjustment and Social Crisis in Nigeria. *World Development* 21 (1):141-153.
Kayode, M.O.
1987 The Structural Adjustment Programme (SAP) and the Industrial Sector. In *Structural Adjustment Programme in a Developing Economy: The Case of Nigeria*. Adedotun O. Phillips and Eddy C. Ndekwu, eds. Pp. 145-155. Ibadan: Nigerian Institute of Social and Economic Research.

Mustapha, Abdul Raufu
   1991 *Structural Adjustment and Multiple Modes of Social Livelihood in Nigeria.* United Nations Research Institute for Social Development, Discussion Paper 26.
The News 11 October 1993.
NewsUpdate 10-11 January 1994 [wire service reports, distributed by electronic mail as NewsUpdate, available on Naijanet, an electronic mail network for people interested in Nigeria].
Newswatch 27 July 1992.
Ohiorhenuan, John F.E.
   1987 Re-Colonising Nigerian Industry: The First Year of the Structural Adjustment Programme. In *Structural Adjustment Programme in a Developing Economy: The Case of Nigeria.* Adedotun O. Phillips and Eddy C. Ndekwu, eds. Pp. 133-143. Ibadan: Nigerian Institute of Social and Economic Research.
Olashore, Oladele
   1991 *The Challenges of Nigeria's Economic Reform.* Ibadan: Fountain Publications.
Olashore, Tunde
   1991 Welcome Address delivered by Prince 'Tunde Olashore, Chairman Ijebu-Jesa Day Celebration Committee on the Occasion of the Celebration of the First Ijebu-Jesa Day on 2 November 1991 (unpublished).
Olukoshi, Adebayo
   1989 Impact of IMF—World Bank Programmes on Nigeria. In *The IMF, the World Bank and the African Debt: The Economic Impact,* Volume 1. Bade Onimode, ed. Pp. 219-234. London: Zed Books, The Institute for African Alternatives.
   1991a Prevalent Misconceptions of the Nigerian Adjustment Programme. In *Crisis and Adjustment in the Nigerian Economy.* Adebayo Olukoshi, ed. Pp. 76-87. Lagos: JAD Publishers.
   1991b The Performance of Nigerian Industry under the Structural Adjustment Programme. In *Crisis and Adjustment in the Nigerian Economy.* Adebayo Olukoshi, ed. Pp. 88-110. Lagos: JAD Publishers.
Olukoshi, Adebayo, ed.
   1991 *Crisis and Adjustment in the Nigerian Economy.* Lagos: JAD Publishers.
Peel, J.D.Y.
   1983 *Ijeshas and Nigerians: The Incorporation of a Yoruba Kingdom, 1890s-1970s.* Cambridge: Cambridge University Press.
Phillips, Adedotun O.
   1987 A General Overview of SAP. In *Structural Adjustment Programme in a Developing Economy: The Case of Nigeria.* Adedotun O. Phillips and

Eddy C. Ndekwu, eds. Pp. 1-12. Ibadan: Nigerian Institute of Social and Economic Research.
Phillips, Adedotun O. and Ndekwu, Eddy C., eds.
  1987 *Structural Adjustments Programme in a Developing Country: The Case of Nigeria.* Ibadan: Nigerian Institute of Social and Economic Research.
Shonekan, Ernest
  1985 *Economic Outlook—1985 vs. 1983: Nigeria's Economic Recovery.* New York: African-American Institute.
Tell   13 April 1992.
Titilola, S.O.
  1987 The Impact of the Structural Adjustment Programme (SAP) on the Agriculture and Rural Economy of Nigeria. In *Structural Adjustment Programme in a Developing Economy: The Case of Nigeria.* Adedotun O. Phillips and Eddy C. Ndekwu, eds. Pp. 177-184. Ibadan: Nigerian Institute of Social and Economic Research.
Trager, Lillian
  1988 *The City Connection: Migration and Family Interdependence in the Philippines.* Ann Arbor: University of Michigan Press.
  1989 *Generating Income and Employment in Rural and Urban Areas of Sub-Saharan Africa.* Paper presented at Senior Policy Seminar on Poverty and Adjustment in Sub-Saharan Africa, Abidjan, 23-27 October 1989.
  1992a *The Hometown and Local Development Efforts: Implications for Civil Society in Africa.* International Conference on Civil Society in Africa. Jerusalem.
  1992b *The Hometown and Local Development: Creativity in the Use of Hometown Linkages in Contemporary Nigeria.* Conference on Diversity of Creativity in Nigeria. Obafemi Awolowo University, Ile-Ife, Nigeria.
  1993 New Wine in Old Bottles: Community Day Celebrations and the Hometown. *Passages*, Issue 6.
  in press Women Migrants and Hometown Linkages in Nigeria: Status, Economic Roles, and Contributions to Community Development. In *Women and Demographic Change in Sub-Saharan Africa.* Paulina Makinwa-Adebusoye and An-Magritt Jensen, eds. Liege: Ordina Editions for IUSSP.
Trager, Lillian and Clara Osinulu
  1991 New Women's Organizations in Nigeria: One Response to Structural Adjustment. In *Structural Adjustment and African Women Farmers.* Christina H. Gladwin, ed. Pp. 339-358. Gainesville: University of Florida Press, Center for African Studies University of Florida.

290 Economic Analysis Beyond the Local System

Usoro, Eno J.
1987 Development of the Nigerian Agricultural Sector within the Framework of the Structural Adjustment Programme. In *Structural Adjustment Programme in a Developing Economy: The Case of Nigeria*. Adedotun O. Phillips and Eddy C. Ndekwu, eds. Pp. 167-176. Ibadan: Nigerian Institute of Social and Economic Research.
West Africa   15-21 March 1993.
World Bank
1987 *World Development Report 1987*. New York: Oxford University Press.
1989 *World Development Report 1989*. New York: Oxford University Press.
1990 *World Development Report 1990*. New York: Oxford University Press.
1993 *World Development Report 1993*. New York: Oxford University Press.
1994 *Adjustment in Africa: Reforms, Results, and the Road Ahead*. New York: Oxford University Press.

15

Rural Workers and the Readjustment of Egypt's Economy: Applying Régulation Theory to Anthropology

James Toth

Introduction

In June 1989, an official delegation from the International Monetary Fund (IMF) arrived in Cairo to negotiate its fifth standby agreement to prevent Egypt from defaulting on its $40 billion foreign debt.

Safe on their own home turf, Egypt's savvy financial negotiators haggled and dickered, stretching out the countless number of committee meetings, postponing the final surrender. Signatures on the final document were delayed. Yet the IMF delegation waited too long to settle. In August 1990, Iraq invaded Kuwait. The United States, eager to keep Egypt a member of its international coalition, reversed its zealous support of the IMF, dropped its incessant insistence on economic and fiscal reform, and sought to relieve Cairo's economic burdens. Egypt's participation in the Gulf war was guaranteed when the United States forgave $7 billion of its $40 billion national debt. Even so, in January 1991, Egypt finally but reluctantly signed a still austere IMF agreement that predictably would result in great social unrest. It demanded (1) higher exchange rates and currency devaluations, (2) higher bank interest rates matching or exceeding the national rate of inflation, and (3) lower budget deficits by eliminating costly consumer subsidies and raising tax revenues. All three actions were guaranteed to result in massive price inflation (Sadowski 1991:214-219).

Within the year, extreme economic hardship was apparent to all. In 1992, Ramadan, the festive lunar month of religious fasting, fell in February, but it appeared haggard and sparse—as if lifted from a page out of Charles Dickens and nineteenth century England. The swell of unhappy faces pressed against the shop windows, looking and longing, but seldom buying, the nuts, fruits, and candies reserved for this joyous occasion. Normally, Ramadan is the exemplar month for night-time feasting, yet this particular spring, the government was unable to keep Ramadan from turning into gloom. Normally, the Ministry of Supply insures that shelves will be well-stocked and prices will remain at reasonable levels. Yet this year, halfway through the month, even government stores of basic necessities ran out. An ominous sign, indeed. More than the usual number of celebrants had to make do without the sumptuous *iftar* (break-fast), the Ramadan cookies, the new clothes. Worried, the government reported that the difficulties from the IMF's "structural adjustments" would take three years to fix (al-Ahram 26 May, 1992).

Workers in the heavy industrial town of Helwan, fifteen miles south of Cairo, decided not to wait. Instead, they accelerated their militant job action. Strikes in the cement and steel factories a month earlier, in January, had indicated just how anxious workers had become about rising prices and stagnant incomes (al-Wafd 18 March 1992; al-Ahali 9 April 1992; al-Ahram 1 May 1992). Meetings in March with Prime Minister ᶜAtif Sidqi were postponed until orders came down from above to convene. Finally, President Husni Mubarak announced a wage package that would temporarily satisfy discontented workers, but which was guaranteed to raise the ire of the more austere IMF officials who were insisting that the government maintain a lid on public sector wages.

Again not surprising, later that summer, strained tensions between Egypt's security forces and angry Islamicists in southern Egypt began erupting in gunfire, police raids, hot pursuit, arrests, and counter-attacks. Initially, the confrontations took place between Egyptian Christian Copts and Muslims, but once government forces entered the fray, sights were turned on them instead. Police raided ammunition storerooms, insurrectionists fought back with attacks on police headquarters. When bombs were found aboard train cars, the government ordered troops to patrol all coaches. Homes of suspected outlaws were blown up. Egypt south of Cairo began to resemble an occupied territory. Soon, fighting began to erupt in the poorer neighborhoods flanking the capital city. Trouble in the northwest Cairo suburb of Imbaba resulted in the arrest of scores of Islamicists.

The IMF structural adjustments were generating horrible consequences in the Fund's zeal to right the wrongs of Egypt's dismal economy. But is it merely a problem in poor timing? The global development of capitalism in the current post-1973 period has proven paradoxical, for at the same time that core economies have contracted—what Bluestone and Harrison (1982) have called "deindustrialization,"—many peripheral formations have actually experienced rapid economic growth. Elsewhere, Newly Industrialized Countries (NICs) began snarling and turning into economic tigers (Lipietz 1987:74). Under such seemingly propitious circumstances, how could Egypt be so unfortunate as to see such plenty pass it by and watch instead its society come to the brink of civil war?

Egypt deserves our attention because it is a country whose national development, position in the new global division of labor, and international diplomatic credibility remain critically contingent on how different segments of its population, and particularly its labor force, endorse or thwart its programs and policies for economic growth. For Egypt is not a Middle East oil exporter nor a member of the NIC club, although it certainly aspires to be (World Bank 1989).[1] It has only sporadically benefited from the influx of First World capital, and its economic adjustment at home has been highly uneven. Instead, it has rented out its large labor force to those countries that have become beneficiaries. Over the last twenty years, emigration abroad has represented a new source of income and ambition for Egyptians workers, and has critically, though indirectly, affected the efforts of even those who stayed behind.

Yet rather than consider Egypt's recent experiences with international emigration or even its recent urban industrialization, I wish instead to focus on those who remained back in the countryside. I concentrate on agricultural production because although farming has declined in stature in recent years, it still remains the largest single sector in Egypt's economy. I turn, then, to the opposite end of the capitalist spectrum and examine a segment of Egyptian rural laborers involved in the process of leaving a feudal-like peasantry and making the transition to permanent waged labor. That is, they are caught in the grip of proletarianization, a process which has not diminished despite the intense "modernization" and capital penetration of the post-World War II period marking the rise of United States hegemony.

What I propose to do in this chapter is to first provide a theory that links the worksite activities of rural laborers with the national and international political economy of the IMF and state economic planners. Then I will examine the friction that exists in agricultural production generated by a gender division of labor that farm employers manipulate in order to reduce labor costs while raising profits. This manipulation is not regarded lightly, however, and both men and women have responded by seeking better incomes and more rewarding employment in other economic sectors. But as workers leave crop agriculture, the yields necessary for food security and export earnings have plummeted to alarmingly low levels.

In recent years, agriculture has not supplied nearly enough food, and importing expensive foodstuffs has drastically inflated Egypt's trade bill. Moreover, since Egypt's industrial sector remains weak, export crops have continued to bear the greatest burden in earning the foreign currency needed to pay for imported food, foreign machinery, and investment dollars. The difference between low exports and high imports has forced Egypt to borrow heavily in order to reduce its budget deficit. As a consequence, Egypt is constantly raising its national debt, but one it finds increasingly difficult to service. The cure, however, may be worse than the disease. For IMF bailouts and structural adjustments have prompted a massive inflation that has generated financial difficulties not only for farm workers but for the entire country. It is no wonder, then, that the reactions of desperate workers, gloomy celebrants, and outraged Muslims have become angry, violent, and vicious.

Régulation Theory

If anthropology is to articulate events like the IMF structural adjustment program with grassroots strikes and insurrections, and bring both together under a single lens, then what is needed is a theoretical perspective that combines anthropology's conventional, microscopic focus on the common, everyday activities of community life with the larger, more macroscopic examination of national and international developments that is found in economics and political science. A number of theories provide the requisite holism. Marxism remains one of the few that offers a dynamic approach by hinging its analysis to "class" as an objective structure and to "class struggle" as a subjective motor force of historical change.

Yet as theoretical practice, Marxism has unfortunately remained faithful to the Kantian roots sustained by the Second International with its parallel pursuit of objective economics and subjective agency. While various interpretations subsequently claimed to combine this dualism under praxis, they instead tilted in favor of either one pole or the other without recognizing that the two are united dialectically. However, in recent years, an approach called Régulation Theory has emerged in Europe, arising from the ashes of an Althusserian structuralism unable to resolve the question of just who creates history and a Sartrean subjectivism unable to determine the economic conditions under which this happens, all nourished since 1973 by a prolonged period of economic decline in the West (Aglietta 1979; Baldi 1972; Boyer 1990; Tronti 1971).[2]

The central problem in Régulation Theory is to understand how contemporary societies change over time. The issue of capitalist transformation, of crisis and breakdown, had once topped the agenda of Marxism before it became distorted by the Russian Revolution's notions of party vanguardism and Western Marxism's ideas of false workers' consciousness. However, Régulation Theory could not simply adopt a social model forged in the more heady days of nineteenth century competitive capitalism. "Bourgeois" economists since John Maynard Keynes had long since developed more sophisticated theories that explained why periods of market crisis alternated cyclically with periods of market stability. Accordingly, there was not going to be just one final breakdown of capitalism but rather a series of economic disasters and crises, separated by periods of relative calm and tranquility. The question then for Régulation Theory is how to account for (1) periods of stability and reproduction, (2) periods of crisis and transformation, and (3) the transition between them.

But Régulation Theory insists that this movement of history be viewed not as Keynes' impersonal aggregation of effective consumer demand nor even as Althusser's passive bearers of structural dictates. Instead, history must be seen as the direct product of human agency *pace* Sartre, but one explicitly mediated by a particular production system and the current configuration of social conditions. Thus history becomes one that is specifically generated by the interaction of society's two antagonistic classes, labor and capital, a rise and fall that comes about as a series of contingent compromises growing out of the daily struggles taking place between workers and managers.

However, this fundamental antagonism does not transform society automatically. Régulation Theory avoids the crass economism of the Second International by rejecting its vulgar assertion that political and ideological superstructures are determined by, or simply reflect, the economic base. Instead, it reverses the equation by arguing that the daily struggles taking place between workers and bosses ("the base") are *"régulated,"* or shaped, by an ensemble of social institutions ("the superstructure") specific to a particular society and history. This means that the fundamentals of capitalism—the separation of labor from property, the wage relationships, and the production of surplus value—do not have the same appearance in all places and for all times. Instead, they are molded and conditioned by different institutional arrangements, such as various property and labor relations, different labor force compositions, diverse hegemonic blocs, and distinct social organizations. This ensemble can include the rivalry among capitalist enterprises, the pressures and demands from political and financial organizations such as governments and banks, the dictates and directives of civil society, and even the customs and habits of social convention. They can embody such distinct organizations as the International Monetary Fund (IMF), United States Agency for International Development (USAID), and the World Bank as well as less bounded cultural constructs like kinship, age, and gender.[3] Together, these institutions "régulate" the explosive struggle that lies at the core of capitalist production.

Thus Régulation Theory analyzes the perpetuation and/or the transformation of the economic, political, social, and cultural patterns of society as the contingent outcomes of the on-going struggle between historically and socially constituted class agents. By means of this struggle between workers and bosses, societies move from periods of quiet calm to moments of intense crises and pass on to establishing new social orders.

Régulation Theory contains two components that connect the microscopic activities of ordinary labor with the macroscopic dynamics of politics, economics, culture, and history. The microscopic involves the labor process which Régulationists call a "regime of accumulation." The macroscopic domain includes the specific ensemble of national and international institutions that comprise a "mode of regulation."[4] The mode of regulation shapes and contours the nuclear struggles that occur inside the regime of accumulation. Depending on the mode's institutional flexibility or rigidity, such struggles may or may not overflow the actual production site to affect the larger society outside.

Analysis begins by examining the labor process that lies at the very heart of capitalism and capitalist production. The labor process is more than just the technical combination of workers, managers, plans, equipment, and skills that together transform raw materials and requests into useful products and services (Edwards 1979). It is also a set of social relationships that establishes an uneasy parity between effort, wages, and prices such that the specific amount of effort workers render earns them a certain amount of wages which, in turn, purchase a given amount of goods and services that reconstitute their skills and ability. Conflicts can erupt in the regime of accumulation when workers appropriate more control over their own laboring efforts, income, work conditions, and consumption than management would otherwise wish. This constant tug-of-war can either intensify and expand or else diminish and die, depending on the superstructural ensemble of social institutions that "régulates" them.

Unlike Althusser's mode of production analysis, Régulation Theory argues against an undifferentiated capitalism, a smooth, timeless totality left undisturbed by historical processes and social agents. Instead, the history of capitalism is represented as a series of phases that unevenly combine specific "regimes of accumulation" and particular "modes of regulation" into what Boyer (1990) has called distinct "modes of development." Régulation Theory maintains that there are two regimes of accumulation, *extensive* and *intensive* accumulation; and two modes of regulation, *competitive* and *monopolistic* market relations.[5] Modes of development are characterized by equilibrium and labor quiescence, but the transition between them is marked by crisis and labor unrest.

Extensive accumulation means generating profits by extending the time labor actually spends working, whether by lengthening the work day or else by reducing dead, unproductive time. This technique of accumulating profits became known as Taylorism. Taylorism began after the initial period of primitive accumulation marking capitalism's birth.[6] Its eponym derives from the popularizer of Scientific Management, Frederick Taylor, whose "scientific" time-motion studies established the most efficient physical movements for labor that could maximize production and profits. His methods included work speed-ups, lengthening the work day, and pushing workers harder, often by employing brutal supervisors.

By contrast, *intensive* accumulation involves making profits through more efficient production techniques by using modern machinery. This has been labeled Fordism. Elements of Fordism, such as the automated assembly line, appeared in the United States as early as 1905, but the entire mode of development did not emerge full blown until after World War II when state welfare policies, labor control mechanisms, and mass consumerism all came together.[7] It is named for Henry Ford, the inventor of the conveyor belt assembly line that could impersonally speed up the labor process despite labor's own wishes. Moreover, efficient production permitted Ford to pay his workers higher wages, which then could be used to purchase the very cars they built. Thus Fordism is synonymous with mass production and mass consumption, high wages, advanced technology, government subsidies, and Keynesian pump priming, planned obsolescence, and legalized unions.

In the United States, the transition from Taylorism to Fordism was achieved through an assorted variety of job actions. Workers demanded higher wages, shorter hours, less despotic supervisors, and union recognition. But companies unwilling or unable to satisfy these demands closed down, moved to less restrictive regions in other parts of the country, or else moved entirely overseas. The growing gap between the overproduction of high-priced goods and the under-consumption of lowly paid workers widened considerably. Without unions, no legal channel was available to articulate labor's demands that could otherwise narrow it. This caused the Great Crash of 1929, which inaugurated the Great Depression of the 1930s that then spread worldwide. The United States was able to recover with the New Deal under Roosevelt, which finally recognized unions, legislated reduced work hours, subsidized unemployment, and expanded markets overseas. Other countries, however, were less fortunate, and instead installed strong fascist forms of state intervention that could traverse the transition. The vast military spending made necessary by World War II witnessed the advent of military Keynesianism. Later the armistice ushered in the period of monopoly capitalism coupled with United States global hegemony. Bought off, labor in the First World remained quiet, basking in the warmth of its new social contract guaranteed by the state and the west's market superiority. In the Third World, however, the intense exploitation of an already pauperized work force ignited a massive number of national independence movements under the leadership of demagogic rulers.

Since the early 1970s, the hegemonic superiority of the United States has vanished.[8] This has marked the beginning of the postmodern or the post-Fordist period, where caught in a transitional phase, it still remains unclear as to what new mode of development will emerge. Unfortunately, Régulation Theory has remained bogged down by such crystal ball gazing and the myopic focus on Fordism in the First World. Considerations of a broader global dimension remain embryonic.

Because this chapter concentrates on the impact made by international banking policy radiating out of the First World on the social dynamics found in the Third World, we must then take this parochial Régulation Theory and apply it instead to non-western social formations. Thus we must outline the different regimes of accumulation and modes of regulation that occur in a country like Egypt and show how labor becomes the agent of their transformation.

Alain Lipietz (1982:33-47) proposed three different regimes of accumulation for Third World economies. These included:

(1) The "export promotion" of raw materials found typically in Third World colonialism. Here labor is subjected to what Lipietz called "bloody" Taylorism: the violent enforcement of low wages, harsh labor demands, arbitrary supervision, and abject poverty by a bloated state apparatus that reverses the lean, laissez-faire political system found in First World Taylorism.

(2) The "import substitution" of Third World industrialization that occurred in the 1930s and 1950s when capital fled a recession-torn metropole. Here, a small, privileged segment of well paid workers is controlled by a peripheral Fordism of secondhand technology. But the home market remains stunted and mass consumption remains limited since most consumers work in an informal sector of small-scale enterprises or a petty commodity sector of peasant production.

(3) The "export substitution" of trading manufactured goods back to First World markets. Peripheral Fordism persists, but unlike before, local industries no longer compete against those in the core but instead coordinate their production with that which is found in the First World.

Today, the peripheral Fordism of export substitution contains three distinct levels of production: (1) conception, planning, and engineering; (2) complex manufacturing with skilled labor and relatively high equipment costs; and (3) unskilled assembly, requiring little knowledge and less investment. Over the two decades since the early 1970s, Level Three industries in the core have shut down—deindustrialized—and have relocated to sites in the periphery to create the "economic miracles" of such NICs as Brazil, South Korea, Taiwan, Hong Kong, and Singapore. Unfortunately, Egypt has not benefited from this peripheral Fordism, thwarted, as we shall see, by a labor force that has felt the intense social polarization such transitions create.

Corporations have taken advantage of cheap labor and market proximity in the Third World to establish factories whose Level Three activities complement Level One and Level Two operations in the core. Financing has come from expanded oil revenues recycled through multinational corporations and international banks. Their principal markets lie in trading with other Third World countries and in re-exporting back to the core. This export orientation still retards the development of mass production oriented toward local needs. Mass consumption is met instead through foreign imports whose high prices exacerbate the national balance of trade and exasperate impoverished consumers. It is within this new international division of labor that we must locate Egypt's rural labor force and begin evaluating the impact of its tense relationship with capital. Régulation Theory provides the conceptual ability to do this.

It remains then to apply this rudimentary theory to those areas in the Third World frequented by anthropologists. Anthropology has made significant contributions to the study of capitalism, but in describing workers, their livelihood, and their communities, and even the conditions under which all these change, rarely has it reached down into examining the minute details of the labor process itself and then considered how production might affect the larger society. The task then becomes one of understanding the common labor activities found in the regime of accumulation and then tracing their linkages to the larger ensemble of institutions found in the mode of régulation that in turn restrain or amplify these core labor struggles. As we shall see, labor's role in creating this history becomes crucial.

En-gendering Egyptian Agriculture

In rural Egypt, the parity between effort, wages, and prices that comprises the agricultural labor process is consistently unbalanced by an endemic gender discrimination that reduces wages and increases effort in an atmosphere of everrising prices. The inflation aggravated by the IMF structural adjustments plainly was exacerbating an already existing situation. But in doing so, it caused the discontent finally to cross that thin line that separates what once were weak and ineffective conflicts from those that now have become sharp and intense.

In 1986, farm workers in Egypt comprised 36 percent of the total labor force—down significantly from fifty percent only ten years earlier.

Yet the number remains more than two-and-a-half times greater than the next largest sector of industrial employment. However, per capita income in agriculture is less than half that earned in industry. It is clear, therefore, that agricultural workers are far more numerous but far more destitute. This means that their cumulative efforts to find better incomes and more rewarding employment ought to be a major force in Egypt's economic growth.

Since the early nineteenth century, Egypt has promoted the export of long-strand cotton as its principal economic resource. This monoculture had kept the national labor force overwhelmingly rural. So that export earnings could remain high, labor costs were cut drastically, and a sizeable portion of the rural work force was unable to survive on what agriculture alone provided. Manipulating the agricultural terms of trade—drastically reducing crop prices and farm wages, and sharply raising prices on consumption, credit, and production inputs—became a formula that generated enormous profits and wealth for the state, private merchants, and large landlords, and bred abject poverty and misery for workers and their families. Further cuts in wages by manipulating gender distinctions made survival even more tenuous.

Egyptian farming has become a sector of small-plot growers. A glance at crude land holding statistics explains, in simplified terms, why today this sector contains such large numbers of workers searching for non-farm employment.

> Of the rural population, half work in agriculture, half do not.
> Of those working in agriculture, half own land, half do not.
> Of those who own land, half own enough, half do not.[9]

Thus only about one-eighth of all rural residents can survive in agriculture on just what farming alone provides. The rest must find jobs in non-farm employment in order to earn an adequate income or to supplement meager farm revenues. Their employers, however, frequently evoke gender differences so that they can predict labor productivity and docility and pay low wages.

In Egypt, farming exhibits a critical gender distinction in its social division of rural labor. Customarily, men have been expected to perform the more strenuous tasks—plowing, weeding, hoeing, thinning, fertilizing, irrigating and certain laborious harvests—and women have been considered responsible for physically easier chores in the homestead, in animal husbandry, but also working alongside men in the fields laboring on such crops as wheat, cotton, rice and animal fodder.[10]

Yet the cultural boundary between men's and women's work has been far from impermeable, and crossovers frequently occur when men do "women's work" and women do "men's jobs." When little non-farm work exists at home, men have been obliged to perform "women's work" at its lower wage rate or when men prove scarce, women do "men's work" but at their former, reduced pay levels. Fundamental to understanding this crossing over gender lines is the existence of wage differentials and sexual stereotypes.

For in Egypt, the separation of tasks and chores assigned to each gender has been buttressed by a consistent record of unequal pay. Economists have observed that for nominally unskilled work, women receive two-thirds the wages of men and children receive half men's pay. Moreover, these proportions have remained historically fixed over time despite growth and decline in the absolute magnitude of the wage itself (Hansen 1969:59-60).

Employers lower their overall wage bill by either (1) hiring women to do men's work while still paying them their previous low wage despite their extra effort, or clse by (2) employing men to perform women's work but paying them women's low wages despite their extra strength. These wage inequities enable employers to divide or decompose the work force and to cheapen it to its lowest possible cost so as to realize greater profit. Discursively, stereotypes centered around personality traits of male aggression and female modesty are then frequently invoked since they presumably predict labor defiance and docility which in turn helps employers avoid strident demands for wage hikes.

However, not content with this lower wage, men frequently engage in casual migrant labor and women, for their part, apply their efforts to home-based animal husbandry. Although men's departures emerge as opposition to wage debasement, it also conveniently removes them from the village and reduces their demands for higher wages. Malcontents are thus shipped out on regional migrant labor trips while local female workers unevenly replace them in the village fields. However, women who find animal husbandry a more lucrative reward for their efforts, are increasingly withdrawing from the labor market, too, and are staying home to work instead (Saunders and Mehenna 1988:214-219; Toth 1991).

Gender differentiation not only reduces nagging wage demands but also undercuts male assertiveness by moderating the latter's wage requests. If men step out of line, employers either threaten to reduce their wages to the level of women's pay or else replace them by women altogether. Mutual resentment of one gender toward the other effectively diverts attention away from those who actually impose wage cuts. Instead, men push women back into the house, justified by beliefs concerning purdah and "natural abilities," and women resist their household seclusion by ignoring male blusterings, banding together and influencing other women—and men—through domestic disputes and manipulations (Collier 1974; Friedl 1989). Discontent is rechanneled into a battle between the sexes.

This gender division of labor allows employers to weaken labor's demands for higher wages and to concentrate their own authority. The stress on gender can significantly divide the rural work force and, very much like the ethnic and racial divisions found in advance capitalist nations, dilute workers' ability to define wages or oppose their decline (Reich et al. 1980).

Where Have All the Workers Gone?

Back in the 1960s, the onset of enormous infrastructural construction projects like the Aswan High Dam and the Tahrir Land Reclamation absorbed such huge numbers of rural workers that it generated severe economic damage to President ᶜAbd al-N_ ir's first Five Year Development Plan (Toth 1991). But over the last 20 years, a different sort of magnet has lured male workers away from farming: those skilled and unskilled jobs found in Egypt's expanding domestic and expatriate construction sector and construction-related industries. Women, too, have begun turning to home-based activities such as animal husbandry and cottage industries, increasing the massive exodus from the waged labor market in crop agriculture (Hansen et al. 1981:59-60). Since the manipulation of gender roles had divided the work force and reduced wages, workers opposing such maneuvers enthusiastically left agriculture and eagerly sought more rewarding jobs in construction and animal husbandry.

Throughout the 1970s and 1980s, departing male workers were replaced by female and child laborers, but only imperfectly. High peaks in seasonal labor demand could no longer be satisfied. Three crops in

304 Economic Analysis Beyond the Local System

particular suffered serious problems: wheat (an import-substitution crop harvested by males), cotton (an export crop harvested by underemployed men supplementing an overburdened work force of women and children), and rice (a popular food crop transplanted and tended mostly by women). Even later, after the 1985 recession began, ex-farm workers were loathe to return to agriculture. The consequences have been catastrophic. Muhammad Salim (1977) and Alan Richards (1991) once measured labor's share of total crop costs as a percentage:

	Cotton	Wheat	Rice
1977	44%	25%	35%
1988	61%	45%	42%

Table 15.1: Agricultural Labor as a Percentage of Total Production Costs (Salim 1977; Richards 1991).

In withdrawing their labor, workers have drastically driven up labor costs for cotton, wheat, and rice. As long as government price policies and the agricultural terms of trade keep the lid on wholesale prices, agriculture remains essentially unprofitable and uneconomical.

Can farm equipment replace workers and maintain productivity? After all, the hallmark of Fordism is that machines will replace laborers and that those displaced will be absorbed into new urban employment (Hopkins 1987:132).[11] But elements of Taylorism still abound in agriculture. Tractors and pumps remain inaccessible for want of lenient credit terms and improved crop prices, or inoperative for lack of spare parts and skilled operators. Low-waged workers continue to be cheaper than expensive imported machinery, although the price of workers is rising. Moreover, labor's integration into the urban labor market remains limited until there is a further commitment of investment funds and a reassessment of capital intensive manufacturing. Expansion of the informal sector and construction employment remain uncertain since these activities remain so dependent on outside capital. So far, farm mechanization has saved the agrarian economy from even greater declines but it has not reversed its production shortfalls.

Long before the enormous rise in oil prices in the fall of 1973, Egyptians had been traveling abroad for work. However, this flow had consisted principally of lower-middle class schoolteachers unable to realize their aspirations for upward mobility (Messiha 1980). This soon changed, however, into an exodus of construction workers instead. After 1967, new investment capital had begun financing economic growth in the Third World. Plant and infrastructural construction required skilled and unskilled workers even before the Organization of Petroleum Exporting Countries (OPEC) tripled its prices. The 1973 price increases, however, sparked by and in support of Egypt's October War, turned the trickle of emigrant workers into a major torrent. By 1976, half of Egypt's labor force in construction was employed abroad (Choucri 1980:83). The sector displayed such a labor intensity and low skill requirement that subsequent domestic vacancies were readily filled by disgruntled male workers moving out of agriculture.

But this regional labor drain was not merely an automatic response to the freely operating forces of supply and demand working impartially across international borders. Instead, it was the outcome of deliberate government policy, which, however, was not formulated in a disinterested fashion but was adopted under intense pressure from numerous craft workers demanding higher incomes and a better standard of living. Egypt's emigration policy proved to be less the "referee's decision" of pluralistic political theories and more the outcome of increased labor agitation coming from skilled workers in the construction trades.

Two policy perspectives on emigration emerged. One viewed emigration as a useful means for eliminating dissent. Urban workers grumbling over low local wages and contrasting them unfavorably with those in the Gulf or Libya could become potential sources of trouble (Choucri et al. 1978:137). A second view, however, concluded that emigration would "sap the society's strength and its most productive elements" (Dessouki 1978). A labor drain would lower the country's surplus of workers which in previously swamping the labor market—or at least in fueling popular mythology—had kept wages low. The threat of labor shortages among skilled workers was particularly disturbing. Production bottlenecks and wage inflation would raise construction costs in Egypt and seriously disrupt the nation's fragile economy. The government's initial response to emigration reflected this second position and all skilled workers were prohibited from leaving the country.

In July 1974, only nine months after OPEC raised its prices, the government announced strict travel restrictions for all craft trades. The Labor Ministry decreed that workers must carry identity cards and legal documents clearly stamped with their occupation and travel authorization (al-ʿAynayn 7 July 1974). Passports, visas, military and security documents became obstacles used to deter emigration (Messiha 1980).

But workers did not accept such restrictions calmly. They bribed officials to overlook identity card stamps, paid others to have their cards altered, and many gave false occupations when renewing "lost" documents. Once their status was "revised" to less critical categories, workers left Egypt in unprecedented numbers and sought and accepted foreign employment.

Challenged by the unauthorized departure of such large numbers, the state finally capitulated and abandoned its initial position. As Parliament members demanded changes in ministry regulations, the only alternative left was to permit open travel. The government repealed visa requirements and made work permits optional (Hansen and Radwan 1982:59-60). Documenting departures was simplified and encouraged many without contracts to leave and find employers once abroad. Those who left vacated positions that ultimately recruited farm workers who no longer willingly tolerated the manipulation of gender traits and the inequities of farm wages but, instead, began seeking local jobs in construction (Halliday 1984).[12]

Employers and officials who had warned that emigration would generate labor shortages and higher wages soon had their worst fears realized. Between 1974 and 1978, construction wages increased three-to-five fold and grew to levels three times higher than wages in agriculture (Hansen and Radwan 1982:59-60). As the new expanding labor market absorbed more construction workers, first for oil exporting nations and then later for their domestic replacements, local companies increasingly recruited those with lesser skills from the ranks of farm workers. Massive reductions in the agricultural labor force since 1973 have had such a disastrous effect on crop production that the consequences have rippled throughout the national economy.

In January 1977, Cairo suffered massive riots and destruction when President Sadat abruptly increased food prices in order to promote domestic agriculture, decrease consumer subsidies, and reduce foreign food imports. The increase failed, old prices were restored, and eventually the conditional IMF loans were even secured—the first of five bail-outs attempting to save Egypt's finances. Yet Egypt's fiscal predicament remained critical, and labor shortages continued to spoil government plans for agricultural self-sufficiency.

In 1982, Egypt transacted one-sixth of all international wheat flour sales (Wall Street Journal 19 January 1983). In 1987, more riots erupted when bread prices rose. By 1988, 47 percent of the wheat consumed in Egypt was imported (Food and Agriculture Organization 1990). By November 1991, imported foodstuffs, including wheat, had accounted for 70 percent of Egypt's total food consumption (al-Wafd 24 November 1991). Farm workers who had once played a critical role in providing cheap foodstuffs were no longer content. The growing imbalance between effort, wages, and prices was generating an intense hostility that no longer could be contained just within the village. A labor market that before 1960 had held such conflict in check was now allowing disgruntled workers to rectify their dismal situation. But their growing exodus soon caused trouble for the entire national economy.

Labor's Role in Egypt's Development

Rising oil prices, emigrant workers, and local labor shortages constitute key components in Egypt's adaptation to the new international division of labor and the current recession. But stunted agricultural production and bloated construction crews are mere symptoms of a yet larger crisis: an arrested capitalist development held in check by the stalemate between labor and state economic planners.

Egypt's economy essentially relies on three pillars—crop exports, nationalized import-substitution industries, and bank credit—to accumulate the foreign currency reserves necessary to balance its trade payments, service its foreign debt, and import capital goods. Departing farm laborers have seriously damaged the first pillar of agriculture. Overworked and underpaid workers employed in fiscally strapped state factories have restricted their output and jeopardized industrial output. And all workers, rural and urban, are now demanding higher incomes to accommodate consumer costs inflated once government subsidies were eliminated as part of the IMF's structural adjustment program. Thus workers critically constrain the state's economic adjustment to the new international order. As workers escalate their demands and apply more pressure, government policies may become even more desperate as the need for economic growth increases.

Recent changes in cotton production and marketing have reduced Egypt's export of "white gold." Labor costs have driven up the expense of cotton production while at the same time, the state has continued to impose price controls on cotton sales in order to subsidize domestic textile production and expand foreign currency reserves. Many farmers have responded by shifting into cultivating other crops such as alfalfa (Mitchell 1991), a crop more profitably sold as feed for meat production and one more easily cultivated by the women and children who replaced men in the fields.[13] In addition, the appearance of synthetic fabrics and the success of cheaper Fourth World competition from countries such as Sudan and Uganda, have reduced the international demand for Egyptian cotton. As a result, the export of this monoculture has declined dramatically.

If cotton exports have failed to earn enough hard dollars, can industrial production succeed? Twice Egypt has sought to create a viable import substitution sector. The first attempt, in the 1930s, entailed private efforts by Talat Harb and Ahmad Abboud who took advantage of economic constrictions in Europe to establish Egypt's first major industries. A second effort involved the massive state nationalizations ordered by President ᶜAbd al-N__ir in the 1950s and early 1960s (Davis 1982; Tignor 1984; Waterbury 1983). Yet in the 1970s, President Sadat's Open Door Policy endeavored to close down the deteriorating remnants of these losing ventures and instead to attract foreign investors by selling off their assets. However, new capital intensive competition from foreign markets, rigid government regulations, and outmoded production facilities have kept Egypt's unsold public sector moribund. Industrial performance has continued to languish.

To encourage foreign investment, the state had pledged a cheap work force whose poverty was moderated by a state program of consumer subsidies. Yet more than just underwriting the consumption habits of the working class, subsidies also permitted foreign investors to reduce wage costs and repatriate higher profits (Fröbel et al. 1981).[14] But since the IMF has forced Egypt to abandon this expensive program, international investors have retreated and consumer prices have skyrocketed. Popular pressure has begun insisting on a corresponding wage increase. Income adjustments will have to be massive, requiring greater productivity to avoid further inflation and more rapid job generation to avoid popular discontent. As their already precarious standard of living becomes further eroded by the steep rise in consumption costs and the added burden of supporting unemployed dependents, workers and their families are becoming even more vocal in demanding higher incomes and more jobs. But the government's success in expanding or creating industries has been very limited. Unable to accumulate foreign currency from either agricultural or industrial exports, it has increasingly turned to foreign finance. Yet, wary of rising labor costs, investors initially were reluctant, although the surfeit of capital flowing into the Third World promised to diminish the weight of this impediment.

At first Egypt attempted to attract foreign investment by relying on its ties to neighboring Arab petroleum exporters. With the collapse of its chief regional rival, Lebanon, Egypt had realistically expected greater investment activity to materialize in the 1980s. Expectations were frustrated, however, as oil revenues increasingly bypassed Egypt and went instead into western banks, first, and then on to more promising and profitable peripheral economies in Southeast Asia and Latin America. Egypt's efforts to encourage Arab investment were further stymied by the 1979 Camp David treaty and its subsequent diplomatic estrangement from regional oil producers. Until reconciliation could be achieved, Egypt relied, instead, on United States assistance, international bank loans, and renting out its labor force.

Throughout the 1970s, revenues from domestic oil production, declining cotton exports, canal fees, tourism, and foreign aid were insufficient by themselves to fuel economic growth. Workers' remittances, however, became a substantial source of foreign currency despite the government's initial reluctance. High incomes earned abroad initially were converted into consumer purchases, real estate, and housing and later were invested in transport and small informal businesses (Khafagi 1983; Assaad 1991). Individual initiatives and national government outlays, together with small sums of foreign resources, financed large economic ventures whose start-up promoted a flurry of construction activity. This conveniently matched the occupations of an experienced labor force increasingly repatriated in the 1980s by permanent unemployment abroad but still averse to agricultural work at home—a tenable position as long as jobs in construction, services, and the informal sector remained abundant.

But despite this increase in capital, much of the private hard currency has fueled "soft" investments in commerce, banking, real estate, and tourism instead of establishing vital industrial projects (Sadowski 1991:214-219). To bridge the gap between shrinking hard currency reserves and the expanding demand for capital goods to fuel industrial growth, the government has been forced to draw upon international sources of credit. Yet by 1990, the national debt had grown to such crisis proportions that Egypt' regional leadership has been severely discredited, which in turn, has undermined serious attempts at regional unity and economic integration (Sadowski 1991:Ch. 7).

Agriculture has become increasingly commercialized, further eroding food self-sufficiency and increasing dependence on foreign food sources. In March 1992, the agriculture minister proposed policies that would turn Egypt to cultivating commercial crops like strawberries, flowers, and luxury products that target the European market (al-Sha'b 24 March 1992). Once current land use policies untie the complex knot of private property ownership, the commercial orientation by urban business people will increase, with the cut flower bouquets and ice-packed strawberries loaded onto Paris-bound planes by the very ex-farmers displaced by such policies.

What awaits them in Europe? Increasingly, no markets and no sales. The consolidation of the Common Market and the opening of Eastern Europe and the former Soviet Union means that what cheap products cannot be imported from semi-peripheral countries like Portugal, Spain, and Greece, will be available from the former COMECON countries where European capital investments promise to establish more vigilantly controlled export facilities. Egyptian trade in luxury crops, in addition to garments and textiles, metal products and furniture, will remain unsold. And when the southern Mediterranean does contribute to core markets, those North Africans and Turks frightened out of Europe by the alarming rise of xenophobic racism will return to their own informal businesses and, with their "advanced market knowledge" of quality and storage, will have a distinct competitive advantage.

Thus squeezed by the ensemble of low agricultural and industrial exports, reluctant investors, international creditors, and constricted markets on one side, and an unbalanced labor process involving disgruntled farm workers, recalcitrant factory employees, and irate consumers on the other, Egypt remains thwarted in establishing a growth-oriented economy and an autonomous foreign policy. The state has not promoted its existing assets and has not yet been able to create new ones. Aggregate investment has yet to establish a sufficient number of economically viable level three industries that complement core production. Its diplomatic independence has become restricted just at a time when the proliferation of hegemonic powers, now including Europe and Japan, and domestic pressures require greater flexibility. Finding a comfortable niche in the new international division of labor is not an easy task.

In Lipietz' terms, Egypt stands poised at the crossroads between competitive and cooperative peripheral Fordism, caught in the uneasy transition from import substitution to export-led growth. But its adjustment to the new global economy and world diplomacy has not so much been through the smooth initiatives of its state officials as by jerks, stammers, and stutters in response to massive popular pressure from its producers and consumers. As discontent grows among male and female workers in agriculture, migrant labor, construction, the informal sector, and many other segments of the economy, Egypt's planners will find it even more urgent but even more difficult to achieve NIC status in an increasingly competitive world.

Conclusion

In this chapter I have attempted to connect the labor activities of rural workers to the larger trends in economic and political development. Régulation Theory provides a perspective that makes these connections transparent. Here analysis begins with the struggles that take place in the labor process found at the heart of the regime of accumulation, at a level at which most anthropologists feel comfortable. These struggles have principally involved contests over wage cuts shaped by Egypt's gender division of labor. Then the analysis rises to the levels found in economics and political science, to focus on the mode of regulation, that ensemble of institutions such as the labor market and state policies which in recent years have intensified the struggles taking place between labor and employers over efforts, wages, and prices. The IMF structural adjustments has plainly aggravated an already desperate situation.

Here, I have concentrated on labor's contribution to Egypt's growing dilemma. In the West, however, as machine production replaces workers or rather, displaces them to the edges of the global economy to such locations as Egypt, scholars like Herbert Marcuse (1964; 1973), Jürgen Habermas (1984), and Jean Baudrillard (1975) have concluded that labor is no longer the source of value and wealth. Their oversight has led to a serious theoretical myopia. While capitalism has become truly global, their intellectual vision remains essentially parochial. Régulation Theory argues that history is the outcome of clashes between the principal classes established under capitalism, labor, and management. Until capitalism disappears—and its end does not appear imminent—then it becomes difficult to argue that this motor force no longer exists.

Rosa Luxemburg once criticized the Second International for ignoring the global dimension when analyzing capitalism. And despite the changes in both capitalism and Marxism, her assessment still resonates today. Anthropology occupies a perfect promontory from which to chart this growth and to document the reproduction and the transformation of capitalism that is taking place throughout its customary domain. Yet the discipline remains fixated on culture studies. As neo-Marxists drop the labor theory of value and as Fordist and post-Fordist economies shift attention from production to consumption, anthropologists have joined the fetishization rather than pausing to analyze it. On the other hand, Régulation Theory can link the economic and non-economic, the cultural, and the non-cultural together in such a way as to begin understanding how world events like IMF structural adjustments can affect the very people that we customarily study at the grassroots level.

Notes

1. According to the World Bank, Egypt is classified as a "lower middle-income" country, along with Morocco, Lebanon, Honduras, and the Philippines. "Upper middle-income" countries include Brazil, Mexico, and South Africa; "low-income" economies include Chad, Haiti, Uganda and the Sudan.

2. Régulation Theory borrowed heavily from the Italian workerist theories developed by Antonio Negri, Mario Tronti, the journals *Potere Operaio* and *Lotta Continua*, and the Italian autonomist movement that lasted two decades from 1960 to 1977. This perspective gave Régulation Theory a substantial focus on labor's activities at the site of capitalist production. However, by 1980, Keynesian theories had eclipsed this workerist approach. What had once been a labor theory of value under the Theory's first theoretician, Michel Aglietta, became a price-theoretic under Robert Boyer, the current doyen of the school. Thereafter, it turned more into a style of radical Keynesianism and away from a concern with workers' agency. Thus, I am concentrating on this earlier period and on those who still remain true to its original principles.

3. I use régulation with an acute accent (*ague*) because it is more than just state regulation since other institutions beside government regulatory agencies are involved. Moreover, structural Marxists had become so obsessed with reproduction that it often turned into a functionalism. However, régulation can also transform society—and sometimes produce quite radical transformations at that. Thus I use the term "régulation" to mean either the reproduction or the transformation of the essential practices of capitalism.

Rural Workers and the Readjustment of Egypt's Economy 313

4. This may be old wine in new bottles. Thus "base" of the Second International becomes the regime of accumulation and its "superstructure" becomes the mode of regulation. The direction of determinacy, however, is reversed.

5. This narrow definition of a mode of regulation appears quite economistic, but can be widened to include other types of institutions, as well.

6. The onset of Taylorism differed from country to country. In England, the core of contemporary capitalism, it had begun as early as the 1830s, but in the United States, after the Civil War in the 1870s. In Italy, for example, it appeared even later, arising at the turn of the century, but was quickly superseded by Fordism, prompting Antonio Gramsci to observe this sudden transformation in his prison notebooks.

7. Unlike Taylorism, the lead this time was assumed by the United States, the new hegemonic giant. Fordism continued until the early 1970s.

8. For an analysis of how this resulted in the Gulf war of 1990, see Toth in press.

9. The cut-off point is between two and three f_ddans, varying with crop prices and the cost of living. A f_ddan equals 1.038 U.S. acres.

10. For a more detailed description of this division of labor, see the bibliographic summary in Toth 1991.

11. In an exhaustive study on mechanization in Egypt, Nicholas Hopkins (1987) could not conclude whether mechanization was supply driven, displacing workers *pace* Fordism and displaying no adverse affect on output, or whether it was demand driven, only partially and imperfectly replacing a growing deficit of workers once they departed.

12. From 1968 to 1972, annual migration rates amounted to between 50,00 and 80,000 individuals. This jumped to 157,000 by 1973. Estimates for 1975 vary from 375,000 to 600,000 to one million. In 1980, anywhere from 500,000 to one million laborers worked outside Egypt. By 1982, two million Egyptians were abroad and by 1985, three million. In 1980, the overall labor force was approximately 12 million people, with 4.3 million employed in agriculture.

13. See above.

14. Fröbel, Heinrichs, and Kreye (1981) concluded that cheap labor is the most significant attraction drawing foreign capital to Third World free trade zones and world market factories. Moreover, since foreign capital also invests under less accommodating conditions (subcontracting, import substitution, regular industrial, and service sector development) the supply of cheap, docile workers becomes even more essential.

References

al-Ahali (Cairo), 9 April 1992.
al-ᶜAynayn (Cairo), 7 July 1974.
al-Ahram (Cairo), 3 November 1985; 1 May 1992; 26 May 1992.
al-Shaᶜb (Cairo), 24 March 1992.
al-Wafd (Cairo), 18 March 1992.
Aglietta, Michel
    1979 *A Theory of Capitalist Regulation: The United States Experience*. New York: Verso Press.
Assaad, Ragui
    1991 Structure of Egypt's Construction Labor Market and its Development since the Mid-1970s. In *Employment and Structural Adjustment*. Heba Handoussa and Gillian Potter, eds. Cairo: American University Press.
Baldi, Guido
    1972 Theses on Mass Worker and Social Capital. *Radical America* 6(3): 3-21.
Baudrillard, Jean
    1975 *The Mirror of Production*. St. Louis: Telos Press.
Bluestone, Barry and Bennett Harrison
    1982 *The De-Industrialization of America*. New York: Basic Books.
Boyer, Robert
    1990 *The Regulation School: A Critical Introduction*. New York: Columbia University Press.
Choucri, Nazli
    1980 Construction and Development: The Effects of Labor Migration. In *Proceedings of the Seminar on Management of the Construction Industry in Egypt, Massachusetts Institute of Technology Research Team on the Housing and Construction Industry*, 19-20 January 1980. Cairo: The Joint Cairo University.
Choucri, Nazli, Richard Eckaus, and Amr Mohie-Eldin
    1978 *Migration and Employment in the Construction Sector: Critical Factors in Egyptian Development*. Massachusetts Institute of Technology Adaptation Program. Cairo: Cairo University.
Collier, Jane Fishburne
    1974 Women in Politics. In *Woman, Culture and Society*. Michelle Rosaldo and Louise Lamphere, eds. Stanford, Calif: Stanford University Press.
Commander, Simon
    1987 *The State and Agricultural Development in Egypt Since 1973*. London: Ithaca Press.
Davis, Eric
    1982 *Challenging Colonialism: Bank Misr and Egyptian Industrialization*. Princeton, N.J.: Princeton University Press.

Dessouki, Ali Hillal
1978 *Development of Egypt's Migration Policy, 1952-1978.* Massachusetts Institute of Technology Adaptation Program. Cairo: Cairo University.
Edwards, Richard
1979 *Contested Terrain: The Transformation of the Workplace in the Twentieth Century.* New York: Basic Books.
Friedl, Erika
1989 *Women of Deh Koh: Lives in an Iranian Village.* Washington, D.C.: Smithsonian Institution Press.
Fröbel, Folker, Jurgen Heinrichs, and Otto Kreye
1981 *The New International Division of Labor.* Pete Burgess, trans. New York: Cambridge University Press.
Food and Agriculture Organization (FAO)
1990 *Production Yearbook: World Development Report.* Rome: FAO.
Habermas, Jürgen
1984 *The Theory of Communicative Action.* Boston: Beacon Press.
Halliday, Fred
1984 Labor Migration in the Arab World. *Middle East Research and Information Project* 8:14, 4:3-10.
Hansen, Bent
1969 Employment and Wages in Rural Egypt. *American Economic Review* 70:308.
Hansen, Bent and Samir Radwan
1982 *Employment Opportunities and Equity in Egypt.* Geneva: International Labor Office.
Hopkins, Nicholas
1987 *Agrarian Transformation in Egypt.* Boulder: Westview Press.
Khafagi, Fatma
1983 Socio-economic Impact of Emigration from a Giza Village. In *Migration, Mechanization, and Agricultural Labor Markets in Egypt.* A. Richards and P. L. Martin, eds. Boulder: Westview Press.
Lipietz, Alain
1982 Towards Global Fordism? *New Left Review* 132:33-47.
1987 *Mirages and Miracles.* London: Verso Press..
Marcuse, Herbert
1964 *One-dimensional Man.* Boston: Beacon Press.
1973 On the Philosophical Foundation of the Concept of Labor in Economics. *Telos* 16:9-37.
Messiha, Suzanne
1980 Export of Egyptian School Teachers. *Cairo Papers in Social Anthropology* 3(4).
Mitchell, Tim
1991 America's Egypt: Discourse of the Development Industry. *Middle East Report,* 21(2):18-34, 36.

Reich, Michael, David Gordon, and Richard Edwards
  1980 A Theory of Labor Market Segmentation. In *The Economics of Women and Work.* Alice Amsden, ed. Middlesex: Penguin Press.
Richards, Alan
  1991 Agricultural Employment, Wages and Government Policy in Egypt During and After the Oil Boom. In *Employment and Structural Adjustment: Egypt in the 1990s.* Heba Handoussa and Gillian Potter, eds. Cairo: American University Press.
Sadowski, Yahya
  1991 *Political Vegetables? Businessman and Bureaucrat in the Development of Egyptian Agriculture.* Washington, D. C.: Brookings Institution.
Salim, Muhammad
  1977 *Iqisadiyat al-Zira'a al-Misriya* (Economics of Egyptian Agriculture). Institute of National Planning, Internal Memo No. 566. Cairo.
Saunders, Lucie W. and Suhair Mehenna
  1988 Unseen Hands: Women's Farmwork in an Egyptian Village. *Anthropology Quarterly* 59, 3:105-114.
Tignor, Robert
  1984 *State, Private Enterprise, and Economic Change in Egypt, 1918-1952.* Princeton, N.J.: Princeton University Press.
Toth, James
  1991 Pride, Purdah, or Paychecks: What Maintains the Gender Division of Labor in Rural Egypt? *International Journal of Middle East Studies* 23:213-236.
  In press No One Likes a Vacuum: The United States-Iraq War and the Search for Middle East Regional Hegemony, 1948-1990. *Critical Sociology,* forthcoming.
Tronti, Mario
  1971 *Operai e Capitale* (Workers and Capital). Turin: G. Einaudi.
Waterbury, John
  1983 *The Egypt of Nasser and Sadat: The Political Economy of Two Regimes.* Princeton, N.J.: Princeton University Press.
Wall Street Journal (New York), 19 January 1983.
World Bank
  1989 *Social Indicators.* Baltimore: Johns Hopkins University Press.

Contributors

Donald W. Attwood
Dept. of Anthropology
McGill University
855 Sherbrooke W.
Montreal, Quebec H3A 2T7
Canada

Richard E. Blanton
Dept. of Sociology and Anthropology
Stone Hall
Purdue University
West Lafayette, IN 47907

Candice Bradley
Dept. of Anthropology
Lawrence University
Appleton, WI 54912-0599

Gracia Clark
Dept. of Anthropology
Student Building 130
Indiana University
Bloomington, IN 47405

E. Paul Durrenberger
Dept. of Anthropology
University of Iowa
Iowa City, IA 52242-1322

Gary M. Feinman
Dept. of Anthropology
University of Wisconsin
5240 Social Science
1180 Observatory Drive
Madison, WI 53706

Thomas D. Hall
Dept. of Sociology and Anthropology
DePauw University
Greencastle, IN 46135

Tania Murray Li
Dept. of Sociology and Anthropology
Dalhousie University
Halifax, Nova Scotia B3H 3J5
Canada

Earl W. Morris
1984 Como Ave.
St. Paul, MN 55108-2023

Arthur D. Murphy
Dept. of Anthropology
Georgia State University
Atlanta, GA 30303-3083

Peter N. Peregrine
Dept. of Anthropology
Lawrence University
Appleton, WI 54912-0599

James Toth
Dept. of Sociology, Anthropology, and Psychology
American University in Cairo
POB 2511, Cairo
Egypt

Lillian Trager
Dept. of Sociology and Anthropology
University of Wisconsin-Parkside
Box 2000
Kenosha, WI 53141

Christina Bolke Turner
Dept. of Sociology and Anthropology, Box 240
Lafayette Hall
Virginia Commonwealth University
Richmond, VA 23284-2040

Richard R. Wilk
Dept. of Anthropology
Student Building 130
Indiana University
Bloomington, IN 47405

Deborah Winslow
Anthropology Program
Horton Social Science Center
University of New Hampshire
Durham, NH 03824-3586

Mary Winter
171 LeBaron Hall
Iowa State University
Amers, Iowa 50011